" 'Yes, we have the body here.' Cayce paused. 'A very sad case. It happened all at once, from a blow, delivered quite unintentionally, during a football game, and not noticed at the time in the excitement of the contest.'

"Ketchum sat on the edge of his chair, his eyes glued on the slumbering Cayce.

" 'I see the color red, blazing red, angry red. His brain is on fire. The convolutions or folds in his brain are red as fire. His mind is distorted, so that it cannot deal with anything reasonably. In time the distortions will become so great, unless something is done soon, that he may well do violence to himself and others.'

" 'Can he be helped,' Ketchum said, 'or is it already too late?' . . . 'It is not too late, but the treatment is drastic, and must be pushed, however hopeless it seems.' "

—*A PROPHET IN HIS OWN COUNTRY*

BOOKS BY JESS STEARN

Fiction
THE REPORTER

Nonfiction
A PROPHET IN HIS OWN COUNTRY:
The Story of the Young Edgar Cayce
THE SEARCH FOR A SOUL:
Taylor Caldwell's Psychic Lives
THE MIRACLE WORKERS:
America's Psychic Consultants
A TIME FOR ASTROLOGY
ADVENTURES INTO THE PSYCHIC
THE SEEKERS
THE SEARCH FOR THE GIRL
WITH THE BLUE EYES
EDGAR CAYCE—THE SLEEPING PROPHET
YOGA, YOUTH AND REINCARNATION
THE GRAPEVINE
THE DOOR TO THE FUTURE
THE SIXTH MAN
THE WASTED YEARS
SISTERS OF THE NIGHT

A Prophet in His Own Country

The Story of the Young Edgar Cayce

by Jess Stearn

with an Epilogue by Hugh Lynn Cayce

BALLANTINE BOOKS • NEW YORK

Library of Congress Catalog Card Number: 74-700

SBN 345-24464-8-175

This edition published by arrangement with
William Morrow and Company, Inc.

First Printing: May, 1975

Printed in the United States of America

BALLANTINE BOOKS
A Division of Random House, Inc.
201 East 50th Street, New York, N.Y. 10022
Simultaneously published by
Ballantine Books, Ltd., Toronto, Canada

Contents

An Acknowledgment

For their unstinting cooperation in bringing forth material never before published about Edgar Cayce, the author wishes to thank the family of Edgar Cayce, his sons, Hugh Lynn and Edgar Evans Cayce, and the family of Dr. Wesley Ketchum, his widow, Katy, and his sons, Dr. Robert Ketchum and Alton Ketchum, together with the Cayce-sponsored Association for Research and Enlightenment in Virginia Beach, Virginia, where the psychic's readings have been catalogued and classified. In the interest of dramatic unity, since such a relatively brief period of the great mystic's life is covered, events have occasionally been modified in sequence and the names of some minor characters altered to avoid embarrassment to those in the present. The period drawn in this book is roughly 1903 to 1910, when Edgar Cayce was becoming fully aware of his powers, largely through his work with the Yankee doctor, Wesley Ketchum, who used him to such great medical advantage during these exciting years.

In appreciation of her constant aid and encouragement, this book, resulting in the main from years of research, is affectionately dedicated to Edgar Cayce's faithful and trusted aide, Gladys Davis Turner. Without her, it would have never reached its present form.

A prophet is not without honour,
save in his own country . . .

—Matthew 13:57

1

The Discovery

Dr. Wesley Harrington Ketchum looked out his second-story window above Latham's Bank in Hopkinsville, Kentucky, and saw the tall, well-dressed figure of a man turn from the walk below into his entrance way.

"Well, Boze," said he to the handyman who was tidying up the office, "we may start the day with a customer of quality."

The black man's eyes gleamed. "I don't told you, Dr. Wesley, that patience was all you needed."

The doctor had returned to his desk, and was ostensibly going over his appointment book. There were no appointments. What patients he had just popped in at whatever time they chose.

"From the looks of him," the doctor said, "he doesn't appear to be very sick."

"You can never tell," Boze rejoined hopefully. "He might have a whole family of sick 'uns."

At that point, the office door opened, and the visitor, a middle-aged man with an air of authority, strode in and turned a sharp eye in Ketchum's direction after acknowledging Boze's presence with a brief nod. He offered his hand and took a chair alongside Ketchum's desk.

"I'm C. H. Dietrich, the school superintendent," he said, "and I guess you're the new Yankee doctor. I've heard good things about you."

1

"I don't know who you could have heard them from," Ketchum said dryly. "The local gentry are giving me a wide berth."

"From the custodian in one of our schools."

"You mean the janitor, don't you?"

Dietrich smiled. "We call them custodians."

Ketchum sat back in his chair and gave his visitor a searching look. "Well, you're my first patient from the so-called upper crust, that is, if you are a patient."

"Oh, yes," said Dietrich, "I have a miserable cold."

"That hardly calls for a doctor, does it?"

Dietrich's keen face lighted up in a quick smile. "Frankly, I'm checking you out, before I turn another case over to you."

Ketchum gave him a suspicious look. "You're not trying to get something on me, are you?"

Dietrich laughed heartily, and his laugh seemed to fill the room.

"You really got your Yankee hackles up, haven't you?" His eyes traveled quickly over the doctor, and he liked what he saw—a medium-sized young man of twenty-six or twenty-seven, with rimless pince-nez glasses, a frank, inquiring look and a peppery manner.

"What can you do for my cold?" he said.

Ketchum got up from his desk. "Come into my clinic, and I'll look you over."

"But I don't need an examination."

"I'm the doctor here," Ketchum said. "Didn't you see the sign on the door when you came in?"

Wryly, reluctantly, Dietrich stripped to the waist, and Ketchum went over him with his stethoscope and palpated his chest. He then looked down his throat, depressing his tongue, prodded his nostrils open with a catheter-like instrument, and rolled back his eyelids.

"You're right," he said. "It's nothing but a cold."

"You're certainly thorough," said Dietrich, getting into his shirt and jacket. "Now, can you do anything for me?"

2

"I don't have any cold cure, but I can make you comfortable."

He reached for a vial and measured some powder out of it into a small box. "Mix a little of this with water twice a day. I'm a homeopathic physician, and I concoct my own medicines, mostly from herbs. We believe in stimulating the ailing system so that it reproduces the symptoms of the ailment."

Dietrich's interest was piqued. "And what does that do?"

"It builds a certain resistance, though the allopathic doctors, the conventionally trained physicians, don't accept this concept, even when it works."

"You're a bit of an iconoclast, aren't you?"

"If you mean I don't accept all I'm told, then you're right. I'm an iconoclast."

Dietrich now came to one of the reasons for his call. "You're open," said Dietrich," "and I like that. Would you see my daughter, Amy? They say it's a cold, but I don't have any confidence in their diagnosis."

"Who are they?"

"Two of the local doctors. Does it matter who?"

Ketchum was lounging against a doorway, eying his visitor with a new curiosity. "You really have been testing me out, haven't you?"

"Yes, I wanted to know what kind of doctor you are. The doctors hereabouts haven't had much luck with my daughter. She's running a fever."

"Why come to me when there are so many better-known physicians?"

Dietrich's dark sardonic face took on an ironic look. "Do you question my judgment?"

"By no means. You're in the best of hands."

Dietrich sat back in a chair, pulled out a cheroot, and gave the younger man an amused glance. "Mind if I smoke?"

"In tobacco country? I'd have to be out of my mind."

"You're quite right about my cold. I had another reason for coming here."

3

"I'll be glad to check over your daughter this evening at home."

"This is a quite different reason."

Dietrich was obviously enjoying himself. His eyes roamed around the well-appointed clinic, stopped at the glistening new X-ray machine for a moment, then moved on to stand near a narrow leather-topped table.

Ketchum followed the other's gaze. "My X-ray is the only one in town. As is my collapsible operating table. I thought they'd be a help since there's no hospital in town."

Boze, dusting nearby, perked up his ears. "Tell about them lamps for aching muscles, Dr. Wesley. They sure make the back feel good."

Ketchum's frown at the interruption gave way to a shrug. "Boze is the perfect hypochondriac. He tries everything." He nodded toward the handyman, with whom he obviously had a genial rapport. "I'll have to try out the operating table on him. That's the only thing he hasn't sampled yet."

Boze's eyes rolled. "No, sir, Dr. Wesley, that's one thing I does without very nicely."

Dietrich smiled appreciatively during the colloquy. "You have enough equipment, Doctor, but southern Kentucky is the wrong place for a Yankee in the year 1903. They're still fighting the Civil War here." He smiled dryly. "Particularly those who didn't fight it before."

Ketchum looked at Dietrich curiously; the superintendent didn't speak like any Southerner he had met since he had hung up his shingle. He loosened up a little. "I came down here several months ago as an assistant to old Doc Young, and when his patients seemed to like me more than him, we mutually agreed to part. Since then, on my own, I've felt what it means to be a Northerner."

"You should have expected that."

"I'm not mad at anybody; the war ended before I was born."

Dietrich smiled. "Not down here it didn't. Anyway,

4

not for the people you call the gentry. They're mourning the loss of a way of life that can never come back. And they blame the people who took it from them. You represent those people."

Ketchum had been studying the other's speech and manner, and the realization finally dawned on him. "You must be a Yankee."

Dietrich puffed leisurely on the long cigar. "I come from across the river, from Ohio, as I understand you do. You have my sympathies, Ketchum."

Ketchum had a glimmer of understanding. "I see," he said. "But, if I may say so, you've done well for yourself."

Dietrich was amused by this unabashed candor. "I married a local girl, and that helped some. But the big thing, when you know these people, is to give them something they can't get elsewhere. Their school system was fouled up, and they needed an outsider to straighten it out. I was it."

Ketchum looked around his clinic. "I can give them the latest therapy."

Dietrich shook his head. "You need more than that."

Ketchum looked incredulously at his visitor.

"You've got to give them a miracle."

"I'm the best doctor in Hopkinsville," said Ketchum boldly, "and I've just passed some statewide examinations to prove it. But I can't perform miracles."

Dietrich smiled, realizing that he had taken the proper measure of his man. "You strike me as a gambler, Ketchum."

Ketchum eyed his visitor warily. "How do you figure that?"

"You wouldn't be here otherwise. You'd have a nice soft practice for yourself in Yankee territory."

There was a tenacity about the younger man that never allowed him to drop anything. "You had a second reason?"

"Yes, you can do yourself and the community a good turn at the same time."

Ketchum's look had become guarded. "I'm listening."

Dietrich's manner became authoritative, as if to announce that the time for sparring had passed. "Now listen closely, Ketchum, and know I am not one to speak lightly."

Ketchum's eyes were riveted on his caller.

"Have you heard of a young man named Edgar Cayce?"

Ketchum shook his head, but Boze's face lit up. "I knows him. He's got the second sight."

The doctor silenced his retainer with a glance.

"Boze isn't far from the truth," Dietrich went on. "Edgar Cayce is the biggest wonder the world has seen in two thousand years. Without knowing a thing about medicine, he can close his eyes, and look into a person's mind and body, describe what is wrong, and say how he can be cured. And he does it while he's asleep."

Ketchum looked at his watch, then got up as if to end the interview. "Take those powders twice daily, Mr. Dietrich," he said briskly.

Dietrich made no move. "Sit down, Doctor, and listen to the rest of it. Don't be a fool."

Ketchum stiffened. "I may be a lot of things, Mr. Dietrich, but a fool I'm not."

"Then don't act like one. Hold out your hands when the manna is raining down."

Ketchum resumed his seat. "I'm sorry, but I can't buy some wild story like that."

"It's not a wild story." Dietrich's voice was cold and incisive. "When every doctor in town and a host of specialists couldn't help her, Cayce saved my daughter's life. She had become a vegetable and he cured her. He said what was wrong, and gave explicit directions to the man who treated and cured her."

"And who was that?"

"An osteopath named Al Layne."

Ketchum's nose went into the air. "Why, those people have no standing. They're quacks."

"Quacks if you like, both of them, but my daughter's

6

alive and well today because of them." Dietrich got up and stretched. "Take these powders, Doctor; I don't believe in medicine."

Ketchum was frankly exasperated. "Why did you ever come to me?"

"Because you might be open enough, from what I had heard, to use Cayce to the greatest advantage, and you have nothing to lose."

Even as a young man, Ketchum had learned that people's motivations told him more about them than their words or actions. "You don't strike me as a man who cares that much about medical matters."

Dietrich smiled at the other's deftness. "You're right, Ketchum. Cayce will not only help sick people, who otherwise wouldn't get help, but if properly handled will be an inspiration to many, many more over the years."

Ketchum shook his head. "You'll pardon me, Mr. Dietrich, if I say that you lose me here."

Dietrich nodded. "There is only one way of explaining what Cayce does." He pointed upward. "Only God could have given Cayce this gift. That is the only explanation there can be."

Ketchum's glance slid away. "In other words, you're selling God."

Dietrich shook his head. "I'm not. Cayce is."

"Well," said Ketchum, "I'm not buying."

Dietrich put out his cheroot with great deliberation. "Think it over. You have my address, and you're coming over to see Amy anyway." He paused. "As I said, Ketchum, what do you have to lose?"

Ketchum smiled mirthlessly. "Just my license, that's all."

Dietrich nodded toward the brassy-looking automatic phone on Ketchum's desk. "Call before you come over, and I'll have Layne there as well. He's the fellow who used Cayce in the first place. And maybe Cayce!"

Too much had come at Ketchum too soon for him to be receptive at this time. "Why can't Layne bring the spiritual message to the waiting world?"

7

"Layne has carried it as far as he can. Somebody with more prestige in the medical field is needed now."

Ketchum gave a hollow laugh. "You couldn't find a doctor in all of Kentucky who's less into the medical field."

"You will be—just give yourself and Cayce a chance."

Ketchum's expression was all too eloquent.

"I understand how you feel," said Dietrich, "because I felt that way myself. But when Layne told me about Cayce, I figured we had nothing to lose, even though I didn't believe in the psychic. I had him bring Cayce through the backyard. I didn't want people to see them coming to the front door. Even then, Cayce was known as the Freak."

Ketchum, normally quick in his judgments, couldn't make up his mind about Dietrich. He seemed clear and cohesive, but what he was advocating was patently nonsense.

"If he had to come around your back door, what would a doctor do with him? Bring him through the cellar?"

"Let me tell you about Amy. When she was two, she came down with the grippe. After apparently recovering, she went into convulsions. She would fall down and her body would become rigid, immovable, until the attack passed. And then we noticed that her mind had stopped developing. She was staying two years old."

Three years later, the doctors decided she had a rare brain affliction that was invariably fatal.

As he recalled, Dietrich had not been impressed by his first glimpse of Cayce. He saw a tall young man, a bookstore clerk, who made no effort to examine the child, just tickling her playfully under the chin when she stared at him.

Dietrich wondered, How can this boy help us when the best doctors in the country have failed? His wonder grew as Cayce removed his coat, loosened his tie and shoelaces and then lay on the sofa, and apparently

8

went off to sleep at Layne's suggestion. After a few minutes, when Cayce was breathing evenly, Layne spoke to him casually, telling him to have before him the body of the child, Amy Dietrich, and to describe what was wrong inside her body.

"I could hardly believe my ears," Dietrich recalled, "when Edgar began speaking. The tone of his voice had changed. Where it had been high-pitched and uncertain before, it now seemed to carry authority.

"We had not told him anything about the case, at his own request, and yet he immediately tuned in that she had had the grippe. He also said that the day before she had took ill, she had suffered a bad fall, and hurt her upper spine. The grippe virus had settled in this vulnerable area, causing the convulsive attacks.

"We suddenly remembered that the day before she got sick Amy had slipped getting out of the carriage and jarred her spine in a nasty fall. But she quickly jumped up and we thought no more about it."

Cayce, speaking in a strong monotone, had then said a vertebra in the neck would have to be adjusted.

At this mention, Ketchum looked at Dietrich inquiringly.

Dietrich explained. "In physiotherapy or osteopathy, the theory is that when a vertebra is pushed out of position, and presumably impinges on a nerve, the whole function of the body may be affected. Manipulation of this vertebra back into place, allowing the energy impulses to again flow freely through the body, is called an adjustment."

Ketchum grunted. "If I accept what you're telling me, Mr. Dietrich, I'd better go back to medical school and ask for my tuition money back."

Dietrich smiled. "Or else incorporate what I am telling you into your practice of medicine."

As Ketchum shrugged noncommittally, Dietrich went on with his story. As Cayce had suggested, Layne made the adjustment of Amy's neck, but there was no discernible improvement. The Dietrichs were agreeable to a second reading, however, since they

9

had been impressed by Cayce's knowing of the grippe and the almost-forgotten fall.

Ketchum was not that impressed. "Somebody might have told him about the child," he said sourly. "After all, Mr. Dietrich, you are quite well-known in the community, and many people knew of your child's condition."

Dietrich shrugged off the doctor's skepticism. "It hardly seems likely that he would have known about the fall, when even we had to be reminded of it."

So Cayce as Dietrich recalled, gave a second reading.

He said the adjustment had not been properly made.

Layne tried again, and Cayce in trance said she would now get better.

"Shortly thereafter," Dietrich continued, "Amy's mind began to clear up, and the vacant look left her eyes. She recalled the name of her favorite doll for the first time since her illness. She called my name and her mother's, and threw her arms around us. In a few weeks, she was like any other normal child of five.

"Subsequently, we had what Cayce called a check reading. Cayce said the condition was removed, and there would be no more trouble. And today, two years later, Amy is as normal as any child of seven."

Ketchum studied the other man for a while, then said seriously, "Mr. Dietrich, I don't know your background except that you come from Ohio, as I do, and have achieved some success in this community. I come from very meager circumstances. I was born in a log cabin, the oldest of eight children, and I worked on the family farm while getting through high school. I whizzed through college, got a teacher's certificate, and taught in the grades for three years, saving enough money for medical school. In Cleveland, where I studied, I took any job I could to earn my way. I worked as a streetcar motorman for eighteen cents an hour nights, getting my sleep when I could. The day I graduated from medical school, I vowed that I would be the most outstanding doctor wherever I was. That was my ambition and I've put myself in hock to prove it."

He gave his visitor a penetrating glance.

"I don't intend to throw away everything I've worked for on some quack, getting myself drummed out of the medical business, to boot."

Dietrich had walked to the door, pausing with his hand on the knob. "You got nothing to lose, professionally, as long as you keep it quiet."

"If Cayce is as great as you say, why not use him on your daughter now?"

It was a logical comment.

"As an essentially conservative man," said Dietrich, "I believe in conservative measures. If you can't help Amy, very frankly I will ask Cayce for a reading. But I don't want to experiment with my daughter if I don't have to."

Ketchum shook his head. "Mr. Dietrich, I'm a practical man. I don't believe in any of this. If I did, nothing would stop me. I'd stand a patient on his head if I thought it would help him."

Dietrich assumed a benevolently paternal tone. "Well, think it over, and if you change your mind, call me, and I'll arrange a meeting with Cayce and Layne. Meanwhile, I'll be expecting you this evening for Amy."

They shook hands at the door, and Ketchum said laconically, "Thanks anyway, Mr. Dietrich. It's good to meet somebody who doesn't think of me as a damn Yankee."

Dietrich smiled. "But I do, Ketchum, I've been down here so long."

Ketchum stared into space for fully five minutes after his visitor had left.

Boze finally broke the silence. "Mr. Dietrich is a powerful smart man," he said approvingly.

Ketchum turned his head a trifle. "Now what does that mean?"

"He don't go shooting his lip without it meaning

11

somethin'. He's a big folks, and big folks stand fur somethin'."

Ketchum waved an airy hand. "I'll take your word for it, Boze."

"You ain't offended, Dr. Wesley?" Boze's broad face registered concern.

Ketchum grinned. "Boze, I can't afford to lose the only friend I have in the state."

Boze's chuckle showed his relief. "I just don't wanna mess up our partnership, that's all. But Mr. Dietrich was sure right about that Cayce fella. He's a wise one, he is."

There was very little Ketchum could do about checking on Cayce, or Dietrich, for that matter. He could make inquiries of the grocer, at the corner coffee shop, of the mailman, or the milkman, if he got up in time. But even these simple people would be careful how they responded. In a community stringently segregated as to black and white, he was even less a part of the white community than Boze.

Later that day, pondering what Dietrich had said, he looked up annoyed once or twice to catch Boze eying him quizzically. "What are you gaping at?" he demanded.

"It's just mighty quiet around here, that's all I was thinkin'."

Ketchum reached into his desk for a thin book listing local subscribers to the Hopkinsville telephone system. He consulted his watch. Dietrich should be home now. Dietrich, like Ketchum, had one of the few phones in Hopkinsville which made it possible to call directly.

Dietrich's voice betrayed no surprise. "I have already alerted Layne," he said, "and I can get him over in an hour."

After freshening up at home, Ketchum decided to walk to the Dietrich house. He seemed to think better while exercising.

Strolling leisurely, he stopped a few blocks from his rooms, at Campbell and Seventh Streets, to watch some children at play. They were engaged in *Civil War,* a popular street pastime among the small fry in Hopkinsville. A dozen children, boys and girls, were ranged on opposing sides. The boys were aiming wooden guns and vehemently shouting, "Bang, bang, you're dead." The five or six boys, Ketchum noted with wry amusement, were playing Confederate roles, while the girls, retreating ignobly, simulated the Union forces. There were no privates in these contending armies, only commanders who were classic symbols of adulation or hate. "I'm Robert E. Lee," fiercely cried a towhead of ten, as he leveled his make-believe weapon at a cowering girl. She promptly burst into tears. "Why do I have to be General Sherman?" she bawled.

Another boy revealed himself as the intrepid Stonewall Jackson. Hoarsely, he gave orders to storm the enemy center. The girls, pink-cheeked and beribboned, recoiled apprehensively in their unpopular cause. "You can't make me a Yankee," a little blue-eyed girl of eight or nine defiantly cried, slamming down her wooden gun in frustration. "I'm going home."

A boy Jeb Stuart, impersonating the immortal Confederate cavalry leader, made an expression of disgust. "You don't expect boys to play those damn Yankees, do you?"

The girl stamped her foot. "Well, I'm tired of being General Grant. And I'm going to tell my daddy. He'll give it to you."

Ketchum almost laughed aloud at this demonstration of how the local community still reacted to the Civil War.

The children looked at him curiously, without seeming to mark his presence. They knew he was the new Yankee doctor, and they were studiously indifferent.

Ketchum braced his shoulders and went on, coming soon in his walk to a cemetery where, over the graves of the unknown Confederate dead, there was an epitaph to Southern gallantry:

"Here lies all of heroism that can die."

Hopkinsville had been captured and recaptured six

times during the War of Secession, and the seeds of partisanship so bitterly sown were still bearing a prolific harvest, as the Yankee doctor was only too aware.

Meditating rather morosely, he walked past rows of stately homes shaded by tall trees, occasionally spotting an old man or woman on a front porch smoking a corncob pipe. Where Seventh Street reached Main, the business thoroughfare, unpaved like other streets, the trees had gradually receded and the hot sun beat down mercilessly on the squat red-brick buildings and the domed courthouse. There was an air of stability about the town. Laid out in 1797, its church spires and old homes seemed as much a part of its stability as the rolling hills and fields that made it all economically possible. The compelling smell of tobacco, faintly acrid, hung as always over the city of eight thousand, reminding Ketchum of the tobacco warehouses in the city's heart and the miles of fields edging out of the city as far as the eye could see.

Ketchum sauntered past the courthouse, at Main and West Seventh, then the Hopkinsville Bank, Wall's Clothing Store, Hoosier's Tailorshop, Hopper Brothers Bookstore, where Edgar Cayce worked, Thompson's Hardware, Latham's Dry-goods, Hardwick's Pharmacy, and Burnett's Shoe Store, occasionally stopping to look into a window. He passed his own office on Seventh Street, above Latham's Bank, and in the dim light could see Boze cleaning up. Boze chose that moment to look out and wave at his employer. Ketchum waved back airily.

Ketchum, as usual, put up a good front. He was fastidiously clad in a gray-striped suit, with a checkered vest, from which the chain securing his father's gold watch, a graduation present, dangled conspicuously. Many pedestrians eyed him curiously, but nobody spoke or nodded. He could walk through the city at any time without meeting anybody he knew.

On street corners, groups of men huddled furtively

together, and their voices dropped significantly with a stranger's approach. But Ketchum could still catch muffled references to the Night Riders and their latest raid. He would have had to be deaf, dumb and blind not to know about the tobacco war which currently saturated the local newspapers. With Christian County the leading grower of dark-fired premium tobacco in the world, practically everybody in Hoptown was concerned with the Tobacco Growers Association fight against the Tobacco Trust. Sporadic violence had broken out throughout the county, and hooded Night Riders periodically burned out farmers who continued to sell their tobacco in defiance of an association boycott.

As a stranger, Ketchum was indifferent to this issue, just as he was to local politics, but he was aware that the economy of the community depended on a fair price for tobacco. Still, his mind was preoccupied with what Dietrich had told him and this man Cayce. It was an odd name, pronounced Casey. But then Cayce, by all accounts, was odd enough to suit his name.

He approached a fine tree-shaded street, with broad well-tended lawns, and his step quickened. He stopped in front of a solid two-story gray house, with a wide verandah that indicated a certain comfortable prosperity. This was Dietrich's house.

As he walked up a flower-edged path to the porch, he wondered wryly whether Edgar Cayce and Al Layne had entered by the front door.

He pushed the bell and heard it chime from somewhere inside the house.

Dietrich greeted him warmly. "The others are here but I thought you'd want to see Amy first."

Dietrich took him upstairs, down a long hall, and into a cheery wallpapered bedroom.

The child, propped up by pillows, was thumbing listlessly through a book of Mother Goose rhymes. Her mother had just brought her some hot soup and crackers.

Mrs. Dietrich was a woman whose youthful beauty had not completely faded. She gave the doctor a searching look, with snapping brown eyes, and drew up a stiff-backed wooden chair to the child's white-postered bed.

He smiled at the wan face and patted Amy's head, feeling the warm dampness of her thick golden curls.

"Just open, and we'll take your temperature like a nice little girl."

He placed the thermometer under her tongue.

The parents appeared nervous as he held the instrument to the light.

"What does it say?" they asked.

He shrugged. "She should be all right in two or three days." He examined her thoroughly, then reached for his black bag, and took out some pills. He wrote the directions on a prescription blank. "Give her these as directed; they'll cut down the fever, and make her comfortable." He patted the child's head again. "I'll give her something, too, to check the infection."

Outside the sickroom, Dietrich turned to him gravely. "What does she have, Doctor?"

Ketchum returned his look evenly. "Diphtheria. The throat and tonsils are symptomatic with membranous growth. But there's nothing to worry about. It's a mild type diphtheria mitis, and a new drug, an antitoxin, should do the trick. It was developed about ten years ago in France and has accomplished wonders."

"You're sure about her condition?"

Mrs. Dietrich, too, was watching him anxiously.

"As sure as a doctor can be."

Somewhat reassured, the Dietrichs led Ketchum downstairs into the family living room. Two men were sitting in heavy leather chairs before a large fireplace with a marble facade. They stood up at the same time and Dietrich introduced the shorter and older man.

"This is Al Layne; he's the man who brought Cayce to me, and saved my little girl's life. And this"—he pointed fondly to a tall, slim, grayish-blue-eyed man with a high forehead and the least suggestion of a stoop—"is the man who did it, Edgar Cayce."

Ketchum's eyes moved from Layne to Cayce and stopped there. There was something distinctive about this young man, who was a year or so younger than himself. As for Layne, he looked like a shopkeeper, with his conciliatory expression and drooping jowls, not at all the professional type that would ordinarily appeal to Dietrich.

In sizing up Cayce, Ketchum saw a lanky young man with tousled hair and a reserved smile. Cayce's voice was high-pitched, and his manner unassuming. He took Ketchum's hand courteously, but was obviously preoccupied with his own thoughts.

"Dr. Ketchum would like to ask you a few questions, Edgar," Dietrich said, with a brief nod.

Cayce gave the young doctor a searching glance, which seemed to say he'd been through all this before.

"I've heard quite a bit about you," said Ketchum, "from Superintendent Dietrich and others."

Cayce nodded, without showing any particular interest.

"Do you have any medical training at all?" asked Ketchum.

The young man shook his head cheerfully. "Not a bit."

"Then how do you know anything about medicine?"

"I don't—at least not when I'm awake."

Ketchum looked helplessly at Dietrich.

The educator shrugged. "It's all up to you, Ketchum."

Ketchum sat down across from Cayce. "Now, tell me, did you help Amy Dietrich?"

Cayce gave him a slow smile. "They said I did. I don't claim anything."

"But Mr. Dietrich said you were able to help when the doctors couldn't."

"That's what he said."

"And how did you do that?"

"I just lay down on the couch, and went to sleep, and Mr. Al Layne, who's an osteopath, asked me a lot of questions."

17

Ketchum's lips curled. "These people are all quacks. They have no standing."

Cayce interposed sharply, "I don't care what you say about me. I've been called a lot of things. But it's not fair to call Al Layne names when he's helping people."

Layne held up a placating hand. "Don't worry about me, Edgar. I'm not important. It's the work that matters." He turned to Ketchum and said lamely, "I'm not a medical doctor myself, but that's probably just as well or I wouldn't have used Edgar."

Ketchum shot a swift glance at Dietrich, who didn't seem disturbed by Layne's admission. Instead he said encouragingly, "Tell Dr. Ketchum what brought Cayce to your attention."

Layne nodded eagerly. "Edgar had lost his voice. The doctors called it aphonia, but giving it a name didn't help any. And, frankly, they didn't know what to do about it." He gestured apologetically toward Ketchum. "Anyway, Edgar had this peculiar ability to transfer his mind into space, so I thought he might be able to look into his own body, just as he could tell that a certain subject had walked off a boat hundreds of miles away, or describe the wallpaper in a room he had never seen."

Ketchum's expression remained a blank, though he had already decided he was wasting his time with a bunch of idiots. "He could do that?" he said with a humoring smile.

"Oh, yes, that was nothing for him. Anyway, since I'm something of a hypnotist, too, I thought I'd put him in trance, and suggest that he peer into his own body, particularly the throat, and tell what was wrong with his vocal cords, and how the condition could be corrected."

As Ketchum listened, unimpressed, Layne described how at this time he had put Cayce to sleep on a horsehair sofa in the Cayce living room, with the psychic's father, Leslie Cayce, and mother, in anxious attendance. At Layne's suggestion, Cayce almost immediately went under. His breathing deepened, there

18

was a long sigh, and he was unconscious. "I could have stuck pins in him, and he wouldn't have known it," Layne said.

In a casual voice, Layne suggested that Edgar examine the interior of his own body and describe whatever malfunction there was in his throat, *speaking in a normal voice*. After a few minutes of silence, Edgar began to mumble, then his voice came through clearly. He was speaking again, even if it was only in trance. As his mother wept gratefully, he explained his condition.

"This body has been unable to speak due to a partial paralysis of the inferior muscles of the vocal cords caused by nerve strain. This may be removed by increasing the circulation to the affected parts by suggestion while the body is unconscious."

The suggestion was promptly made by Layne, and the response was almost immediate.

"Edgar lay there, breathing evenly, his face composed. Suddenly, the upper part of his chest and throat turned pink, and then a deep crimson, reflecting the increased circulation."

After a few minutes of this invigorating blood bath, Cayce announced, "The condition is removed now. Suggest that the circulation return to normal, and that the body awaken."

Layne did as he was told. The color faded, the skin resumed its normal hue. Cayce sat up, opened his eyes and reached for a handkerchief. He coughed into it, giving up quantities of mucus streaked with blood.

"I can talk now," he said. "I'm all right." He had apparently cured himself, as Layne had hoped.

Through Layne's long narrative, Cayce had fidgeted uneasily, occasionally darting a nervous glance at the impassive Ketchum to see how he was taking it all.

Ketchum's face was a mask.

Dietrich now turned to the doctor. "What do you make of it, Ketchum? Amazing, isn't it?"

Ketchum was finding it difficult to be polite. "Even if it happened as Layne said, he wasn't helping anybody else," he said with a shrug.

Layne held up a hand. "I don't blame you for being skeptical, Doctor. But it seemed to me then that if Edgar could see into one body, he could see into all. 'If you can see inside yourself while you're asleep,' I said, 'why can't you see inside somebody else?'"

He suggested that Cayce attempt to give him a physical reading, and diagnose a chronic condition.

Edgar, as usual, was willing to try.

Cayce's father, known as the Squire for his lordly ways, put his son in trance, as he had seen Layne do it, and asked him to look into Layne's body, making a diagnosis and recommending a remedy.

Cayce spoke for fully fifteen minutes. When he came out of it, finally, a jubilant Layne cried out in approbation. "You gave me a perfect rundown of my long-time abdominal symptoms, and prescribed medicines, diet and exercise as a corrective. I can hardly wait to try your therapy."

Cayce looked curiously at the notes Layne had jotted down, frowning over anatomical terms he had never heard of, at names of medicines he didn't realize had existed, and of exercises he had never been exposed to. He shook his head in bewilderment. "I know nothing about anatomy, nothing about drugs or chemistry. I've never worked in a drugstore or a hospital. Where could all this come from?"

Layne believed Cayce was clearly clairvoyant. But naming it still didn't explain it.

As he neared the end of his story, Layne's gaze traveled around the room and stopped inevitably at Ketchum.

"And do you know, Doctor, a week later, following the regimen suggested by this boy"—he pointed at Cayce—"I was rid of my stomach distress for the first time in years."

Ketchum was beginning to think he was in the paranoia ward of a state asylum. Nothing seemed to be rooted in reality. "Everything comes out of something," he said with a look at Dietrich. "Now this gift of Cayce's, if it exists, where does it come from? How do you account for it?"

Dietrich exchanged glances with his wife. "As I told you, Ketchum, it is a God-given gift."

Ketchum was now showing his impatience. "Mr. Dietrich, I'm a man of science. That doesn't wash with me. What do you have to say about that, Cayce?" He turned sharply on the psychic.

Cayce started at being addressed unexpectedly. "I don't know what to make of it," he said lamely.

Ketchum was determined to show up this fraud. "Can you think of anything that would account for a quality that makes you different from other men?" There was a faint note of disdain in his voice.

Cayce looked at him uncertainly. "Doctor, I want you to understand I'm not pushing any of this. I'd just as soon be left alone. But if God gave me anything that can help people, it may be wrong for me to withhold that help."

The constant references to God infuriated Ketchum. "Where does this God idea come from?" he said in a cold voice.

Cayce hesitated, then looked around helplessly until he caught an encouraging smile from Dietrich. "May I tell you all of an experience I had as a boy?" he said diffidently.

With a restraining look at Ketchum, the school superintendent said pointedly, "I think we can all learn something listening to Edgar."

"Yes, I might as well hear from *him*," said Ketchum tartly.

The years slipped away, and Edgar Cayce's eyes shone as he recalled the experience so long ago that had changed his life. He was thirteen then and had been reading the Bible every day for three years. He would go into the woods beyond his family's farm, where he had built a small lean-to fashioned of saplings, moss, bark and reeds from the edge of a nearby brook. He dug himself a well, purifying the water so he could drink it. And there, curled up in the woods, with the fallen leaves for a pillow, he read his Bible with an excitement never to leave him. A moving panorama of fascinating figures passed wondrously before him: Joseph and his coat of many colors; Noah and the Ark; David and his slingshot, with which he slew the giant Goliath; Lot's wife turned to a pillar of salt; Daniel in the lion's den; Esther and Ahasuerus; and Haman hanged high for his infamy. And of course Jesus, counseling the confused, healing the sick and the halt, raising the dead.

One day at dusk, he apparently fell asleep as he was poring over the story of Manoah. In a dream as vivid as any reality, he looked up and saw a woman standing before him. He blinked incredulously. He thought at first it was his mother, but as he looked closer saw that it was a stranger. She spoke gently: "Your prayers have been answered. Say what it is you want most, so that I may give it to you." He was struck speechless, but after a while managed to say, "I would like to be helpful to other people, especially children when they are sick."

The vision was so dazzling that he turned his head away for a momentary respite. When he looked up, the Lady was gone, and he found himself wondering in a half-daze whether it had been a dream or reality.

Deeply shaken, he ran home and told his mother of the visit from the Lady, and her promise. "Do you think I have been reading the Bible too much?" he asked.

His mother took the Bible from his hands and looked at this strange boy of hers compassionately. "It doesn't matter whether it was a dream or not," she said. "It was still a vision, and you were being told something."

She turned to the Gospel of St. John and read softly, " 'Verily, verily, I say unto you. Whatsoever ye shall ask the father in my name, he will give it you. Hitherto have ye asked nothing in my name: ask, and ye shall receive, that your joy may be full.' "

Still confused, he asked her to explain.

Edgar's mother, deeply spiritual herself, had always recognized that quality in her son. "You have always wanted to help others, and this may be what the lady

22

of the vision meant by your prayers having been heard."

After that, Cayce's clairvoyance began to manifest itself. Encouraged by Layne and Dietrich to continue his story, he described the ensuing changes in himself, how he could fall asleep over a book and, on awakening, remember everything in that book. He would dream of events, and those events would occur. Sometimes he saw death and destruction, and shuddered at what he saw.

"It got so, after a while," he said, "that I deliberately tried to block things out."

As he came to the end of this singular story, Cayce looked around sheepishly. "I wish there was somebody who could explain it all to me. I just don't know what to make of it."

Ketchum had listened with growing petulance. "I don't know what to make of it either, but I don't see how any of this can be of any use to any doctor in his right mind."

At Ketchum's tone, Cayce's face reddened, and he started to get up, but Dietrich restrained him with a look. Now, for the first time, Mrs. Dietrich, who had been a silent witness throughout, spoke up, looking Ketchum in the eye and speaking with the fervor of a convert. "Edgar Cayce saved my daughter, when the best brains of medical science confessed their failure. I will always be grateful to him, and will never allow him to be downgraded in my presence—by anybody."

Ketchum moved his shoulders slightly. "I wasn't downgrading the boy," he said in an indifferent voice. "I just can't substitute visions and daydreams for evidence. Mr. Dietrich, as an educator, I am sure, understands that."

Mrs. Dietrich was not one to retreat. "What better evidence is there than what happened to my daughter?" She looked at Ketchum challengingly. "Ask me whatever question you like. I have no visions for you, Doctor, only facts, stemming from our wonderful daughter's illness and cure."

23

Ketchum crossed his legs carefully, preserving the crease in his freshly pressed trousers. As a plain speaker himself, he liked plain talk. "All right," he said, "let us explore for facts. Who were the doctors you went to first?"

"There were a number of local physicians. When they couldn't diagnose Amy, we consulted Doctors Walker and Linthecum in Evansville, Indiana, and Doctor Hoppe, the nerve specialist in Cincinnati, Ohio. But she grew constantly worse."

"How long had your child been afflicted before you consulted Edgar Cayce?"

"About three years."

"Tell me, as fully as possible, the way in which your child was afflicted and how it affected her health?"

"For three years she was a hopeless imbecile, and the specialists assured us that it would be but a very short time until she died. They said there was no similar case on record that had been relieved. At this time, my husband and I were expecting her death almost momentarily. When Mr. Cayce diagnosed the case, her mind was gone. She was helpless."

"And what did Cayce do?"

"In trance, he prescribed osteopathic treatment, and after the eighth treatment by Mr. Layne my child's mind was fully restored; her health began to improve. In six weeks she was perfectly well and strong with no defect at all. She entered school immediately, joining the class she would have normally been in, and led her class at the finish of the term."

Ketchum picked his way carefully. "Now what did the Evansville doctors say the trouble was specifically?"

"They said the trouble was at the base of the brain. Mr. Cayce put it back of the frontal bone."

"You haven't as yet mentioned what this diagnosis of Cayce's was."

"He said the trouble came on with a spell of grippe, aggravated by a lesion from a fall. Nature, trying to

24

protect itself against the disorder, formed membranous tissue on the brain."

"And what was the cause of this membranous growth?"

Showing unusual knowledge, born of her daughter's infirmity, Mrs. Dietrich recalled every detail of that memorable day.

"Mr. Cayce said the neck muscles leading from the fifth cervical vertebra were congested. This drew the spinal cord to one side, damming the flow of blood in this area, until it reached a spill-over point where it would spurt against the brain, resulting in a convulsion, and causing the protective membrane to form. The pressure point was no larger than a thumbnail, and when the muscles were relaxed in the neck area, the blood would flow normally and she would be healed.

"Edgar Cayce described every bruise, every sore spot, the scratches on her body, though covered fully by clothes. He examined every organ minutely, in this unconscious stage, and could even report what happened internally during her convulsions."

Ketchum's frown deepened, and he decided to backtrack out of this dubious ground into some area of reality.

"When did Layne first see the child?"

"The day before Cayce's diagnosis."

"Did Layne treat her?"

"No, he looked at her for a while, observing her behavior. He said he could relieve her nervousness temporarily, but couldn't cure her because he didn't know the problem, and that nobody else did, including all the specialists that had nodded their heads over her so wisely."

Ketchum was more and more frustrated. He had met a Tartar in Mrs. Dietrich. But with this reference to the vulnerable Layne, he now turned on the man he obviously felt was a quack. "Are you a licensed physician?" he asked sharply.

Mrs. Dietrich stiffened resentfully at the question, but the good-natured Layne didn't seem to mind.

"I'm an osteopath."

"And how many years did you study to get your license?"

"For some time."

"What was the school?"

"The Franklin School of Osteopathy."

"Did you attend regular classes?"

Layne hesitated in embarrassment. "Most of it was through correspondence," he said finally.

"You became a therapist through the mails?"

"Not exactly. I had studied physiotherapy and had practical knowledge of the human anatomy."

"But you went to no regular college, had no regular professors, attended no regular classes?"

Layne regarded his interrogator imperturbably, as though used to such questioning. "That is true, Doctor."

Mrs. Dietrich intervened at this point. "Dr. Layne also has the gift of magnetic healing." She seemed to enjoy referring to Layne as Doctor.

Ketchum's head popped up. "And what is that, pray," he asked scornfully, "this magnetic healing?"

Before Layne had a chance to speak, Mrs. Dietrich hastened to explain. "There is an energy flow from his hand, with a healing quality. You can actually sense the heat from his hand over an injured area, freeing the magnetic forces in the body. He is a natural healer, with a God-given gift." She smiled grimly at Ketchum. "Unlike some doctors, who only have degrees to show what they can do."

Ketchum appeared not to have heard, as he resumed his barrage. "Now tell me, Mr. Layne," stressing the Mister, "how you happened to be called in on the Dietrich case."

"On the recommendation of a patient I had treated." He smiled. "The regular doctors had given up on him, just as they had on Amy Dietrich."

Ketchum had the uneasy feeling that the other man was laughing at him. "What about this magnetic healing of yours?"

Layne drew a deep breath. "Some day all of med-

26

icine will recognize that body and mind are an intricate electrical or magnetic field. When this field is interfered with or impeded in any way, the magnetic flow of body currents is impeded, and disease develops. Edgar Cayce was able to see into Amy's body with his peculiar X-ray power, and tell us where this obstruction was, and by a simple adjustment the magnetic flow was restored. I don't have a magnetic healing force, actually, but the body does."

A smile crossed Ketchum's face. His gaze moved from Cayce to the Dietrichs, then to Layne again. A sudden idea had struck him, which would effectively rebut all the nonsense he had listened to for the past hour. In an innocent voice, he said, "Since Amy is again ill, I suppose that nobody would object if I asked this wonder boy to look into her body now and make a diagnosis. And then maybe Layne can do a magnetic healing."

Dietrich held up a protesting hand. "But you apparently had no difficulty with the case."

Ketchum was his jaunty self again. "Well, I could always use a backstop."

Mrs. Dietrich bristled as she had before, when Layne was questioned sharply. Layne looked uncertain. Only Edgar Cayce seemed unruffled.

"If nobody minds," he said mildly, "I'll see what I can get for little Amy."

The Dietrichs slowly nodded their assent, and Cayce stretched out on a nearby sofa, loosening his tie and collar and slipping off his shoes. Layne moved to the head of the sofa. He quickly proceeded to put Cayce in trance with the suggestion that he find the body of seven-year-old Amy Dietrich, herself too ill and too young to request the reading, but which was requested for her by her parents.

After a few moments, the slumbering Cayce repeated the question in an undertone, and said, "Yes, we have the body here."

"Good," said Layne. "Now examine this body and tell what is wrong with it."

Cayce's voice was never more clear and resonant.

"This body, that of a child, is suffering from a systemic condition, which manifests itself in a high fever and a membranous infection of the throat, especially the tonsils."

"And the ailment?"

Cayce hesitated but a second. "Diphtheria," rolling the word off his tongue. "Diphtheria mitis, a relatively mild form of the disease."

Layne looked around happily. "And what should be done to correct this disease and make the body well again?"

"Rest, more rest, keeping the body warm and relaxed, and it will respond to whatever treatment is indicated."

"And what would that treatment be?"

"That which is called toxin antitoxin, a new method of treatment for this disease, but very effective. The body will then recover."

In his elation, Layne didn't bring Cayce out of his unconscious state right away. He turned to Ketchum, triumphantly. "Well, what do you say to that, Doctor?"

Ketchum, with all eyes on him, motioned to the slumbering figure with scorn. "How do I know that somebody didn't quietly tell him about my diagnosis, and that he isn't faking the whole thing?"

2

Tests

The Hopkinsville Literary Club, in a gala opening of the new social season, had chosen hypnotism as the subject of a public demonstration. And young Edgar Cayce, employed mundanely enough during the day at Hopper Brothers Bookstore, had been asked to participate in the exhibition. Even after Al Layne had asked him he had demurred, but had finally yielded to the cajolery of his father.

Convinced now of his son's unique gift, the Squire was his principal booster. He had a popular forum that none could deny. In his general store, among the barrels and the boxes, the men talked of politics and tobacco, and the ladies discussed fashions and food, and rising prices. People bought yards of cloth, barrels of flour, sacks of rice and potatoes, apples, herbs, tea, medicine—everything they did not raise on their farms. With every dollar's worth of goods, they were entitled to a scoop from the whiskey barrel, which sat in a corner with a dipper over it. It was a pleasant world.

Often, the Squire was so engrossed in elaborating on his son's strange ability that he neglected the customers on the other side of the counter. His father, Thomas Cayce, had been noticeably psychic, dowsing successfully for water all over southwestern Kentucky. But this genetic facility traditionally skipped a generation, and the Squire deplored having to earn an ordinary living as a farmer, part-time magistrate, and then a storekeeper.

In his son, he enjoyed a vicarious stimulation, a glamorous excursion into a world where he could claim distinction as the parent of somebody unique. It did not matter that many of the people he regaled about his son's gift had not the slightest idea of what it was he was talking about. Indeed some were beginning to think the father as daft as the son. On a typical occasion, the Squire, stroking his handlebar moustache, had cornered Mrs. Henry Jones in his notions department and treated her to a discourse on Edgar's powers.

"As a boy," said he, "Edgar was a real dullard in school. He was constantly daydreaming. When he was twelve he was still in the third grade, and everybody was laughing at him. We didn't know what was wrong. So one day I thought I would help him with his lessons. My brother, Lucian, was teaching and said the kid couldn't even spell *cabin,* though he had practically built one for himself. So he made the boy stay after school and write the word five hundred times on the blackboard."

Mrs. Jones looked around frantically, but the Squire's blocky body left her no avenue of escape.

"I went over his lessons with him," he went on imperturbably, "but as soon as he closed the spelling book, he couldn't remember a thing."

The Squire had Mrs. Jones backed into a corner, and was poking a finger under her nose for emphasis.

It was late, the Squire recalled, and he thought it would be best to end the embarrassment and get to bed. But Edgar was eager to go on, almost as though he wanted to prove something.

"Let me rest for five minutes," he said, "and I'll know my lesson."

That was the day the lady of the vision had told him he could do anything he wanted to.

The Squire had laughed good-naturedly and gone into the kitchen for a glass of water. When he got back the boy was curled up in a chair, with his head resting on the pillow, the spelling book under it.

The father shook him. "Wake up, it's time for bed." He had given up on the lesson for the day.

Edgar started up, rubbing his eyes, then smiled. "Ask me the lesson, I know it now."

To humor the boy, the Squire asked him to spell a few words that he had missed before.

The Squire was amazed at the response.

"He could spell them all, and then he began telling me what words were next to the words I had given him. He even described the pictures, and told me the pages they were on. He seemed to be reading right out of the book."

Mrs. Jones had finally relaxed. "And how much," she asked, "is this silk pattern by the bolt?"

The Squire shook his head, temporarily defeated, then went on to the next customer undaunted. He would not be satisfied until all of Hopkinsville, the state and the country were aware of the prodigy who bore his name.

It had really begun long before that, on a day that was to be the saddest in young Edgar's childhood. He had watched wide-eyed as a horse stumbled into a pond, throwing his grandfather and trampling him to death in his panic. The boy, riding on his grandfather's lap, had been safely thrown clear by the falling rider.

His grandfather's funeral had meant a traumatically lonesome day for the boy. He slipped away from the funeral by himself and went to play under the maple trees back of the family farmhouse. He was four then, and for the first time he saw his little playmates. They were nice little boys and girls, and he wondered why other people didn't see them. He would talk to them, and they would talk back. His father came out of the house, frowning as he looked around, and asked who he was talking to. When Edgar turned to point them out, they were gone, returning only after his father went inside.

"That boy," the father had said impatiently, "is

31

like an old man. He's not only as solemn as a graybeard, but he's forever seeing things that aren't there."

Now, with his new appreciation of his son, the Squire wasn't so sure that Edgar really hadn't seen something and he recalled out of Scripture, "Thou hast hid these things from the wise and prudent, and hast revealed them unto babes."

In his newfound pride, the Squire took the family en masse to witness Edgar's performance at the Literary Club. There was Annie, the oldest, called Sister. She was shorter than average, with dark gray eyes and light brown hair. Ola was next, a tall, slender dark-haired girl in high school, then Mary, ready for high school, and Sarah, the baby, still in pigtails. They all adored their older brother, for his thoughtfulness and good humor. He was relaxed and easy with them, recognizing the love and affection behind their occasional banter.

Edgar's mother, Carrie, had chosen not to go. She winced at the prospect of her son's being made a public spectacle. "I want him back in as good condition as he is going," she enjoined the Squire. "Don't let anybody trifle with him while he's asleep."

There were perhaps three hundred persons at the benefit affair. Edgar had arrive early with Al Layne, who was to hypnotize him, and was standing by a raised platform similar to a stage with a handful of solemn-faced men, who were questioning him closely. They were all doctors.

After seeing that his daughters were comfortably seated, with a good view of the proceedings, the Squire joined the group. Layne quickly introduced him to the various doctors—Benson, Robinson, Quinby, Sanders, and Smithers—all of whom briefly nodded, then went back to their interrogation. They were Cayce's jury for the evening.

"Gentlemen, gentlemen," said the Squire, protesting the sharp questioning, "this is not a courtroom, and my son is not a defendant. He just happens to be the greatest psychic in the world."

Dr. Smithers, a tall, bespectacled man with a gray beard in the fashion of Robert E. Lee's, gave the Squire a jaundiced look. "We are merely seeking information."

The Squire preened himself the least bit. "Well, as the lad's father, perhaps I can answer your questions," he said in a humorous vein. "You know, I was in on the beginning of this."

"That won't be necessary," said Dr. Sanders, a tall, impressive-looking man of forty-five or so. "The demonstration should tell us whether the young man is a fake or not."

Edgar Cayce had been listening with rising indignation. "Look," he said sharply, "Al Layne asked me to help the Literary Club, and that's the reason I'm here, and the only reason."

The youngest of the doctors, Philip Benson, something of an amateur hypnotist himself, attempted to placate Edgar. "All we are trying to do, Mr. Cayce, is establish the ground rules. After all, if there is anything to what you do, it could be a very interesting research project for medical science."

"That may be so," said Cayce, "but I'm not interested in what you call medical science. I'm only interested in the Literary Club raising enough money so they can get some new books for the public library. That's the extent of my interest."

Alarmed at Edgar's mounting agitation, Layne took him soothingly by the arm and, with a look at the crowd now filling the auditorium, asked, "Gentlemen, don't you think it's time we started?"

To the delight of the spectators, Cayce stretched out on a couch placed on the stage. Layne, with the jury of medical men standing just behind him, proceeded to put Edgar into trance. Soon his subject's eyes were closed, and he was breathing slowly and rhythmically, his chest rising and falling evenly.

The doctors looked on suspiciously. To narrow the possibilities of collusion, the physicians, establishing the ground rules, had decided not to release the name and address of the subject until Cayce was thoroughly

33

under. "In the interest of science," said Dr. Benson loftily, "we want to make sure there is no chance of anybody filling him in with clues before the event."

Layne had smilingly assented.

Now, with Cayce clearly unconscious, Layne turned to the doctors and asked them to pick out a subject at random. "Any of your patients will do," he said. "It doesn't matter who."

After looking inquiringly at the other doctors, Benson gave Layne the name and address of a student ill in a college dormitory nearby.

"Do you want any other information?" he whispered.

Al Layne, shaking his head, repeated the name and address aloud. "Tell what is wrong with this body, giving its condition." There had been no request for a remedy or cure, only the nature of the illness, and considering the public exposure, Layne thought this just as well.

As the audience leaned forward for each word, Cayce was silent for a few seconds, and then, to the vast relief of the Squire squirming in a front row, said in a clear voice, "Yes, we have the body here. This is a young man, with a normally healthy constitution. He has been seriously ill, but is presently recovering from typhoid fever."

Every eye in the auditorium looked to Dr. Benson for his reaction.

Dr. Benson blinked. "Ask about his condition," he said faintly.

Layne repeated the question.

"There is still some fever, particularly in the evenings," said Cayce, "and considerable weakness, but the body is strong and will soon be on its feet."

Layne turned inquiringly to Benson.

"Ask the temperature and the pulse rate."

Layne hesitated, questioning the fairness of so specific a request, for something so variable, but then plunged ahead with a shrug.

Cayce paused but a moment. "The body's pulse

beat at present is 96, the temperature 101.4 degrees."

The doctors regarded each other wonderingly, as a number of spectators whistled incredulously.

The Squire, sitting next to his daughters, allowed his eyes to travel around the room, beaming his pride at every familiar face.

But the doctors were not yet through with their ordeal of fire.

Sanders had been following the proceedings with an amused smile. He now consulted in an undertone with the doctors, and as a consequence it was decided to dispatch a committee of three to check the patient's pulse and temperature.

As the attending physician, Benson necessarily headed the delegation, the two others having been selected at random from the crowd.

As Cayce slept on, Sanders stepped forward to announce, "Since the dormitory is but two or three miles away, the committee should return in fifteen minutes with the desired information."

The doctors turned back to the slumbering figure. Two or three got to wrangling over Cayce's state of consciousness, disagreeing whether it was a hypnotic trance or a dream state, or whether he was faking completely.

Huddled in conference before the couch, they effectively screened the prostrate Cayce from the throng. As Layne looked on horrified, one of the doctors drew a long surgical needle from a black leather bag and deliberately thrust the needle into the sleeping man's arm. There was no visible reaction. He then stuck the needle into Cayce's hands. Still there was no response. "Well, he ought to feel this." The doctor scowled, sticking the needle sharply into the soles of Cayce's stockinged feet. There was not the slightest response.

Still not satisfied, one of the doctors ran a penknife under the nail of Cayce's forefinger, raising the nail from the flesh. There was no sign of blood or of pain. Cayce still breathed rhythmically, his head to one side,

35

his chest motion indicating the regularity of his respiration.

With Layne still vainly protesting, another of the doctors produced a long hatpin, such as the ladies of Hopkinsville featured in their Sunday finery. Layne leaned over to grab the fearsome instrument, but Sanders adroitly interposed his body as his colleague forcibly thrust a hatpin though Cayce's cheeks. Still he made no response.

"He's a tough customer," said the doctor callously.

By this time, the Squire, though back a distance from the platform, was beginning to sense that something unscheduled was going on. He got up quickly and climbed the few steps to the platform in time to see the doctor yank out the hatpin.

Furiously he seized the doctor by the shoulder and twisted him around. "How dare you touch my son!" said he, fighting back an impulse to strike out forcefully.

With a scornful glance for the doctors, the Squire asked Layne to end the session by suggesting that Cayce come out of his sleep, feeling refreshed and not remembering anything he had just said or done.

Cayce was suddenly roused from his slumber. He started to sit up, and immediately sensed the excruciating pain in his arms, hands and face. He turned angrily on the doctors, who began to fumble apologetically for excuses.

"It was all for science," said the doctor with the hatpin.

"Science be damned," cried the young Cayce. "You claim to be scientists, but at best you're technicians. You have no desire for knowledge, only the desire to limit the universe to your own limitations. You will never accept anything that interferes with your own smugness and conceit. I am through with doctors, and I will never give another reading unless that person needs help and believes in me."

He quickly put on his shoes, tie and jacket, jumped down from the dais, and started to stalk out of the auditorium.

His father tried to restrain him. "Edgar, aren't you going to wait till the doctors come back from the dormitory?"

Cayce, not remembering, of course, had no inkling of what his father was talking about. "I don't know who they are or what they're after," he fairly shouted, "but I don't care if they never get back."

He swung up the aisle and had almost reached the door when a familiar figure he had no reason to be fond of sprang up from a back row and said with a grin, "Well, Cayce, I guess those doctors were really needling you."

As some of those nearby laughed, Cayce recognized Wesley Ketchum, and scowled darkly. "You're no better than the rest," he said curtly.

"Whew," said Ketchum, "he's madder than a hornet."

Cayce had retired to his bedroom long before the Squire arrived home with the four girls. The girls trooped off quietly to bed, and the Squire, seeing no light in Edgar's room, went off to sleep as well.

Edgar Cayce was up early and at the breakfast table when his father came in with a big smile and sat down next to him.

The Squire looked up at his wife, who was loading the table with food. "You should have seen Edgar last night, he was sure something." He threw an arm around his son's slim shoulders. "You should have waited, Edgar. That committee of three that went to the dormitory to check you out came back just ten minutes after you left. And do you know what?" His voice held a note of great portent.

Edgar regarded his father glumly. "I don't care what, I just want to be left alone."

Carrie Cayce's pretty face showed her concern. "What happened to Edgar?" she asked, turning to her husband almost accusingly.

"Why," said he enthusiastically, patting little Mary on the head as she sat down, "why, Old Man just picked out this boy he had never seen as having typhoid fever, and then got his temperature and pulse rate right on the nose—101.4 degrees and 96 pulse beats. You should have seen the excitement in that crowd."

Mary, listening avidly, now put in innocently, "Daddy, what did all those people around us mean by saying that Edgar had done some sort of trick? I didn't see Edgar do anything like that."

Edgar got up abruptly. "I'm just fed up with it all."

They made no effort to stop him as he vigorously marched off to open the bookstore.

That day, while waiting on people and dusting off the bookshelves, Edgar Cayce came to a determination. He had seen a Bible on a table and he opened it, looking for guidance. "I say unto you, love your enemies, bless them that curse you, do good to them that hate you, and pray for them which despitefully use you and persecute you."

He put the Bible down with a grimace.

All right, God, he said to himself, I'll do as you say, but I'm going to do it my way. I'm going to teach the young people to be better Christians, not just pious churchgoers, and I'm going to do it right in church, where it should be done. I have no interest in scientists. What do they know of the human heart and soul, these cynical unbelievers who can see no farther than their noses?

His lips must have been moving in correspondence with his thoughts, for Harry Hopper looked at him with a surprised grin. "Give 'em hell, Edgar, like they say you did last night. I missed it, but I understand you put on a helluva show."

Cayce groaned inwardly. "If it's of any interest to you, it's my last performance. Like Sarah Bernhardt, I'm giving up show business."

Hopper's grin broadened. "The divine Sarah seems to keep coming right back."

Cayce left the shop earlier than usual that afternoon and walked the few blocks to the Christian Church, an offshoot of the Presbyterian Church, where his family worshiped. He had been toying for months with an idea, and though he would never have the

38

education for the ministry, he could preach in his own way, without a pulpit. He had no patience for ritualistic differences, which seemed to divide Christians from one another just as drastically, and irretrievably, as Christians were divided from other faiths.

The gulfs between Christians particularly didn't make any sense, for hadn't Christ said that all men were brothers, and they should love one another, irrespective of race, religion, class or quality? "Be ye therefore perfect, even as your Father which is in heaven is perfect."

The Reverend Mr. Smothers was not expecting anybody. He looked up in surprise. He knew the Cayce family as he knew others in his congregation, by their appearance before him in their best clothes, one day a week, on Sunday.

On his way over, Edgar had carefully framed in his head the manner in which he would present his proposal. Now, as they exchanged glances, he completely forgot what he had planned to say.

"What, Edgar," said the minister, "can I do for you?"

That which was uppermost in the back of his mind came out unexpectedly. "Do you mind my not having any education?"

The reverend's eyebrows raised inquiringly. "Why should I mind?" he said gently. "Jesus was a carpenter, and the apostles were simple fishermen. I am sure that was all for a reason."

Edgar took heart as he peered closely into the eyes of the kindly, middle-aged man he seemed to be seeing for the first time.

"And what was the reason?"

The minister rested his narrow face, with its thoughtful eyes, on a column formed by his hands. He seemed to recognize intuitively that he did not have to tailor what he wanted to say. The earnest young man would comprehend.

"The narrow intellectuality of the day had rejected the God of Abraham, who had demanded sacrifice, courage and faith of his people, and cynically replaced him with a God of materiality and riches. The apostles, in their simplicity, were not of this materialistic world, and so quickly understood a message which dwelt on the spirit, and the brotherhood of man, while condemning the hedonism that made a mockery of God's worship."

Edgar was entranced, wondering why the minister had never spoken like this from the pulpit. "You remind me of an evangelist, the way you spoke then, the way your eyes lighted up."

The minister gave him a wan smile, and uttered with a sigh the word of a disgusted Jehovah:

" 'Mine are a stiff-necked and stubborn people.' "

Cayce nodded. "I just can't imagine the rich people of this town giving up their wealth like Jesus said: 'Go thy way, sell whatsoever thou hast, and give to the poor, and thou shalt have treasure in heaven.' "

The minister brightened up considerably, apparently recognizing in the young man before him a strangely kindred spirit. "Jesus," he explained, "didn't want everybody to give everything away they had worked so hard for. As you know, he pointed out that the workman was worthy of his hire."

Edgar had been raised a rigid fundamentalist, to accept everything in the Bible literally as laid out. "What was he trying to do then?"

"He was trying to make man realize that money and its pursuit were not the end-all, and the emphasis should be on heavenly qualities."

"In other words there is nothing wrong with making money in itself?"

"Not as long as you don't do it at the expense of your fellow man and your own soul." The minister was obviously relishing what was an unusual discussion for him. " 'And the disciples were astonished at his words,' " the reverend intoned softly. " 'But Jesus answereth again, and saith unto them, 'Children, how hard is it for them that *trust* in riches to enter into the Kingdom of God.' " He accented the word *trust* as he quoted from the Gospel. "That means not to rely heavily on their riches, and make it a dominant consideration."

He looked up at Edgar with a flustered smile. "I've been so busy sermonizing that I haven't learned what I can do for you."

"Even if you can't help me," said Edgar gratefully, "it was worthwhile coming here today."

The reverend crossed his tweed-clad legs and looked inquiringly at his visitor.

No matter how he tried to school himself, the young Cayce blurted out anything of importance that he felt especially strongly about. "I want to be a Sunday School Teacher, and teach the young people, and anybody else who might be interested. I want to tell them all about the Bible, about David and Goliath, Joshua and Jericho, Manoah, Jonah and the whale, and most of all about Jesus, and what a wise and wonderful man he was."

The minister nodded thoughtfully. "I think you could do very well. You seem to know the Bible, and you have the desire to help."

"I want to teach here, in this church."

"I don't know why not," the minister said slowly. "I think you would attract people with your enthusiasm."

"You don't think it presumptuous on my part?"

"Quite the contrary. I find you very modest and humble." He sighed. "You might attract some I have not been able to reach. The young often heed only the young."

"Thank you, Reverend." Cayce's voice rang with grateful sincerity. "And when could I start?"

"This Sunday, if you like. In the evening, when we normally have vesper services."

He warmly shook Cayce's hand.

"I would call that a deal, and think we should pray on it together."

A frown ruffled the younger man's brow. "Would you say that all men were the same to Christ, whatever their place in life?"

The minister's face revealed his wonderment. "But

of course. If Christ didn't stand for the brotherhood of man, then he stood for nothing."

Cayce drew what encouragement he needed from this. "Then you think, as I do, that all men are the same before God?"

"But of course." The reverend's perplexity deepened.

Cayce let out a deep breath. "I am glad of that, Reverend, because I would like to open my classes to all people."

"Of course," the minister repeated.

Edgar looked at the older man closely, noting the traces of life's cruel disappointments etched in the delicate filigree about the eyes and mouth.

"I am glad to hear you say that, Reverend, because"—he drew a long breath—"I cannot teach the Lord's word unless it is truly received by all men as God intended and Christ preached."

Comprehension suddenly dawned on the minister as he not only put together what Cayce had been saying, but connected it with the nervous, almost defiant attitude he had found equally baffling. "What are you trying to say, Edgar?" he asked quietly.

Edgar spelled it out. "All people would be welcome, rich and poor, young and old, the sick and the well, and"—he paused—"the black and the white."

The Reverend Smothers studied him silently for a minute or so. He was a Southerner himself, of an old Virginia family, bred in the aristocratic tradition of the Randolphs and the Carters, the Lees and the Jeffersons.

"You know, Edgar," he said at last, "what the custom has been about black and white hereabouts for two hundred years."

"Abraham Lincoln was born in Kentucky."

"And so was Jefferson Davis," said the minister dryly. "But that is beside the point."

"And what is the point?"

"That the people would not stand for it. I would have to give up the church or it would give me up.

The Negroes do have their own churches. God isn't denied them."

Edgar was carried away with his cause. "Then what we have been saying about the brotherhood of man is meaningless?"

The minister's face had a look of gentle sorrow. "No, Edgar, it only means that twentieth-century man is not yet ready in every area for Christ's word."

"Can he pick and choose when and where he is ready?"

"Man isn't perfect. He only strives for perfection." The minister's voice had lost its resonant timber; he seemed tired.

Edgar Cayce gave him a challenging look. "But can't we, thinking as we do, carry that word forward as we know it?"

The minister eyed his visitor speculatively, then got up and paced thoughtfully around the small rectory. When he sat down, a gleam had come into his eyes, a look almost of amusement. In his exuberance, he clapped a hand on his visitor's knee. "You know, Edgar, if you can go along with me, we may be able to work it out."

Cayce looked at him inquiringly, not knowing what to say. "I'll do whatever I can to help."

"I have an idea." The minister now seemed to be enjoying himself thoroughly. "In our church, we have a choir loft, but no choir, right?"

Cayce nodded at what seemed self-evident.

"So we announce a new Sunday School class, with you as the teacher, and we introduce a new choir, a black choir, to sing the old hymns and spirituals as a background to your class."

Edgar looked at him doubtfully. "They won't really be in the class."

"Oh, yes, they will, they will hear every word you say. We'll put benches in for them."

"But why can't they just come there and sit like the rest?"

"Because that's all you would then have in your class. This is the year 1903, in Confederate country,

Edgar. Give it another fifty or a hundred years, and they may be ready. But right now, let's be thankful for any kind of a start."

Edgar stubbornly adhered to his scriptural orientation. "Well, if they can sit upstairs, why not downstairs as well?"

The minister shook his head. "They wouldn't even be allowed upstairs if they weren't there presumably working in your behalf."

"You mean like house servants."

"Exactly." The minister pressed his hand. "Do it, Edgar, go along with me, and we will open an important door for the Lord in the hearts of man."

Cayce considered the other man reflectively, recognizing at length the depth of commitment it took to evolve even this proposal. "It's a compromise," he said tenaciously. "Would the Lord approve compromising his word?"

The older man gave him a benign glance. "Edgar, there is no human achievement without some compromise. Don't you remember when they tried to trap Christ about his allegiances and he replied, 'Render therefore unto Caesar the things which are Caesar's, and unto God the things that are God's'?"

Edgar suddenly realized that a new dimension of Christianity, stultified by custom and tradition, had opened for this man of the cloth, and he was reaching out for support. Edgar's mind was made up. "I'll be happy to teach in your church," he said, "particularly with such a choir to back me up."

They smiled knowingly at each other, and clenched hands in a firm and understanding grasp.

To herald the unprecedented step, there was no blowing of trumpets about integration or amalgamation. Both Cayce and the minister, being Southerners, knew of the special affection Southerners of a certain class had for what they termed their colored folk. Unlike Northern abolitionists and liberals, who called for emancipation and equality while keeping their black friends at a healthy distance, the Southerners of the day had no objection to rubbing elbows with the black

44

race, once the lines of demarcation were clearly established. The choir loft, in this case, was the line.

There was only one announcement, and the minister made it that Sunday from his pulpit. "We are honored to announce that Sunday School classes for all will be inaugurated next Sunday, and will take the place of the usual vesper services. Edgar Cayce, a youthful and dedicated Christian who is a member of our own congregation, will teach the class." He paused to allow a slight stir in the congregation. "For years, you have wanted a choir to help solemnize our services, but we have not had enough young voices to make this possible. Now the Lord has heard our prayers, and the Sunday classes will have a choir. Edgar Cayce has persuaded many of our colored friends to add their voices to the Lord's. They will occupy the choir loft"—he pointed upstairs to the back of the church—"which has been so long without song."

A murmur of uncertainty ran through the congregation. There were a few horrified glances.

The pastor held up a hand for silence. "Our colored friends," he said dryly, "will enter by a separate door that will take them directly to the loft, and they will leave by the same door."

And so in Edgar's church was born the doctrine of separate but equal prayers, acceptable by him only as a step in the right direction.

That next week, Edgar was busy sending word through friends in colored town for a strong turnout. He had run into Boze as that versatile gentleman was coming out of Ketchum's office and promptly enlisted his support. Boze's head had bobbed rapidly in gleeful assent. "Why, Mr. Cayce, I'll have all my folk there, and the choir from the Methodee church. They're powerful singers." He gave the psychic a respectful but quizzical look. "You sure changin' things 'round here, Mr. Edgar."

"Tell the people it is all right," said Edgar earnestly, "the Lord will welcome them."

Boze's white teeth flashed. "But how about congregation? Has the Lord done tol' 'em?"

45

Cayce smiled. "They got the message, Boze, they got the message."

Edgar's inaugural class was a gala occasion in the Cayce family. As he had for the demonstration in hypnosis, the Squire jauntily collected his four daughters and brought them en masse to the session. This time, Edgar's mother also joined the group. "My boy," she said proudly, "will have something special that we can well listen to."

The Squire was a trifle nervous. "I hope Edgar doesn't get into his visions and those little people of his."

His wife gave him a confident smile. "Don't worry about the boy, he knows which side of God he's on."

Edgar had meditated long what he should talk about. He knew that many who were not regular churchgoers would be there, the Hopper brothers, Ethel Duke, who taught school and was a friend of sister Annie, Al Layne, and, of course Boze and his delegation. Boze had promised also a violin, to supply the music for the choir. "I'm not bad, Mr. Cayce, not bad at all."

As he had before, looking for help, Cayce opened the Bible at random. His finger fell on the tenth chapter of St. John. He read it and smiled. God had given him the inspiration for his first lesson.

As he sat near the altar, with the Reverend Smothers next to him, lending moral support, his eyes ran over the throng. They filled every pew and the loft above. He could even make out Boze, hanging over the rail with his violin so that Edgar would know that everything was ready. He could see his father and mother in the front row, with his sisters, and the Hopper brothers, looking at him curiously; behind them Al Layne and his wife, and his friend Jefferson Pope; and as his eyes traveled farther back, he saw Ethel Duke, who he somehow felt was to play an unnamed role in his life; and, back of her several rows, the now familiar face of a man who seemed fated somehow to follow after Edgar Cayce—the Yankee doctor, Wesley Ketchum. He supposed that Boze had told his employer about the class, and he had nothing better to do. He didn't recognize the young lady Ketchum was with, but she was pert and attractive and seemed to go well with him. His glance roamed back to the loft, and ran over the faces of the colored people who had come to church this day with their white coreligionists.

He saw Boze smiling expectantly, waiting for the prearranged signal. Cayce's arm rose. The congregation hardly knew what to expect, but suddenly all eyes were turned to the loft, for with a muted violin background, hardly discernible, there came the haunting refrain of the old slave hymn, "Swing Low, Sweet Chariot." Cayce listened with the others, moved as they were by a song reflecting the enduring faith of a Job-like people:

> "Swing low, sweet chariot, coming for to carry
> me home,
> Swing low, sweet chariot, coming for to carry
> me home.
> I looked over Jordan, and what did I see, coming
> for to carry me home?
> A band of angels coming after me, coming for to
> carry me home."

The voices rose in unison, striking a chord in every heart.

> "If you get there before I do, coming for to carry
> me home."
> Tell all my friends I'm coming too, coming for
> to carry me home.
> The brightest day that I ever saw, coming for to
> carry me home.
> When Jesus washed my sins away, coming for to
> carry me home.
> I'm sometimes up and sometimes down, coming
> for to carry me home.

But still my soul feels heavenly bound, coming
for to carry me home."

As the voices slowly faded and died, Edgar felt
a lump in his throat and, looking around the church,
saw many dabbing suspiciously at their eyes.

Edgar approached the altar. From thinking again of
the lady of the visions his thoughts moved to the
Gospel of St. John and the Greater One of whom he
wrote. The crowd, looking at this curiously intent young
man, was hushed. There was not even a rustle of
clothing, nor the sound of a cleared throat or a
cough.

Edgar began evenly, without any sign of the stammer
that sometimes marked his speech.

"Some two thousand years ago," he said, "a man
was born of God to show that we were all of that self-
same God. He was the first universal man, just as
David, who slew Goliath, and rose from a humble
estate to become a powerful king, was the first Western
man in the Bible. He was a simple man, with little
or no schooling. He worked with his hands as a
carpenter. He had few friends and many enemies, but
he persevered in his mission, having undying faith in
God the Father, even as he died on the Cross."

The words just seemed to flow out of him, far beyond what he had read in St. John earlier that day.

"Yes," he found himself saying, "Christ is in all
of us, and that is why he is Christ reborn. If what he
had to say two thousand years ago ended that day
on the Cross at Golgotha, there would be no reason
for any of us to be here in this church today. But
because his message lives in us, and is needed today
as never before, Christ lives in us."

His eyes wandered over the crowd, seeing every
face minutely, black and white alike. "Jesus said it
all, far more eloquently than anyone else ever could.
And John, most beloved of his disciples, wrote it down
so that we can talk about it, and see how it applies
to everything we do, even to this auspicious meeting

48

taking place here today. Our Savior said so wisely, so sweetly, so prophetically:

"I am the good shepherd, and know my sheep, and am known of mine.

"As the Father knoweth me, even so know I the Father: and I lay down my life for the sheep."

Cayce's eyes moved upward, finding his mother with tears of joy in her eyes, and traveling to the choir loft once again, as though his message was especially for them. His voice rose, quavering the least bit, before it boomed out:

" ' And other sheep I have, which are not of this fold: them also I must bring, and they shall hear my voice; and there shall be one fold, and one shepherd.' " In the loft, heads bobbed as if in understanding assent. There were low, barely audible murmurs of Amen and Hallelujah. Cayce could see Boze's shining face.

His eyes seemed to take in everyone individually, including the minister who had been raptly watching him.

"I want you all to go home and think of what Jesus said then, and how we can make it work in our lives." He held out his hand to the Reverend Smothers. "And I want the good reverend to stand up and be recognized before you and his God for what he did here today, knowing the love and foresight that went into his decision. For he stands here today, in the place of Christ, not only the shepherd of his own flock, but of every sheep that will hearken to his word."

Again he clasped the hand of the man who had made the day possible. "Thank you," he said fervidly.

The pastor turned to his flock. "That's the best sermon I ever heard in this church. Now, may God bless you all and help you to remember always the undying words of our Master:

" 'Love one another.' "

The session was not quite over.

Cayce again held up an arm, and fifty voices rose

49

in a hymn, born of the division between the States, but which now had a similar inspirational meaning for all who believed in freedom. The voices, in an ever rising crescendo, carried into the street outside the church, moving all who heard.

> "Mine eyes have seen the glory of the coming of the Lord.
> He is trampling out the vintage where the grapes of wrath are stored.
> He hath loosed the fateful lightning of his terrible, swift sword.
> His truth is marching on.
>
> He has sounded forth the trumpet that shall never call retreat.
> He is sifting out the hearts of men before his judgment seat.
> O, be swift, my soul, to answer him; be jubilant, my feet.
> Our God is marching on.
>
> In the beauty of the lilies, Christ was born across the sea,
> With a glory in his bosom that transfigures you and me.
> As he died to make men holy, let us die to make men free,
> While God is marching on."

No sooner had the last tender note of the "Battle Hymn" faded away than the Squire rushed over to his son, who was busily accepting congratulations, and began pumping his hand. "Old Man," he said, "you're some kind of genius. Before you're through, you'll be pastor of this church."

3

Love's Sweet Dream

In his teens, Edgar Cayce had a dream which was to shape his whole life. The dream was so vivid, and yet so baffling, that he confided it to his mother, just as he had his vision. As he recalled the dream, he was walking through a grove of small, cone-shaped trees. There were white starflowers covering the ground. A girl walked arm and arm with him. Her face was veiled; he could not make out her features or expression, but there was an unmistakable impression of love and understanding between them. Arms interlaced, they crossed a stream together and encountered a naked, winged masculine figure, who carried a cloth of gold.

"Clasp your right hands," the figure told them.

Over the joined hands he laid the cloth of gold.

"United you may accomplish anything," he said.

As he disappeared, they walked on and came to a muddy crossing. They were hesitating, wondering how to cross without soiling their clothes, when the figure reappeared.

"Use the gold cloth," he commanded.

They waved the cloth and were immediately transferred to the other side. Next, they came to a steep cliff. With the knife he found at his feet, Edgar cut steps into the side of the cliff and drew his mysterious companion up after him. Higher and higher they climbed, but the summit eluded them and was still out of sight when the dream ended.

Cayce's mother, Carrie Major Cayce, was psychic without ever having discussed within the family the strong impressions constantly flowing through her.

She was in the kitchen kneading some dough when Edgar told her about his dream.

"Can you tell me what it means, Mother?"

She laughed. "That's easy. It's about the girl you will marry one day. She is your destiny mate, a soul mate you have known before and will know again."

Not knowing of reincarnation at this time, Cayce wasn't sure what she was talking about. But without explaining, his mother hurried on with her interpretation. "This girl is veiled because you haven't met her yet. But she is waiting for you somewhere. Already your souls, reaching out subconsciously for one another, are in love and happy together. When you meet, as you will, you will immediately recognize each other. Your souls are destined to be together always."

Unable to relate to any of the girls he knew of his own age, Cayce found it hard to believe that somebody perfect was in store for him.

"Will I meet her soon?" he asked.

His mother sensed how lonesome her son was, and his need for somebody special to ease this loneliness. "I only know what the dream tells me." She smiled encouragingly. "It will be well worth waiting for."

"Is that all in the dream?"

"Yes," she said. "You cross the water together—that is the proposal or engagement. The cloth of gold is the marriage bond, and your faithfulness to that bond will see you through every difficulty. The cliff represents an uphill struggle. It is your way, step by step, of providing for your family, and for finding your own niche in life. The end, the summit, is not in sight, because there is no limit to what you can do, once the preparation—the steps—are properly laid out. You can climb them as far as you will."

For the next few years, Edgar had tried to imagine

this girl. He would lie awake nights, staring into the dark, trying to frame her into the picture of his mind. Sometimes, she would be tall and blue-eyed, other times dark and petite with velvet brown eyes. She was always gentle, and she always had a comforting smile for him. But as in the dream, he could not quite assemble her features. Everything he saw was fragmentary. Meanwhile, he felt very little urge to date the eligible young ladies of Hoptown and was known as a loner. He didn't participate in sports or frequent the bars that the young men of Hopkinsville patronized. He stuck to himself, reading his Bible, and aspired to read every book in the downtown bookstore where he worked as a salesman.

Having never got beyond the ninth grade, he was sensitive about his lack of education. He had alternately toyed with the idea of being a preacher or a doctor, and then would laugh at himself. How could he give himself these airs when he hadn't even finished high school? He had a knack for taking pictures, an artistic flair for photography, but how would that realize his inner yearning to fulfill the life of service held forth by the lady of the vision?

He was too young then to recognize that the most insignificant-seeming events are often major turning points in the lives of man.

This one morning he wandered down to the creek near his home looking for a wayward cow that he milked as a daily chore for his mother. On the bank of the creek, he almost stumbled across a man half-reclining on the grass, who had been immersed in a book. The stranger looked up with a smile, and Cayce's attention was instantly caught by the book. It was the Bible.

There was something about the man's penetrating gaze and his smile that made the shy young man suddenly feel at ease. They chatted for a while and then Cayce said, "That is my favorite book. I read it through once every year."

The stranger, a well-dressed, middle-aged man, with a commanding presence, gave the young man an appraising glance. "Have you ever thought of being a minister?" he asked.

Cayce was taken aback. "I don't have the education," he sputtered, "but I have had some unusual experiences!" He hesitated, suddenly self-conscious. He felt himself reacting strongly to this stranger, wishing to tell him things that he had not been able to discuss freely before. He was impressed by the way the man spoke of Christ, almost caressing his name.

"Are you a man of God?" he asked.

"I am the evangelist, Dwight L. Moody, and I am speaking at the tabernacle in town."

Cayce comtemplated him thoughtfully for a moment, wondering whether the evangelist had any answers to any of the things that had been troubling him for so long. And so he asked, "Do you believe in visions?"

Moody gave him a sharp glance and patted the Bible at his side. "This is not a fairy tale. It speaks of visions. One came to Paul, who was Saul, on the road to Damascus, and this prosecuting agent of the Jewish Sanhedrin became the most fervid convert to Christ. God tells Aaron, 'If there be a prophet among you, I the Lord will make myself known unto him in a vision.' "

Cayce was electrified by the other's ardor; it seemed as if a magnetic current were passing between them, giving Moody's each word and gesture a special urgency.

"Have you ever had any visions?" Cayce then asked.

A smile crossed the great evangelist's face, almost as if he had been expecting the question. "I think this may have some meaning for you. One day I was in Cleveland. The crowds were great, the reception tremendous, I had never had greater response. And a voice said to me, 'Close the meeting and go to London.'

"The voice was too insistent to be denied. My representatives argued, but I felt I had no choice. And they were particularly exasperated since I could give no reason for my decision to close the meeting.

"I went to London, not knowing a soul there, and wandered the streets, hoping to discover some reason for my being there. Without knowing why, my steps took me to the slums. The houses were dreary and shabby, but one day my eye was caught by a window box radiant with geraniums. I stopped to admire them, and then floating out of the window, I heard a child's sweet, pure voice singing 'Sweet Hour of Prayer.'

"I entered the tenement, walked down a narrow hallway and through an open door into one of the flats. A little lame girl was sitting by the flower box, singing,

" 'May I join you?' I asked."

The little girl stopped singing and a light came into her eyes. It was the light of recognition. "You are Mr. Moody, the great evangelist," she said, "and you have come in answer to my prayers. I knew God would hear. Ever since I saw your picture in our newspaper, I have been praying for you to come to London."

Moody realized then with a strong inner conviction that God had guided him to this small child for a reason. "I got down on my knees and prayed for that little girl—and thanked the good Lord for directing me there. That was the beginning of my meetings in London."

Cayce listened spellbound, but with the old misgivings. "But how can I even teach Sunday School when the congregation knows so much more than I?"

The evangelist tapped the Bible lightly. "Christ didn't pick his apostles from among the intellectuals, but from among simple fishermen. The pedants, the professors, the so-called scientists would have had nothing to do with him."

Moody smiled. "If you are meant to do great things, and I think you are, he will show you the way." He opened his Bible at random and read: " 'That if two of you shall agree on earth as touching any thing that they shall ask, it shall be done for them of my Father which is in Heaven. For where two or three are gathered together in my name, there am I in the midst of them.' "

His smile brought a glow to the young man's heart.

"You see," said Moody, "all you need is somebody agreeing that you can help them, and the good Lord will do the rest."

Thrilled beyond words at this message, Cayce was encouraged to inquire about that deep, insatiable yearning which filled so much of his daily thoughts.

"Is it wrong of me to feel that I need a companion before I can do anything with my life?"

Again the evangelist smiled. "Of course not, and it will happen as God wants it to happen, when you least expect it. Just have faith. It shall be as Ruth once said, 'Wither thou goest, I will go; and where thou lodgest, I will lodge; thy people shall be my people, and thy God my God.' "

Cayce had been sorry to see the man get up to go. It was a meeting he would always remember and treasure. The evangelist had urged he have faith, and the right thing would happen when he was ready for it.

"Go about your life, living each day to the fullest, doing the best with what you have where you are."

He was thinking of this on a day, like any other, as he stood behind the bookstore counter with proprietor Harry Hopper. It had been a slow morning, and the Hopper brothers, Will and Harry, appeared to hold him personally responsible for the lack of business. Weren't they paying him twenty dollars a month, throwing in a new suit of clothes so that he could make a good appearance?

He was peering out the window, as if to coax some of the passing traffic into the store, when he saw a buggy pull up in front of the store with two young ladies. One in a fluffy white dress that trailed almost to the ground daintily alighted and made for the entrance.

Edgar quickly recognized her as Miss Ethel Duke,

a friend of one of his sisters. In deference to this acquaintanceship, Harry Hopper picked up a feather duster and wandered back to the rear of the store where the stationery and miscellaneous school supplies were kept.

Ethel Duke was a personable young lady, barely out of her teens, with a rosy face, dewy blue eyes and upturned nose. She gave Edgar a friendly, outstretched hand and asked warmly, "And how have you been, Edgar?"

"Fine, and what can I do for you?"

She smiled archly. "I don't want to disappoint you, Edgar, but this is hardly a business call."

His face dropped.

"Now, don't take it that hard."

"Not at all, Ethel, I'm happy to see you."

She beckoned him with a finger, her eyes gleaming merrily. "Come outside, Edgar, there is somebody I want you to meet."

As he looked flustered, she sighed in mock dismay. "Now don't worry about Harry Hopper. Your job is safe. I will buy something, I promise."

Edgar's embarrassment deepened. "That's not necessary," he said.

He followed her into the street, to the waiting carriage. Ethel pointed to the pretty girl who had been sitting next to her and who was now regarding them with an inquiring look.

"This is the one and only Edgar Cayce that you have heard so much about," Ethel said humorously. "And this, Edgar, is my cousin, Gertrude Evans."

Edgar looked up and saw a slip of a girl in a frilly white dress, with shimmering brown eyes and a pale oval face like a cameo.

He stood as if transfixed for a moment, too startled to speak.

He had seen her somewhere, he was sure of it, and suddenly it came to him. He had seen her many times, in the daydreams he had spun out of his fantasies. She was the petite beauty with the velvet brown eyes.

57

He looked up to see the two girls eying him closely. There was a look of amusement in Gertrude's eye.

"Has the cat got your tongue, Edgar?" Ethel said.

He reddened to the roots of his hair. "How do you do?" he finally blurted out, as both girls laughed.

He recovered sufficiently to join in the laughter.

"You certainly were miles away," said Ethel, without realizing how many miles.

He was afraid to speak for fear of stammering. He had never before been so conscious of anyone as he was of this slip of a girl lightly holding the reins in her hand. He watched her out of a corner of his eye, while appearing to address himself to Ethel Duke.

His gaze finally returned to the girl whose brown eyes were twinkling at him good-naturedly.

"How do you do?" he again blurted out.

"That's better," said Ethel Duke. "You're coming right along."

Ethel Duke now came to the purpose of her call. "We're having a lawn party at Gertrude's home tonight—the old Salter place on the Hill—and we'd like the honor of your company, Edgar." She smiled roguishly. "Now isn't that formal enough for you?"

Still watching Gertrude covertly, Cayce finally stammered out, "At what time?"

"Eight o'clock," Ethel answered.

He stood on the walk, watching the buggy disappear down the street, then waved, though the vehicle had already rounded a corner and there was nobody to wave back.

In almost a stupor he walked back to the store.

"Where is the Salter place?" he asked Will Hopper.

"About a mile east of town, up on the Hill, just before you get to the looney bin." He smiled at the faraway look in young Cayce's eyes. "Now don't get the two places confused, Edgar. We don't want to lose our star salesman."

That evening he was too excited to sit down to dinner. He was full of questions about Gertrude and her family. His sisters, Annie and Mary, rallied him good-naturedly, but his mother as usual told him what she could.

"Gertrude's grandfather is Sam Salter. He's an architect, and he helped build the Western State Hospital, for the mentally ill, and he had a part in building South Kentucky College. He is a hardworking, Christian gentleman. He built a fine home on ten acres, and Gertrude lives there with her mother and her mother's sisters. Her father died early."

Edgar could have taken the family rig that night, but instead he chose to walk the two miles or so from his own home. It would give him more time to think, and wouldn't throw him so precipitately into a situation he welcomed and yet was apprehensive about. All day, as he waited on people, the dark-eyed oval face had intervened. With nervousness approaching agitation, he proceeded now on foot to the house on the Hill. He had no idea how he would relate to her, even how to begin a conversation. He was fully aware of his own drawbacks as a social creature. He was shy, almost backward, ungainly in movement, with a craggy face that in no way could be considered handsome. What if she paid no attention to him? But—he grasped at straws—why else had he been invited if not to get acquainted with her? But of course that was Ethel Duke's idea, not Gertrude's. She may have been too polite to withdraw the invitation, even after meeting him. His heart was pounding as he strode down Seventh Street toward the Salter place. As he neared the house, his courage almost deserted him. But he remembered what the evangelist had said about having faith. And there was also that compelling familiarity.

The moon shone down, casting the house in a silvery silhouette, and Japanese lanterns bobbed in the night breeze. As he approached, the sound of laughter and conversation almost made him turn on his heel. But the thought of that face drew him on. He came to a gate, took a footpath, and walked under great oak trees and towering maples. He circled the house carefully, following the sound of music. Tables had been set out on the back lawn, and they were heavily laden with lemonade and punch, sandwiches, cakes, cookies and fruit. Ignoring the benches and chairs, thirty-five or forty young people were sprawled comfortably on the grass, sitting on suit jackets or shawls.

Others were dancing on a terrace extending out below the verandah, braving the sultriness of the midsummer evening. Two young men were energetically playing the violin, and a third was strumming a banjo in a spirited rendition of Stephen Foster's "Beautiful Dreamer."

Cayce looked around helplessly.

At this moment Ethel Duke spied him hesitating at the edge of the lawn and took his hand. She brought him over and introduced him to Gertrude's mother, an amiable-looking woman with a faint resemblance to her daughter, and to Gertrude's aunts, Kate, the older, and Carrie, a beautiful girl with limpid brown eyes, only slightly older than her niece. Ethel got him a lemonade and then somehow guided him through the crowd to Gertrude. She was flushed from dancing. She was lovelier even than he had remembered. He couldn't take his eyes off her, and when she looked up, he flushed in embarrassment. She smiled and gave him her hand. She was in a white silk gown that swept to her ankles, and her shoes were white. She was a picture of chaste purity, with the red rose in her hair matching the red of her lips.

They looked deep into each other's eyes, and he had an overwhelming feeling that he had always known her. He had never experienced this overpowering sensation of familiarity before. And he knew, knew in this instant, while marveling that it should be so with somebody so obviously unattainable, that she felt this as well.

He desired to be alone with her, and as if reading his thought, she said, "Shall we walk down to the carriage house?" Her hand reached out for his, and he held it self-consciously. Near the carriage house was a small arbor, or summerhouse, where they could sit and still look out through the open sides at the moon and clearly hear the murmur of the trees.

His fears of not establishing a rapport were soon dissipated. Whereas he was quiet and introspective, she was open and communicative, plying him eagerly with questions. She wanted to know everything there was about him.

Was he always going to work at the bookstore? Did he have any great ambitions? Was there anything special he wanted to be?

He started to say that he would like to be a minister, but was afraid she would laugh at this as a presumption on his part. Instead he related how he had gotten his job at the bookstore by just making himself useful, not mentioning that the suit he had on was the first reward of his labors.

She looked at him quizzically. "People find you a little strange, don't they?"

He sighed. "I suppose so. I never played ball, cards, gossiped about girls, or roughhoused. So I guess that makes me strange."

"You don't have many friends, do you?"

He was tempted to confide about the playmates he had when he was small, but was again dissuaded by the fear she might laugh. He couldn't stand the thought of her thinking him ridiculous. "I guess I'm not very much," he said lamely.

At that, unexpectedly, the fire came into her eyes. She took his hand impulsively. "I don't ever want to hear you saying anything like that again, Edgar Cayce. You're a pretty important person, and the world will know about you one day."

He thought of the dream of the gold cloth, and his walking arm in arm across the creek with a girl, and suddenly her face emerged, and it was the same dark-eyed oval face that was now peering at him so intensely.

"What's wrong, Edgar?" said Gertrude with a worried frown. "You look as if you just saw a ghost."

He drew a hand across his eyes. "The prettiest ghost anybody ever saw," he said without explaining.

As they walked back to the party, arm in arm, he

felt ecstatically convinced that he had met the girl of his dream, the girl who would one day climb that cliff with him.

After that night, Cayce became a regular caller at the Salter home. He liked to anticipate Gertrude's wants and bring her small gifts, a book usually—*The Winning of Barbara Worth,* which he thought suggestive, or some novel by E. P. Roe, her favorite author. His psychic gift manifested itself in the romance. Like any suitor, he could visualize from a distance every lineament of his beloved's face. But he could also close his eyes, as he stood behind the bookshop counter or supped at night, and could actually see Gertrude flipping through a book he had given her. Other times, he could sense her pulse beat and read her thoughts, feeling incredibly that she loved him as he loved her. It was at times a disconcerting experience, to travel into the heart of somebody he loved, and he felt like a Peeping Tom. But his conscious mind still couldn't always accept what his subconscious told him.

Although the Salters thought Cayce odd, as the rest of the town did, they came to love him for his gentle ways. In turn, he came to consider the Salter place a second home. He quietly enjoyed the idiosyncrasies of Gertrude's two aunts, who carried their personal rocking chairs from room to room of the big house as they moved about. He liked the feeling of the massive oak cabinets, tables, and sideboards scattered about the family rooms, and he loved to sit in the big kitchen with the family, and cozy up to the pot-bellied stove that spread its heat unevenly through that part of the house. The stove had a history, which Edgar had shared as a spectator one night. Grandmother Salter, a strict Methodist, constantly lectured on the evils of cards, dice and liquor. Because of his abstinence, the young suitor was a favorite of hers, and she frequently extolled him as a model of Christianity, much to his embarrassment. One night, Grandmother Salter found a deck of playing cards in Uncle Will Salter's pocket and called the family together in the big kitchen for a sermon on the score of gambling.

As Edgar tried to escape with Gertrude, she summoned him imperiously back into the room. "You, too, Edgar," she called. "The devil is always after unsuspecting converts."

As she finished her discourse on the wickedness of gambling, she opened the door of the red-hot stove and with a flourish tossed the cards onto the flaming coals.

Edgar was quietly enjoying the performance when the cards, being largely celluloid, exploded on contact with the flames and with a loud report blew off the door of the stove, flinging it across the room.

Mrs. Salter gave a satisfied smile. "You see," said she, "the devil just gave his last gasp."

Sam Salter believed in complete democracy in his home. Whenever a controversial subject came up at the dinner table, he insisted that each person present, to the smallest child, have a right to express his opinion.

The family cheerfully accepted Edgar as one of them. He would listen to them argue about the weather, the menu, politics, the sermon at the Methodist Church, patterns for dresses, happy that they included him in their discussions, even though he merely sat and listened most of the time.

Once the discussion centered on God.

"Do you believe in God?" Gertrude's younger brothers, Hugh and Lynn, asked Edgar one night.

"Of course he does," Grandma Salter replied.

"We want to hear it from Edgar," the children chorused.

Edgar looked up and down the table, and he saw Gertrude's eyes softly trained on him, encouraging him to express himself for once.

He spoke without conscious thought, the words slipping off his tongue. "God is a universal force, he is in everything fine we think or do, and we are part of him as children of his universe. We belong to him, and he is ours, a fortress in time of trial, a garden of roses in our joy and jubilation."

Gertrude's eyes were moist. "Why, Edgar," she said, "that's beautiful."

The small fry were not so impressed.

Young Lynn had a sly smile. "But, Edgar, the Bible says that man is cast in God's image."

Edgar Cayce's gray-blue eyes regarded him solemnly. "And that is true. But like so much of the Bible its meaning is symbolical. God is perfection, and man as he nears this perfection approaches a Godlike image. The closer he is to perfection with Christ, the closer to God, and to God's image." With an unaccustomed glow, he quietly quoted from his favorite book! "Be ye therefore perfect, even as your father which is in heaven is perfect."

There was a silence for several moments; then Sam Salter said with a brief bow from his chair at the head of the table, "Thank you, Edgar. We have had a lesson from you tonight, not only philosophically, but in humility." He looked sternly at his two grandchildren. "A lesson some of us would do well to adopt."

At this time, Gertrude had no clear idea of the idiosyncrasies of Edgar's mind. The young Cayce himself was not fully aware, either, of his susceptibility to hypnotic impressions, nor had he learned to guard his almost somnambulistic subconscious from the most casual suggestion. He had stayed at Gertrude's a little later than usual one evening, talking, as even brief partings were becoming increasingly difficult. After he nodded off drowsily in a corner of the big sofa, Gertrude had to let him nap for a few minutes before the long trudge home.

"Go to sleep, Edgar, and rest a while," she said.

Edgar's head fell back limply, and he half-sprawled on the couch. Gently she elevated his feet from the floor to the couch, wanting him to rest comfortably, and with a look of endearment at the slumbering figure went up to her room.

When she came down to breakfast in the morning,

her brothers were giggling, and her mother gave her a disgusted look.

"What did you do to Edgar? He's still stretched out on that sofa, sleeping."

Gertrude's eyes widened. "Edgar sleeping—here? Why, he only lay down for a nap. Why haven't you awakened him?"

This brought a new burst of giggling from her brothers, Hugh and Lynn.

"Lord knows, they tried," said her mother, "but he just wouldn't wake."

Gertrude, with her brothers trailing after her, marched into the living room.

There was Edgar, his mouth slightly open, his breath softly rhythmical, still sprawled out as she had left him.

She shook him by the shoulder, gently at first, then more vigorously. He made no response, no noise, no word, no movement. Her brothers seemed to be richly enjoying the spectacle.

"It's no use," they said, laughing behind cupped hands. "Edgar's really out of this world."

She turned on them sharply. "It's no laughing matter."

She hurried into the kitchen to express her concern.

Her mother threw up her arms. "I don't know what's to be done with the boy."

"We'll have to call Dr. Janson. There must be something wrong."

The boys had followed after their sister. "It could be sleeping sickness," they said helpfully.

Dr. Janson, duly called, arrived within the hour with his little black bag. He surveyed the supine figure with a dispassionate eye and asked, "How long has he been like this?"

"For twelve hours anyway," Elizabeth Salter said.

Gertrude's brow was ruffled with worry. "Is it anything serious, Doctor?"

"Now let's not get excited," said the doctor soothingly. "The boy just probably needed the rest."

65

He took Edgar's pulse, rolled back his eyelids, opened his mouth with a tongue depressor. Then he pronounced his verdict. "There doesn't seem to be a thing wrong with him," he said.

"Nothing wrong?" exclaimed Mrs. Salter. "Nobody sleeps like that."

The doctor left, mystified. "If he doesn't wake by nightfall, give me a call."

As she stared at the doctor's receding back, Mrs. Salter's face reflected her bewilderment. "We had better notify his parents," she said. "They'll want to take him home."

Gertrude's soft brown eyes melted. "Mother, why can't we take him to the spare room? He shouldn't be carted around when he's like that."

Mrs. Salter bowed to the appeal in her daughter's eyes. "All right," she said.

With the boys helping, they half-walked, half-carried the sleeping figure to the guest room just off the living room.

Within a few minutes of being notified, the Squire came racing over. He scratched his head as his eyes traveled over the recumbent form. "That boy beats all," he said.

"Can't you do anything?" said Gertrude imploringly.

"I can shake him," said the Squire.

"We tried that," said Gertrude impatiently. She gave the Squire a curious look. "You don't seem at all worried."

"Oh, no," said the father, with a tinge of pride, "something strange is always happening to Old Man. He'll come to when it's time."

"Can't you do anything?" she repeated.

The Squire knit his brows. "I could get Al Layne here—he's the hypnotist—but he's out of town. But don't worry, he'll wake up. He always has."

Edgar slept through that day and night, and the next day. He was still sleeping, breathing evenly and strongly, by the time the Salter family was getting ready to sit down for dinner. He had been unconscious now for nearly forty-eight hours.

Gertrude's brothers refused to take his sleeping state seriously. "Edgar just wants to become one of the family," they said with mischievous glances at Gertrude.

She flushed and got up from the table. "I don't think that's nice at all, when poor Edgar is dead to the world, suffering from heaven knows what."

"Now, now," her mother put in consolingly, "the doctor didn't seem upset when he was here today."

Tears brimmed in Gertrude's eyes. She ran out of the room and into the bedroom where Edgar was lightly snoring.

In mingled frustration and anxiety, she cried aloud: "Edgar, wake up. Wake up, Edgar."

The sleeping figure, to her great amazement, started to stir. There was a deep sigh, and then, lo and behold, Edgar sat up, dazedly rubbing his eyes.

The first thing he saw was Gertrude's face. "It must be late," he said, "I better be getting home."

"Late, Edgar! Why, you've been sleeping here for two days."

"I can't believe it." He checked his watch. "Why, it's only the dinner hour."

Her relief was so great that she started to laugh through her tears. "Edgar, you've been here so long my family was thinking of adopting you."

She thought for a moment, and a great light dawned. "Edgar, you went off to sleep when I said, 'Go to sleep,' and you woke up when I said, 'Wake up.' I've got to be careful what I say to you."

"Only when I'm drowsy, Gertrude dear."

Edgar's peculiarity, as it was euphemistically known on the Hill, manifested itself in many ways. Despite the consignment of Uncle Will Slater's playing cards to the flames, Gertrude's brothers were inveterate card players, usually holding off until Grandma Salter had safely retired to her room for the night. Hugh and Lynn were constantly importuning Edgar to join them in the popular new game of bridge, which had recently succeeded whist as a parlor pastime. But Edgar had no interest in cards, or any other game that required total concentration.

"Are you too good for cards?" Lynn prodded.

"No, I just find them dull."

Gertrude looked up, annoyed on this occasion. "Why don't you two boys find some other partners, and let Edgar relax?"

The boys continued to tease him. "But they say Edgar can just fall asleep over a book, and remember every word in it. Just think what he could do if he sat on a deck of cards."

Edgar took the jibing in stride. He was used to it. "I just don't think it would be fair, boys."

"Fair?" cried Hugh and Lynn together. "Let us decide that."

Sitting around the big kitchen table, they playfully dealt our four hands, giving Gertrude and Edgar, as well as each other, thirteen cards.

"Now pick up your cards," said Lynn, "and we'll show you how the game goes, Edgar."

The cards were lying face down on the table.

"As I said," Edgar observed casually, "it wouldn't be fair."

"We'll give you a handicap of five hundred points," said Lynn smugly.

"That's not what I was driving at," Edgar said mildly.

"Oh, come on, Edgar, don't be a spoilsport, pick up the cards, and we'll show you how to play. You can't lose anything, we're not playing for money." The boys looked around apprehensively. "Not in this house."

"I don't have to pick them up," Edgar said quietly.

He had long been the good-natured butt of the brothers, and had decided it time to give them a little lesson.

Gertrude thought the baiting had gone far enough. "Edgar, don't pay any attention to them. They're impossible."

"Oh, there's no problem, Gertrude." He turned to the brothers. "You agree that I could not have looked at the cards?"

"Of course, we dealt them out."

He singled out Lynn, the leader. "You pick up the hand you dealt me, all thirteen cards, fan them out, and"—he paused dramatically—"I will tell you, in order, from left to right, what each card is—ace, deuce, king, and so forth."

Lynn's jaw dropped. "I don't believe it."

"Well, pick up the cards." Edgar's voice was challenging now.

As Gertrude and her brother Hugh looked on entranced, Lynn carefully sneaked the cards into his hand, making sure that none was exposed.

"Ready?" said Edgar.

"Ready," said Lynn.

Closing his eyes, Edgar quickly began to read off the cards, stopping after he reached the thirteenth card, a king of hearts.

Lynn's chin had dropped, and he seemed dazed. "You didn't make a mistake," he said, "you called every card in order." He looked at his brother, and his brother looked back. Both had the same idea at the same time.

"Edgar, we'll back you against the greatest bridge players in the world. All you have to do is learn the game."

Edgar smiled good-naturedly. "I'll never play cards with anybody, boys. It wouldn't be fair."

Through being in love, Edgar's sensitivity grew. Extremely aware of his own feelings of desolation at times, his sense of compassion for others mounted accordingly. Loneliness wasn't the only concomitant of man's essential isolation. One could also suffer, he found, by discovering heights of happiness in the distance, then not have the strength to scale these heights and claim the prize.

Everyone, as he began to see it, lived in two worlds, the world of self and that even more mystifying world of friends, acquaintances, strangers and loved ones.

When Gertrude turned away from him a moment, her mind caught by a vagrant thought that did not concern him, he would feel miserably isolated. When she and her brothers laughed together over childhood escapades, he would sit in aching silence, suffering because she was reliving a world that he was not a part of. And yet he was not selfishly possessive. He wanted for her only that which he knew was good for her. He worried about her constantly. Constitutionally, she was not strong, though she didn't like anybody fussing over her. She had dropped out at South Kentucky College because of recurring respiratory ailments, settling in her lungs and bronchial tubes. When the weather turned harsh, she had bouts with the flu and a dry hacking cough. She was not the ideal convalescent. She found it hard to sit still or rest in bed. She loved walking the dogs, riding horseback, taking an airing in the family buggy.

Because of her susceptibility, he felt especially protective, nurturing a growing desire to take care of her. For her part, she drew him out and made him feel he was actually somebody. He wanted to tell her all this, and more, but the proper time never seemed to present itself. She was either in a jocular mood, or there were people around, or his throat tightened up unaccountably just as he was about to communicate.

One evening, finally, the stage seemed ready. He had resolved to delay no longer. If she refused him, it would mean that the dream which had encouraged him was only a mirage, and he might as well face up to reality. After dinner, Edgar and Gertrude had the living room to themselves. They were on the sofa, facing each other, and she was baiting him good-naturedly about getting on in the world. He saw his opportunity.

"Under certain circumstances," said he, "I think I could do very well in business."

She smiled encouragingly. "In what circumstances?"

He took her hand. "You know what circumstances."

"I'm not the psychic, Edgar." There was a tender look in her eye that escaped him in his agitation.

He gulped and plunged ahead. "I have very little to offer, except my love. But I would like that to be yours always."

Her dark eyes stared soberly into his. "You have much to offer, and nobody knows how much better than I."

He looked at her hopefully. "I have no direction without you, Gertrude, no aim, no purpose. You make it matter what I do."

Her eyes were the least bit dewy and she smiled. "I know what you are trying to say, Edgar, and I am honored. I know that I love you, but I don't know whether I have it in me to be the partner you need. I don't know if I have the strength."

He had taken heart in a recent recurrence of the cloth-of-gold dream. The veil had lifted, and he had seen the face clearly. It was Gertrude's.

"If it isn't you, then it will be nobody," said he. "You are the lady of the veil."

She looked up with quickened interest. "What lady?"

He told her of the dream, and its interpretation, and her emergence from behind the veil.

Touched, she placed her hand gently on his arm. "Edgar, what other girl could have a suitor like you? I am sure there would never be a dull moment."

He looked up eagerly. "Then you will?"

Her eyes sparkled mischievously. "Don't you, who know so much, know that?"

"Not about myself, Gertrude, never about myself—not about the two of us. I can't be detached about you."

"Nor I about you." She frowned thoughtfully. "Marriage is God's way of bringing a man and woman together. Two people learn to forget their separate wants, and get to know what they want together. They get over their selfishness, even about each other, through having children and sharing the child in the joys and tribulations of its growth."

She had struck just the right chord, saddened as he was at times by their thoughts diverging along different channels.

"When will you know?" he asked.

"I just need a little time to consider everything."

"If you consider everything"—he laughed rue-fully—"you'll never marry me."

"Oh, Edgar, don't be so self-effacing. You're a very distinguished man."

He smiled for the first time. "If you say so, Gertrude."

"I see so much more in you than you do yourself. There is nobody else in this world like you, Edgar."

"That may be a good thing."

She shook her head in mock exasperation, rising from the sofa with the gesture. "Edgar, you certainly don't oversell yourself."

She took one hand in both of hers. "Come back Sunday night," said she, "and you will have your answer."

For three days he moved about in a daze. The Hopper brothers murmured of lovesick calves behind cupped hands but nevertheless commiserated.

Sunday finally came, and Edgar trudged off toward the Hill as if headed for the gallows. It had started to rain, but the drops felt cold and vitalizing, and he felt at one with nature, even if a little bedraggled. As he halted at the Salter gate, he recalled the first visit months before. He braced his shoulders and held his head high, though his knees were quaking.

Gertrude came to the door. She wore her familiar smile. His watchful eye could see no difference in her attitude. Her first concern was his wet clothing, and she made him get into some dry things of her brothers.

She mopped his face with a large handkerchief. "Edgar," she said, "you'll be the death of me yet."

As if by prearrangement, there was again nobody in the comfortable living room. Edgar fumbled for his pipe, but didn't light it. For a while they sat together silently, gazing at the glowing fireplace and listening to the rain rattle on the roof.

"I'll have a hard time keeping my pipe lit on the way home if this rain keeps up," he said.

She smiled impishly. "Are you thinking of going home presently?"

The young suitor's aplomb suddenly deserted him. He put the pipe away and took her hand, looking deeply into her eyes.

"Gertrude, I have to know."

"But, Edger," said she, "you should know, everybody else does."

He looked at her silently, not knowing what this signified.

Her laughter was like the peal of a bell. "Edgar, I love you, I always have. I always will. I wouldn't have kept you in doubt if I hadn't known what the decision would be. But I had to talk it over with my family, as we discuss everything. But"—her hand pressed his—"now there will only be you and me, and I will be your lady of the veil. We will climb that mountain together."

4

Cayce Helps Out

After his marriage, Edgar finally fulfilled a long-time ambition, opening a photographer's studio at Main and Seventh Streets. It was a second-floor walkup, next door to Hopper Brothers Bookstore, occasioning the facetious comment that he was getting up in the world. While he was short on equipment, Edgar was long on enthusiasm and talent. His subjects were mostly mothers with children, though he photographed an occasional street site, warehouse or barn.

He enjoyed photography because it indulged a certain creative flair and because he liked people, particularly children, with whom he felt wonderfully at ease. His own little friends had disappeared long before, and the void was now filled by the children of Hopkinsville.

Chance, or fate, had led him into photography, just as it seemed to have directed him to clairvoyance. When he was afflicted with aphonia, unable to use his vocal cords, he had turned to the study of photography. It was something he liked that he could do without using his voice. Gertrude had encouraged him to leave the bookstore.

"You should be your own master, Edgar, as you have originality and employers don't always appreciate new ideas unless they think of them themselves."

In Hopkinsville, he was a familiar and well-liked

figure, despite a certain reserve on first meeting people.

Even those who thought him a little strange were indulgent. He was one of them. For Ketchum, whom Cayce thought about without quite knowing why, it was hardly the same thing. It just was not Wesley Harrington Ketchum's town. He was always the last to hear any news, whereas the average physician in a small community knew everything first, from the five new kittens at Mrs. Henry's to the Harrisons' maid eloping with the plumber's helper. Ketchum had the uneasy feeling at times that he was poised on the brink of a canyon. If he fell in, nobody would even know he was gone. He had his father to thank for the expensive equipment that made his clinic the most modern in Hopkinsville, with its new X-ray machine and heat lamps, all unique. But all these advantages were going to waste, along with the special talents the young doctor had brought from the North. He could not very well advertise, as the local doctors would have been only too happy to post him for his breach of medical ethics. He could have spoken before some of the fraternal organizations, but nobody asked him.

His friendship with the pretty schoolteacher, Katy deTuncq, whom he had been squiring about, had ripened, but their relationship had little bearing on his practice. As a resourceful, capable man, it was particularly galling that he had no chance to show his skill. When he did offer his services, as luck would have it, it turned out badly. There had been an outbreak of fever in Shantytown, in the dilapidated black section by the railroad tracks, and he had ridden over with Boze one day to see if he could be of service.

Another doctor had already been there. He had checked over the sick in their miserable tar-paper shacks, with gaping holes in the roofs and floors, written out a few prescriptions and gone his way.

After visiting three homes, Ketchum had been appalled. He didn't dare tell even Boze what he suspected. Instead, he went directly to the health office in Hopkinsville.

The Health Officer, a Southerner like every doctor in Hoptown but Ketchum, looked at him in hostile disbelief. "Sanders was over there, and saw nothing like that."

Ketchum was adamant. "I don't know Sanders, but I do know typhoid fever when I see it, and those people should be quarantined. The drinking water's obviously contaminated, it didn't look very clear to me."

As it turned out, it *was* typhoid, and Ketchum, who had no friends in Hoptown but Dietrich, had now earned himself an enemy—Dr. Sanders, who promptly attacked the younger doctor as a prying busybody from the North and threatened to shoot him on sight.

But there was one favorable consequence of the Sanders attack. It brought Ketchum a certain amount of publicity, which got him known to the very wealthy and prestigious Davises.

The Davises' only son, nineteen-year-old Clifford Junior, was desperately ill. Months before, during a football game, the youth had walked off the field, then fainted. On being revived, he appeared to have regressed to childhood. He could not think or speak intelligibly. His condition had baffled every doctor in town, as well as specialists in Louisville, Nashville, and the Mayo Clinic in Rochester, Minnesota.

Clifford's mother contacted Ketchum only with her husband's grudging consent. As had the other doctors, Ketchum found the boy in perfect shape physically, but mentally deficient. He couldn't comprehend the simplest question. His eyes were dull and glazed, his jaw hung slack, his attention constantly wandered. He was about as responsive as a head of lettuce. And yet he was the best-looking young man in Hopkinsville.

Junior's mother came right to the point with Ketchum. "Can you help? And if you can, will you take the case? Otherwise, please don't waste our time."

Ketchum didn't have the slightest idea what was

wrong with Clifford, but would have been the last to admit it. "You don't mind my being a Yankee?" he temporized.

Mrs. Davis was a pleasant-looking woman with a formidable bosom. "I wouldn't care if you were General Grant, if you could cure my boy. But in all frankness, I think you would have to be a Miracle Man to do it."

As they talked, plans for the boy's treatment were whirling through his head. "I wouldn't take the case, unless I had a free hand," he said boldly.

She gave him a piercing glance. "Doctor, money is no object if you can help my son. But if you're just trying to squeeze money out of us, we'll drive you out of here like we did the Yankees."

Ketchum was about to correct this version of the Civil War when common sense restrained him. He took her measure with his shrewd blue eyes. And he liked what he saw. "You have nothing to lose, madam. I expect no fee unless I cure him, though, of course, there will be expenses and perhaps a consultation or two."

She liked his frankness. "You're a cocky one, aren't you?" she said, with a smile.

Seeing at least surface parallels with the Dietrich case, Ketchum's thoughts had turned to Cayce, and then he groaned, remembering how he had ridiculed the psychic. Nevertheless he still thought of him, skeptically, as only a last resort. He turned first to a former teacher, a famed neurologist in Cleveland, who might take a special interest in making a former pupil look good.

Ketchum left hopefully for Cleveland with Cliff and the Davises' hired hand, Sam, a giant black and son of a slave, long devoted to the Davis family.

In Cleveland, Ketchum was doomed to disappointment. The neurologist could only shake his head sadly. "This is a typical case of dementia praecox—a form of insanity developing usually in late adolescence and characterized by loss of interest in people and things. He can only get worse."

He warned of the patient's growing violence, until he had to be put away. "If I were you, Ketchum, I'd have the attendant sit next to him on the train, and I'd sit behind him, just in case he goes berserk before you get home."

This was a harsh blow for Ketchum. "What can I do?" he implored.

The neurologist saw but one solution. "Only one thing. Recommend that he be put away. It will have to be done sooner or later, before he hurts himself or somebody else."

Secretly dismayed, Ketchum decided to keep the diagnosis to himself for a time. On the train back to Hopkinsville he considered the meager possibilities. He could take his patient to New York or Philadelphia for further consultations, with the verdict in all likelihood the same. Or he could use Cayce. This was his only chance, and a slim one. He debated to himself how to approach the psychic. As an emissary, Dietrich would only tend to stir up unpleasant memories. He rummaged about in his head for a connection and remembered Dr. Thomas House, a mild-mannered little man, from a local medical meeting. He had been one of the few doctors to show Ketchum any friendliness, and, as he understood it, he was related somehow to Cayce.

That night, back in Hopkinsville, he called House on the telephone.

The doctor was not at all encouraging. "I wouldn't touch Cayce with a ten-foot pole," he said emphatically. "Even in the family, some of us consider him a freak. I'm only connected by marriage, you know," he added, as if this somehow absolved him.

Having nowhere else to go, Ketchum was persistent. "Just bring us together, that's all I ask. The responsibility is clearly mine."

"Just stroll over to his studio; he's not hard to meet."

Ketchum quickly recapitulated his last meeting with the Freak. "I need a little help in smoothing things over."

House was a stalwart of conservatism. "Look, Ketchum, you've got two strikes against you down here as a Yankee, and with Cayce it'll be three strikes and the ball game."

Ketchum chuckled into the phone. "It's already the ninth inning, with two outs and two strikes on the batter —me."

"Just be patient, and some of us who don't mind Yankees too much will send you a case or two."

"That's not all of it, Doctor."

House growled into the phone. "I know, you're going to cure all the incurable cases. I've heard about Cayce curing Dietrich's little girl. You just know it was spontaneous remission. Of course, my wife thinks he's great, but she's prejudiced. Edgar recently married her favorite niece, and that," he sighed, "puts him in the family."

The next morning, as was not uncommon, Edgar's father was in the studio when House walked in unannounced with the young doctor.

Before they had time for anything more than courtesies, Cayce came loping out of the darkroom with a dripping negative in his hand. He looked around in surprise, seeing Dr. House, then his gaze stopped at Ketchum.

"Do you want your picture taken?" he asked crisply.

Ketchum held out his hand in conciliation. "I had Dr. House bring me over so I could apologize."

"No apologies are necessary," said Cayce, squinting into the light to better read the negative.

"I was a little rough that time, and I want to make it up to you."

Cayce eyed him suspiciously. "You mean, you're giving me another chance."

The Squire had, with difficulty, held his tongue, but seeing a chance for some form of medical recognition, he now assumed the role of peacemaker. "Dr. Ketchum has a real interest in your work, Edgar. You should be flattered. Just think what it would mean if the medical profession got behind you."

79

Cayce gave his father an indulgent glance. "That will never happen, not in a million years."

Ketchum jumped in eagerly. "It could happen, if there were enough cases to make it statistically revealing."

Edgar took a deep breath. "The doctors aren't interested in the same thing I am. I just want to help sick people, and the doctors want to know how it works, without caring what it does."

Ketchum nodded wisely, adjusting his pince-nez firmly to his nose. "But if you're the real article, why not let the whole world know it?"

Cayce regarded him ruefully. "If I remember correctly, I've already given a demonstration for you."

Ketchum had the grace to look embarrassed. "But what harm would it do to give another demonstration? Repetition at will is the scientific way of proving something."

Edgar sighed. "I want to help all I can, but I can't work against all this skepticism. It gets me down."

"You can't blame me for being skeptical."

"I don't blame you, I just can't work with you."

Ketchum's sensitivity came to the fore. "Because I'm a Yankee?"

Cayce looked at him in some surprise. "I don't see any horns on you, Ketchum. I'm just tired of experiments, and doctors who say they want to be shown, when all they really want is to show how smart they are."

The Squire stepped in diplomatically. "Now, Edgar, these men here, Ketchum and our own Dr. House, are men of learning, and we can learn something from them."

"I don't question that," said Cayce. "I just don't see where learning has much to do with me."

Ketchum still had no understanding of the other man. Thinking that Cayce was inflating his ego at his expense, Ketchum was already beginning to regret his impulse to see him again. But he thought he might as well make use of the time already consumed to show up this country bumpkin. His voice was deliberately unctuous. "Why not give a demonstration that will show more clearly than a dozen explanations what you are capable of doing?"

Cayce shook his head. "You've got me wrong, Doc. I don't have any ego about this. It is a gift of God's and I am only an instrument."

Ketchum whistled to himself. Now, he thought wryly, he's bringing in God, like he owns him. Aloud, he said, "How about giving me another chance? I'm really vitally interested in what you can do for people."

"This is not a game with me," said Cayce. "If you can produce somebody with a need I'll read for them. And the request for a reading must give the name and address of the subject."

Ketchum was agreeable. "I'll be right back with a request. Don't go away."

By this time, Dr. House, nervously checking his watch, had made his escape.

Ketchum walked down the street to the Latham Hotel and returned in a few minutes waving a sheet of paper.

"Is it genuine?" Cayce asked, without troubling to look at it.

Ketchum nodded vehemently. "This person has a real physical problem."

Cayce loosened his clothes, took off his shoes, and stretched out on his black leather couch. Ketchum gave the signal and a young lady with nondescript features appeared with a shorthand pad. The Squire proceeded to put Cayce in trance, then with some surprise read off the name and address on Ketchum's paper. He asked the sleeping psychic for a disgnosis and cure.

When Cayce came to, Ketchum was standing triumphantly in the middle of the room, his thumbs in his vest, teetering back and forth on his heels, and grinning broadly from ear to ear. "That reading would fool anybody but me, Edgar," he said sardonically. "If you tie up with me, we'll make a ton of money touring the sticks, taking in the gullible."

Cayce looked up from lacing his shoes. "What are you trying to say?"

"That man you were reading for was me."

Cayce's face expressed its disgust. "Don't look like that," said Ketchum, "I have a need. I've been examined by six of the best doctors in Ohio, and I'm going to be operated on next week for appendicitis."

"And what did I say?" Cayce turned to his father.

"You mentioned appendicitis." His father appeared uncomfortable in the face of Ketchum's confidence.

"Yes, he mentioned it," Ketchum interposed, "but he said I only think I have it. Well, I have it, believe me."

Edgar looked puzzled. "What did I say was wrong?"

"You said I had stumbled over a box, and hurt my back. And that a good osteopath could fix me up." He was smiling jubilantly. "That's a hot one, appendicitis from a fall."

Edgar's annoyance was beginning to show. "Well, if I was wrong, what are you so happy about?"

Ketchum's eyes were popping in excitement. "Can't you see? You're just one of a kind. You're a mentalist. You pick up things in people's minds. Now you got appendicitis somehow, but you dismissed it because you didn't know how to properly relate it to me."

Edgar gave his visitor a sour look. "How do you know that?" he asked abruptly. "I'm beginning to think that you're the fake."

"Now there, there, Old Man," put in the Squire diplomatically. "The doctor didn't mean anything by it. He's just trying to make sure he's on the right track."

Now that he was sure he had solved the riddle of Edgar Cayce, there was no containing Ketchum. He turned to the stenographer, who was seated at Cayce's typewriter. "Type out your notes, while I try to convince this fellow that he can make a fortune just going around the country reading minds. We can make a million, Cayce, traveling the country from theater to theater. I can bill you as the Amazing Edgar."

Cayce snapped on his tie angrily. "I don't care what you think, I know I'm right. You only think you've got appendicitis." He had never before expressed himself so forcibly about his own prowess. "I'm sick and tired of these readings," he said with a scowl, and stomped out of the room.

Ketchum eagerly took the typed pages from the stenographer. "Don't worry about your son," he told the Squire, "I know how to handle him. He's a cool one, that boy. But I've got his number. Can you imagine saying somebody should hold my feet while the osteopath fixed my back?"

Before the uneasy Squire could comment, Ketchum rushed out the door and down the street to the office of Dr. James E. Oldham, the osteopath specifically recommended in the reading. It took him only minutes to get there.

The gray-haired Oldham looked up from his desk to see a young man brush past his secretary and stand before him, hand outstretched in a genial gesture.

"I'm Ketchum," said he, "the new doctor in town. The local doctors don't like me any more than they do osteopaths, so I guess we got something in common." Conveniently forgotten was his own classification of all osteopaths as quacks.

Oldham's blue eyes twinkled behind his steel-rimmed glasses. If he was surprised that an M.D. should call on him professionally, he didn't show it.

"No Yankee comes calling on a Rebel without something more substantial in mind than friendship," he said pleasantly.

"Doctor, I thought you might look me over. I've been feeling poorly." He held his hand to his stomach. "I've got the miseries."

Oldham led him into a treatment room. "Just get naked to the waist, climb on that table, and we'll soon find out."

As he disrobed, Ketchum asked casually, "Ever heard of a fellow named Cayce?"

Oldham laughed. "There's scores of them in

Christian County. You can't sneeze without blowing on a Cayce."

"Edgar Cayce is this boy's name."

"Oh, sure, everybody knows him."

"Strange, isn't he?"

"Some say so."

"Does he know anything about medicine?"

Oldham cocked a jaundiced eye at his visitor. "Whatever he knows, he picked up from being treated when his voice gave way. The boy has a photographic memory."

Ketchum was now on his back, and the doctor was peering over his spectacles at him.

"You see this paper, Doctor." Ketchum held up his notes. "Well, that faker, Edgar Cayce, gave me what he calls a reading today, and his diagnosis differed from that of a half-dozen reputable men of medicine. He's a mind reader, that's all he is."

"The boy has a smattering of medicine," Oldham said, pressing his hands exploratorily over Ketchum's ribs. "But he shouldn't be telling people what's wrong with them."

"That's what I think, and that's why I'm here. Examine me, and tell me what you find. I won't say a thing to influence you."

He turned on his stomach, and Oldham examined his spine, checking the configuration of the vertebrae from the neck to the lower spine.

"You've had a pain on your right side, haven't you?"

"That's right."

"And you have thought that you had appendicitis."

Ketchum instinctively stiffened. "My God, that's practically what Cayce said."

Oldham's hands focused on two vertebrae in the lower spine. "There's been an injury here, probably from a fall, and it's caused pressure on the right side. This is commonly mistaken for appendicitis. That's probably how Cayce made his mistake."

84

"But he didn't make a mistake, if you're right. He said the same thing you did."

"It must have been an accident," said Oldham glumly. "The boy doesn't really know very much."

He called his wife from an adjacent room. "She'll hold your feet while I twist your spine back in line."

Ketchum almost bolted up in amazement as the treatment suddenly took the turn Cayce had suggested. Maybe the boy did have something salable. He grunted as the osteopath gave his lower back a quick wrench.

"Two dollars," said Oldham as Ketchum got to his feet.

"I guess you never heard of professional courtesy," Ketchum said sharply.

"Not for Yankee," said Oldham. "They pay."

It was well worth it. For the first time in months, the painful ache in Ketchum's right side was gone.

That evening, he sent Boze to the Squire's house and asked that he please call on him with his son as soon as possible. He wanted to make amends. The Squire, with his exaggerated respect for doctors, was overjoyed. But he had a difficult time convincing Edgar, finally invoking the Bible to win him over to a final reconciliation.

"If Christ could turn the other cheek after what they did to him," said the Squire, "you certainly should be able to overlook the little thing Ketchum did, particularly when he wants to make it up to you."

Edgar shrugged unhappily. "That's what he was supposedly doing before. I don't like doctors, they're know-it-alls."

"This fellow is different," said the Squire with unconscious humor, "he's smart."

The Squire knew how to get around his son. But when Edgar strode into Ketchum's office, a step behind his father, his face was a noncommittal mask.

Ketchum ushered him into a chair with flattering courtesy. "I don't blame you for being mad, the way I have doubted you," he said contritely. "But I have to admit now that you know more than those six Ohio doctors rolled into one. And you know more than Oldham. He doesn't realize the gift you have, that's how little he knows."

Leslie Cayce looked up brightly. "You see, Edgar, there are doctors who will acknowledge that you're not a fake."

His son said sharply, "I'm not so sure they're not fakes. If they could convince me of that, maybe I'd join them."

"This afternoon," Ketchum said, "I was half-ribbing you about touring in a sideshow. I'm being serious now, Edgar, when I tell you that working together we can help a lot of people and make a mint doing it."

Cayce picked up his black fedora. "I'm not interested in making a lot of money."

"And why not, Edgar?" his father put in.

Edgar considered for a moment mentioning the exalting vision of the lady, then thought better of it. "Somebody important wants me to help people who need help whether they have money or not."

"And who is that?" Ketchum said patiently.

"Somebody you wouldn't care about."

Ketchum restrained a quick retort, saying placatingly, "I wish you would think it over. We could help a lot of people who might not otherwise receive help. We could come to a regular agreement. I'd do something extra for you, too, like getting a lot of new camera equipment for your studio."

Cayce looked at him suspiciously. "Where would you get the money for something like that?"

"I have ways of raising it, provided I have an arrangement with you."

"I don't like the idea of taking pay for helping people."

"Think about it," Ketchum said. "What good is a gift if nobody profits by it—other people, as well?" he added hastily, as Edgar gave him a cold glance.

"If you have somebody that needs help, I'll try to help them. I don't need any pay or presents for that type of reading."

"You may think differently when you have a family on the way," Ketchum said. "See what your wife thinks about it."

Even without this suggestion, Cayce would have discussed Ketchum's rather vague proposition with Gertrude. She surprised him with her practical approach. "It would be nice, Edgar, so long as you didn't tarnish your gift, to have something laid by for a family."

He was puzzled by her unaccustomed prudence. "But that's quite a ways off yet, Gertrude."

She blushed to the roots of her hair. "Is it, Edgar?"

He suddenly stopped wiping the dishes she had just finished washing. "Do you mean. . . ?"

"Yes, Edgar, that's exactly what I mean."

His arms reached out and drew her to him closely.

"Anything you say, Gertrude," he said emotionally. "Now, Edgar, don't go selling your soul to Wesley Ketchum for me."

"Just my ability. And as Ketchum said, it may help people who can't otherwise be helped."

At this time, neither Gertrude nor Edgar had any clear idea as to how a psychic should be properly rewarded for his services and still preserve his integrity. It was all too new. There were no rules except those of common sense, dictated by experience and Cayce's own subjective impressions.

"As long as you didn't get into commercial projects," said Gertrude, "you would remain spiritually motivated and not risk the chance of losing your gift. For since the power apparently comes through the subconscious mind, the conscious mind would tend to get in the way of a clear channel."

Edgar Cayce had no idea his wife had given this much thought to his clairvoyant powers. "What makes you say that the conscious mind would be a disturbing factor?"

"The desire for gain is one of the most conscious motivations there is. Just look around you, and you will clearly see that."

"Then how can I charge people for readings on their health problems?"

"You're not doing it for money, you're doing it to help them, and the payment is only incidental. You have the right to earn a living, when you are doing good, just as a minister does. And you don't need Ketchum to do it."

Edgar Cayce devoted many soul-searching hours to this problem of how best to handle his gift. "I just can't see myself charging people to make them well. Can you imagine Christ and the disciples taking money for healing the sick and maimed who came to them? Not that I'm comparing myself to them, but their lives should certainly stand as a guide."

Gertrude knew that her husband was reaching out for counsel in his dilemma; otherwise she would not have continued the discussion. "Jesus and the disciples," she said with a smile, "did not have wives and families to support."

He did not break his concentration by returning her smile. "It seems to me," he said with a ruffled brow, "that if a person wanted to make money with this gift, it would be preferable to use it commercially, on the stock market, or the races, or even looking for buried treasure, something impersonal like that, where you weren't hurting anybody else, or taking money from anybody directly."

"But you don't know that for sure, Edgar. So you might wind up hurting yourself." She considered for a moment how she could make her point in terms that he would readily relate to. "Christ," she said finally, "was against commercial projects."

He looked at her curiously. "How do you figure that?"

"Didn't he drive the money-changers out of the temple?"

"But that was on sacred ground," he protested.

She gave him a tender look. "And don't you think that the lady of the vision made your mind and soul sacred ground that day she came to you?"

He smiled as he realized how she had backed him

off into a corner. "You really have given me something to think about."

"You would have come to it by yourself, and it's still a decision that you alone can make. It's your gift, and you alone will have to pay for misusing it. So make up your own mind, Edgar, dear, in your own time."

The decision to throw in with Ketchum wasn't easy, and Cayce needed time to work out certain safeguards in his own head. Ketchum, faced with an immediate problem, could do little more than wait. He had discussed none of this with the Davises, merely saying he was resolved to try his own treatment. Pressed for particulars, he took refuge in professional vagueness. Cayce was still his only hope.

After a week passed without word from Cayce, Ketchum decided to call on him one day. Their offices were but a block apart on Seventh Street and the visit was impromptu. As usual, Cayce was busy with his picture-taking, being very patient as a bratty nine-year-old subject kept looking out a window to her mother's dismay.

Cayce waved cheerfully to his visitor. "I'll be right with you. Sit down somewhere."

Cayce crouched over the tripod camera. "Look at my hand," he commanded. The child turned, without thinking, facing the camera.

He pressed a bulb and the shutter clicked.

The picture was finally taken, and the mother gave her daughter an approving smile.

"How much will that be, Edgar?"

"Five dollars, Mrs. Quackenbush, if you have it handy. Otherwise, you can drop it off sometime."

Mrs. Quackenbush poked through her purse. "Would two dollars do for now, Edgar?"

He nodded amiably. "Of course, Mrs. Quackenbush."

Gertrude had walked into the studio, and was frowning unhappily. She appeared not to notice Ketchum. "Edgar, we just can't handle the grocer the way your customers handle you."

He kissed her lips closed. "Why, I've known Mrs. Quackenbush all my life."

"And she knows you."

Gertrude, noticing Ketchum's amusement, quickly cut off the discussion.

Edgar turned to the doctor. "And what can I do for you?" he asked, drawing up a chair for his visitor. "I haven't quite made up my mind about the other matter."

Ketchum had his approach worked out. "I'm not rushing you, it's just that I have a very special case of a boy who's in real trouble. The doctors haven't been able to do a thing for him."

The word *trouble* had a way of perking up Cayce. "Tell us about it," he said with a glance that took in Gertrude, "without any details, as I wouldn't want to be influenced by conscious information."

Very briefly, Ketchum described the case, and gave the Davis boy's name and address. "If you don't help him, he may spend the rest of his days in a padded cell."

Listening silently, Gertrude said with a shudder, "You're going to have to help that boy, Edgar."

Cayce gave Ketchum a shrewd glance. "You're really working on me, Doc; first my father, and now my wife."

"Will you read for the boy?"

Cayce took off his hard white collar, and stretched out on the couch. "I need a rest anyway," he said with a grin.

Gertrude stood over him, and was about to put him in trance, when she noticed his eyes were already closed and he appeared to be sleeping.

Ketchum looked chagrined. "Does that mean you can't put him under now?"

"He is under—all he has to do at times is close his eyes."

In a casual voice she proceeded: "You have before you the body of Clifford Davis, Jr., of Hopkinsville, Kentucky—North Main Street. Now go over this body, and tell us what you find."

As usual, Cayce repeated the suggestion in an undertone, beginning with the name and address, then, word for word, reiterated the request for information.

"Yes, we have the body here." He paused. "A very sad case. It happened all at once, from a blow, delivered quite unintentionally, during a football game, and not noticed at the time in the excitement of the contest."

Ketchum sat on the edge of his chair, his eyes glued on the slumbering Cayce.

"I see the color red, blazing red, angry red. His brain is on fire. The convolutions or folds in his brain are red as fire. His mind is distorted, so that it cannot deal with anything reasonably. In time the distortions will become so great, unless something is done soon, that he may well do violence to himself and others."

"Can he be helped," Ketchum said, "or is it already too late?"

Gertrude relayed the question.

"It is not too late, but the treatment is drastic, and must be pushed, however hopeless it seems."

"And what is this treatment?"

"Specific treatment, put to the limit."

"Anything else?"

"That's enough."

Ketchum looked helplessly at Gertrude. "What's specific treatment?"

"I'll ask him."

Cayce mentioned the administration internally of a little-known but potent solution. "Equally important is giving the right dosage daily, stepping up the dose as the body becomes used to the treatment. Start with ten drops and bring it gradually and specifically to thirty-five drops a day, then to sixty drops if necessary."

"It sounds homeopathic to me," said Ketchum.

Gertrude looked interested. "Is that a type of medicine?"

"Oh, yes, the remedies are administered in minute doses, increased with time. This kind of treatment

91

will induce in a healthy person the very symptoms you find in the ailing patient."

"In other words, fighting fire with fire."

Ketchum gave Gertrude a surprised look. "In a sense, yes. The medicine Edgar proposes would simulate dementia praecox in the ordinary person, but as the drug wears off, the symptoms will disappear."

Gertrude now suggested that Cayce regain consciousness. "The vitality of the waking body will be restored, and the body, perfectly normal and balanced, will wake up and resume its usual function and awareness, not remembering anything that was said."

Cayce sat up and began rubbing his eyes. "Was I any good?" he asked.

Ketchum shot him a quizzical glance. "I still say you're either the most interesting man in Kentucky or the worst fraud."

Cayce gave him a gloomy look. "I don't care whether you believe in me or not—as long as I help somebody."

"What do you know about the brain and its convolutions?" asked Ketchum.

"Convolutions?" said Cayce. "What's that?"

"Did you ever hear of the cerebrum or the medulla oblongata?"

Ketchum laughed until his sides shook. "Wouldn't it be something if you were putting us on?"

Gertrude found herself bridling indignantly. "There's something about you, Doctor, that makes me remember what the good Lord said about patience being a virtue."

Ketchum stopped laughing. "Don't take me seriously, Mrs. Cayce, I'm all for your husband."

On leaving the studio, Ketchum went directly to the downtown drugstore with the prescription that Cayce had recommended.

The druggist, a tall, spare man, with steel-rimmed glasses, gave the new doctor a curious look. "That's an old wives' remedy for the loonies," he said. "Where did a young doctor like you ever come across something like that?"

"What do you mean by the loonies?" Ketchum asked.

The pharmacist looked at him in surprise. "Somebody who is nutty, cracked, insane. And this potion is calculated to soothe the beast in man."

"When was the last time you made it up?"

He threw up his hands. "Never said I did. My old granny used to go out in the fields, gather up the wild plants, and crush the juice out, and give a steady dose of it to my gramp every spring when he got the crazies."

The light dawned on Ketchum. "So that's where the boy got it from."

"What boy?" said the druggist.

"Just a figure of speech. Will it take long to put it together?"

"Just a few minutes. It's an elixir, very concentrated. The main ingredient is from a plant that used to grow wild around these parts." He gave Ketchum a searching glance. "I just don't understand how you got hold of it."

He disappeared into a back room to return shortly with a dark solution in a four-ounce bottle, with a dropper attachment. "If the patient's not completely balmy, this will do it."

He frowned. "Who's it for, Doc? I need a patient's name on the prescription."

"Put my name on it," said Ketchum. "I think I'm getting the loonies."

Back in his office, he telephoned the Davises.

Clifford Davis, Sr., answered, then summoned his wife to the phone. "It's that damn Yankee," he said, with his hand over the mouthpiece. "I don't know why you're bothering with him."

Regina Davis gave her husband a baleful look. "We've run out of doctors from your daddy's regiment of Kentucky volunteeers, that's why.

"Yes?" she said flatly into the phone.

"Can Sam bring the boy in tomorrow after nine?"

Mrs. Davis' voice was noticeably cool. "Another consultation, with another specialist?"

"No, I'm handling it myself. Let Sam bring him in."

"What do you intend to do? So far, you haven't accomplished any more than anybody else. Just more time and money."

"I'll need the boy in here three times a day for a while, morning, noon, and evening. That's all I can tell you."

"All right, but every doctor in Christian County tells me I'm mad to have anything to do with you."

"And what have they done for you?"

"Nothing, and that's why I'm sticking with you for a time."

Boze was already in the office, tidying up the treatment room, when Sam arrived with Clifford the following morning.

Sam was in overalls and a pair of old scuffed shoes, his big toe sticking out prominently. "Mrs. Davis done told me I should stay with her boy, and watch what all you do with him, Dr. Ketchum."

Ketchum nodded at Boze, who was slouching in the doorway. "Boze is helping me, and you'll be helping him."

"What does Boze know about a sick man?" said Sam scornfully.

"We need perfect quiet, and Boze is going to stay out here in the reception room, and make sure nobody interrupts, while I work in the clinic with the boy."

Even as a young doctor, Ketchum had quickly learned that the average layman is favorably impressed by the complexity of treatment. And there was obviously nothing impressive in administering drops to a patient. He stressed the importance of Sam's assignment. "I just can't have any disturbance. When the telephone rings it must be answered right off."

Sam pointed in disbelief to the telephone instrument, with its bright brass receiver. "I got to talk to that machine?"

"When it rings," said Ketchum.

Young Cliff made no effort to follow the conversation. He sat listlessly in a chair, looking vacantly out a window. As the doctor motioned him into the inner room, he regarded him mutely, without any sign of understanding.

"Take him by the arm, Sam," Ketchum ordered, "and sit him down on the stool in the clinic."

After Sam had performed his mission and returned to the anteroom, Ketchum sat down opposite the uncomprehending young man and measured off ten drops into a half-glass of water.

"Drink that, boy, it'll put hair on your chest."

The youth defiantly shook his head, muttering darkly.

Ketchum resorted to strategy. He acted as if he were about to quaff the mixture down, then smacked his lips in mock enjoyment.

At this, Clifford impulsively lunged out, wrested the glass from the doctor's hand, and gulped the contents down in one swallow with a smile of sly satisfaction.

Ketchum patted the boy's head approvingly. "If there's anything to that Cayce," he said, "you're going to make me a very happy man, Cliff."

That was only the beginning. Twice more that day, Sam returned with the heir to the Davis fortune. As directed by Cayce, Ketchum increased the dosage to eleven drops, then still another drop, to twelve in all, in the evening. Each time he went through the charade of taking the mixture for himself, and each time with a lunge the boy grabbed the glass and gulped down the solution.

With no improvement evidenced, the dosage was gradually increased until the patient received twenty drops at the start of the day and forty drops at the finish, in the evening.

Worried now, Ketchum brought another bottle of the elixir, and by the second week the dosage had been increased to sixty drops. There were still no results, good or bad.

With no prospects of relief in sight, whatever faith

Ketchum had in Cayce was rapidly dwindling, but he still had nowhere else to turn. Hoping for some explanation, he looked up Cayce again.

Cayce shrugged his shoulders, and regarded him imperturbably. He found it hard to empathize with this doctor who was so different from himself—brash while he was reserved, pompous as he was humble, sophisticated while he was artless. Two more unlikely men could hardly have got together.

"I have never made any claims," Cayce repeated stolidly. "And I can't help it if it doesn't work, since I don't know why it works."

"Just give him another reading to find out why the treatment isn't helping him," Ketchum pleaded. "You wouldn't let that poor boy down, would you, Edgar?"

Gertrude had walked into the studio, and now viewed Ketchum with her usual mistrust. "Are you sure, Dr. Ketchum, that it is the boy you are concerned about?"

The doctor gave her a piercing look. "Exactly what do you mean by that?"

"To be at his best, Edgar needs to be properly motivated."

Ketchum held her gaze evenly. "It seems to me there's plenty of motivation in this case."

"Too much, perhaps," she said.

By now, Edgar was also regarding his wife curiously. "I don't understand, either."

"I think Dr. Ketchum does."

Ketchum bristled the least bit. "Dr. Ketchum doesn't," he said emphatically.

"Have you examined your own motivation?"

"Sure, I want to help the boy, first, last, and foremost."

"I suppose you do," she said grudgingly, "but you are also looking to help yourself—and that may be the difficulty."

Ketchum did not agree. "Everybody's looking to help himself, that doesn't affect this situation. It seems to me that Edgar's motivation is the main thing."

Cayce had been following the discussion with in-

terest. "You know, Gertrude," he interposed mildly, "Jesus never asked whether the sick were worthy or not. He just helped whoever came to him."

As usual, Ketchum had brought out the worst in Gertrude. "Yes, and look what happened to Jesus," she said tartly.

Cayce reached out with both hands and took her hand. "Yes," he said softly, "he died for our sins, and our salvation. Let us remember that."

With a muffled gasp, she turned and ran out of the room.

Cayce followed her flight with a sigh. "Sometimes, Ketchum, things become confused and it's hard to know what is best. But I feel it is better to believe the best of people and be deceived, than to go around not trusting anybody."

In a few moments Gertrude came back into the room as if nothing had happened.

"I am going to give a check reading for young Cliff Davis," Cayce told her. "Will you help me?"

Gertrude had regained her composure. She sat relaxed by the couch as Cayce loosened his clothes and stretched out luxuriously.

"It's one way," he joked, "of getting a few winks during the day."

Gertrude passed her hand lightly over his brow and gave him a look of infinite tenderness. "You will go to sleep," she said, "and your inner consciousness will delve into the body of young Clifford Davis, who is presently at his home on North Main Street in the town of Hopkinsville."

Cayce locked his hands across his stomach and looked at the ceiling. His gaze grew dreamy and a glaze covered his eyes, signaling the beginning of the trance.

As his lids closed, he began to murmur inaudibly; then his voice became resonant. "We have the body," he said with authority.

"Go over the body," said Gertrude, "check out the disturbance, and tell us why the treatment as given

has not had the desired results, as indicated in the first reading."

Ketchum edged forward to the couch as Cayce cleared his throat.

"The treatment, as given, is correct," he said after a pause. "But the body's system is such that it is not as recepive as some and more has to be given. Have confidence, and continue the treatment."

Ketchum whispered, "Ask how long it will take."

"How much longer must the drops be given before the body recovers?"

Cayce shook his head. "As long as necessary."

Ketchum groaned. "That's just where we were before."

Edgar's chest was rising and falling rhythmically, in harmony with his breathing.

Gertrude began to take him out of it. "The patient has disappeared," she said. "You will not see him. Not remembering a word you have said here, you will wake up, fresh, invigorated, ready to resume your normal work in the studio."

Cayce yawned, opened his eyes, then jumped off the couch, bursting with energy. "Well"—his glance went from his wife to Ketchum—"did it amount to anything?"

Ketchum shrugged his shoulders. "You said to keep doing what we were doing."

"Then do it," Cayce said.

Back in his office, Ketchum sat disconsolately behind his desk and reviewed not only the Davis case, but his whole situation as well. He was certainly not setting the world on fire, he told himself grimly, and perhaps it would be wise to pull up stakes and move on to greener pastures. It was a smart man who knew when to cut his losses, and that was all he had. He looked at the calendar on his desk. There were ten days remaining in the month. That was it.

Later that day, he got Mrs. Davis on the telephone. "If I don't help your son in a week, I'll be leaving Hopkinsville."

"You may as well," she said unsympathetically.

"Nobody will want a Yankee doctor no better than one of our own."

And so the routine of the ascending and descending drops was resumed. Cliff would gulp down the solution, then stare vacantly into space, occasionally laughing aloud for no apparent reason.

"He's as crazy as a loon," Ketchum told Boze, and Boze would flash his white teeth in a knowing smile.

"Ev'rybody knows that."

Looking at Clifford's childlike face, contrasting so incongruously with the powerful body, Ketchum was ready to agree. All his frustration was suddenly directed against the man who had failed him. He said wearily to nobody in particular, "I was right about that freak Cayce in the first place. He's a pious fraud."

Boze rolled his eyes, as if at some sacrilege. "Don't talk like that, Dr. Wesley. The good Lord may turn you to salt where you stand."

Ketchum eyed Boze in some surprise. "And what do you know about that freak?"

Boze shook his head vigorously. "He's got the secon' sight. Once, they say a black man kill this white man, an' Mr. Cayce closed his eyes, an' told how it wasn't a black man at all. He told how these two white men argued, and how one picked up a shovel an' smashed the other. Then one sees the black man comin' along an' put the blame on him. Mr. Cayce saw it all just like it was happening."

Ketchum was still skeptical. "All right, but he's not helping the boy."

"He will, he will. That man can do anything."

A week later, Ketchum gave young Cliff his last treatment. The boy was as oblivious as ever.

"Take him home, Boze, he won't be back. The week is up"—he consulted a train schedule—"and so am I." He slumped wearily into his chair.

"Up where, Dr. Wesley?"

Ketchum clapped his handyman on the shoulder. "Up the creek, Boze. And that's way up."

He took his childlike patient's hand and shook it.

"Well, Clifford, you can't say we didn't try. You defied science, and the supernatural. But, bless you, a man never had a more patient patient than you."

Clifford's face creased in an India rubber smile. He tried to speak, but only gibberish came out.

Ketchum turned to Boze. "Tell Mrs. Davis the Yankee won't be bothering her any more."

Boze gave him a sympathetic look. "I still got my money on Mr. Cayce."

"Well, don't put any of mine on it," said Ketchum, "or I won't have the fare back to Ohio."

That night Ketchum was too tired even to go home. He stretched out on his office couch, pulled a blanket over himself, and fell off into a troubled sleep.

A few hours later he was rudely interrupted. The sun was barely blinking through his office windows when the telephone on his desk began to ring insistently. He fumbled for his watch in the half-dark. It was six o'clock. Who could be calling at this ungodly hour? "Yes?" he growled into the receiver.

The voice on the other end was bright and cheery. "Good morning, Miracle Man."

He came to with a start. The happy voice was that of Mrs. Clifford Davis.

Not fully awakened, Ketchum was still trying to collect his thoughts, as he asked, "What happened?"

There was a catch in the mother's voice, and then a pause.

"This morning," she said in a wavering tone, "my son came down to the kitchen, and just as if nothing had ever been wrong, he stood in the doorway and said with his old smile, 'Good morning, Mom, what do we have for breakfast?' "

5

The Dalton Matter

The Davis case had been helpful, but not as Ketchum had hoped. There was a tendency on the part of the citizenry to block out uneasily on mental cases and not relate them to the ordinary ailments that beset man. Though some few patients came Ketchum's way, the Davis case was by and large a ninety-day wonder.

"I don't understand you people," the doctor told the psychic. "Here, I accomplished this wonder, the mother herself describes it as a miracle, and only a few hypochondriacs and women with nothing better to do turn up."

Cayce restrained a smile. "It could have been worse, Ketchum. If young Davis hadn't recovered, the family might have sued you for malpractice."

Ketchum had been watching the young photographer putter about his studio. "What do you mean, Cayce?"

"Well, you were giving that boy practically a lethal dose of those drops."

"Hell," said Ketchum, "that was your idea."

Cayce chuckled. "Oh, so *that* was *my* idea."

Ketchum joined in the laughter. "You win, Cayce, you always win."

Cayce shook his head. "There aren't any winners or losers, Ketchum, just players, playing out our string with whatever tools the good Lord sees fit to give us."

Ketchum looked at the other man doubtfully. "You believe what you want. I've got to get back to the office, and drum up some business. It's got to get better, it can't get worse."

"Don't worry, Ketchum, you're going to be rich beyond your fondest dreams."

"Is that what God wants for me?"

"If that's what's needed to keep you here. You are an instrument of the Lord, Ketchum, like it or not."

Cayce was smiling, and Ketchum was not sure how serious he was.

"It may come in a phone call, a letter, a personal call," Cayce went on, "but opportunity will come."

Ketchum was intrigued in spite of himself. "What makes you so sure?"

"Just go about your business, God will do the rest."

Ketchum answered tartly, "I hope God knows my rent is overdue."

Cayce smiled tolerantly. "His eyes mark the fall of even the smallest sparrow."

Ketchum took a look at his watch. "Save that for church, Cayce. I have to run along."

Boze was waiting when Ketchum walked through the door. He triumphantly held up three fingers. "You done got that many patients in there." He motioned to the waiting-room. "There must be some powerful magic goin' for you, Dr. Wesley."

Ketchum nodded at two elderly women and a forlorn-looking man sitting in the hardwood chairs. "I'll be right with you," he said cheerfully, disappearing into his inner office to wash his hands.

As he dried his hands, the telephone rang, and Boze picked it up. Ketchum saw his eyes boggle with excitement. "Come get it, Dr. Wesley. It's Mr. Dalton, the contractor man. He's gotta be the richest man in the whole world."

The voice on the other end of the phone was clear and authoritative. "This is Dalton. The Davises told me about you some time ago. Never thought I'd call a Yankee, but one of my men tumbled into a pit at the brickworks and he's in a dead faint."

"Maybe he hurt himself in the fall," said Ketchum.

"Not a bruise on him."

"He may have been overworking."

"He just started." Dalton's Southern drawl sharpened. "Look, Doc, I thought I was doing you a favor."

"Keep him warm, and as soon as I can, I'll be out."

Ketchum stepped out to the waiting room. "I have an emergency," he said. "Be back in an hour."

One of the ladies bristled. "My rheumatism won't wait for no man."

She flounced out ahead of the doctor, who passed her on the stairs.

"Just sitting in my office seems to have cured you," he said pleasantly.

Her nose went up in the air. "What would you expect of a Yankee?"

Ketchum got into his rig, a black buggy, with a rather sorrowful-looking horse, and drove off with a flourish as if he had a racing champion for a mount.

Five minutes later he drew up to the brickyard. At the edge of one of the pits, a small knot of men were grouped about a prostrate figure. As the doctor briskly stepped forward, they quickly gave ground for him.

Ketchum took a quick look at the man. He noted the pallid countenance, the irregular breathing, the general look of debility, and thought with dismay, He's a goner. He stooped down and felt the man's pulse, drew his stethoscope from his little black bag, and pressed it to the man's chest.

"He's barely alive," he muttered to himself.

He rolled back the eyelids, examined the man's eyes, then unlaced his shoes and rubbed his feet. There was hardly any circulation. The man was in a coma.

He turned to a giant of a man, well over six feet tall, weighing more than two hundred and fifty pounds, carrying an air of supreme authority. He correctly guessed his identity. "We'll have to move him, Mr. Dalton. Have you got a road wagon you can spare?"

Some straw was thrown into the bottom of a wagon, and the unconscious workman, Frazier, was stretched out on it, and his own jacket thrown over him for warmth.

"Get him home in bed, and I'll be around after a while," Ketchum said. "I have to pick up some instruments."

The man and the woman were still waiting when he got back. He disposed of them quickly, then got on the phone and called Cayce at his studio.

"Edgar," he said, "there's a man sleeping in a house on Elm Street, sounder than you ever have, and I don't know what's wrong with him. Time is of the essence."

Cayce looked at the clock. It was almost noon, and he had a luncheon date with Gertrude. "All right, but there's nobody here to give the suggestion. So you better come over and conduct the reading, as you have watched my father do. I'll take the phone off the hook, so we won't be disturbed. Maybe it will work."

Ketchum raced down the block to Edgar's studio.

Cayce was ready for him. He lay down on the couch, his clothes loosened, thoroughly relaxed. He smiled reassuringly at the excited Ketchum. "Calm down," he said. "There's nothing to it. Just make believe you're the Squire. The rest is easy."

Though Cayce had now reached a point where he put himself under very easily, Ketchum, in his anxiety, quickly suggested, "You are asleep." He then proceeded to give him the subject's name and address, asking for help. He breathed a sigh of relief as he saw Cayce's lids close and his breathing become deep and rhythmical.

With new confidence, Ketchum now got down to the heart of the matter. "Examine the body of this workman thoroughly, and discuss what is wrong inside the body, and what can be done to help it."

Cayce hesitated the least instant, then said firmly, "Nothing can be done for this body. It is too far gone."

Ketchum was appalled. What was he to tell Dalton? At least, he should have some diagnosis to justify this solemn prognosis. "What is wrong with this body; why did he pass out and stay in coma?"

"The body had been in a bad state for years, not receiving the proper nourishment. It is suffering from malnutrition, in an advanced stage. The life forces are low. The body has too long had a steady diet of pork and hominy grits, without the needed greens which supply the vitamins and minerals the body needs for continued health. It should have had turnip greens, green beans, spinach, asparagus, with vegetables cooked but lightly so the minerals don't run off in the water. Also vegetables raw, carrots, radishes, scallions, lettuce, and the like."

"What can be done for this man now?"

Cayce shook his head. "Nothing; it is too late for this body. We can only hope that it will have learned its lesson for the future."

Ketchum was too absorbed with the immediate problem to latch on just then to Cayce's apparent implication of another lifetime. In any case, he had no interest in reincarnation. "What would you call this disorder?" he asked with his usual practicality.

Cayce hesitated a moment. "Pellagra."

"Pellagra?" Where had he heard that foreign-sounding word before? Of course, Italy was full of pellagra, an insidious form of malnutrition, nearly always fatal.

He was almost bursting with excitement at this revelation. "Thanks, Old Man," he cried, forgetting in his haste to take the sleeping Cayce out of trance. "I'll see you later."

Ten minutes later, Gertrude strode into the studio and found Cayce asleep on the couch, the telephone still dangling uselessly from its cord.

"Wake up, Edgar," she cried, remembering when he had slept for two days, "wake up, it's time for lunch."

But this time the suggestion didn't work. For unknown to Gertrude at this time, Edgar Cayce could only be awakened by the person who had given him the original suggestion. In the same way, the only person who could communicate with him in trance was the person he had responded to originally.

Fortunately, Ketchum recalled his oversight before he got back to his office and quickly retraced his steps. He stopped short on seeing Gertrude, who was looking down helplessly at her prostrate husband, but quickly recovered his composure. "I forgot something," he said urbanely, and then proceeded to bring Edgar out of his trance.

"Wake up," he said, "feeling refreshed and vigorous, not remembering anything that you said."

Cayce slowly sat up and rubbed his eyes, looking dazedly around the room. His eyes moved slowly from Ketchum to Gertrude, then fell on the dangling telephone. He got up and put the phone back on the receiver.

"Was I able to help that fellow?" he asked.

"What fellow?" said Gertrude. "All I know is that when you didn't turn up at the sandwich shop, I telephoned from there and the line seemed to be busy. So I came rushing over and found you dead to the world."

Ketchum didn't have the time or inclination to stand around and explain. "Thanks again, Old Man," he called out as he swung out the door.

Gertrude stared coldly after his retreating form. "That Ketchum," she said, between her teeth.

"Now don't get upset," said her husband placatingly, "or you won't enjoy your lunch."

Dalton's workmen had left by the time Ketchum got to the Fraziers' place. Mrs. Frazier, a sad-eyed woman with a sallow face, greeted Ketchum with a wan smile. Two small boys with tousled blond hair lurked shyly behind her full skirts, their interest in the unaccustomed commotion in the household reflected in their widened eyes.

Mrs. Frazier's whole body drooped from a lifetime of expecting the worst and not being disappointed. She could be expected to sag just a little more with any fresh blow. "He shows no sign of coming to," she said despondently.

Ketchum sat down by the bed. His patient was still unconscious, looking more dead than alive. Routinely, he checked the pulse, respiration, palpated the chest. He opened the man's mouth, looked at the tongue, rolled back the eyelids. Mrs. Frazier's tired eyes were listlessly following his examination.

"I believe," Ketchum said solemnly, "that your husband has an advanced case of pellagra. He may not recover."

Mrs. Frazier looked at him dry-eyed. "Who will support the family?" she asked of nobody in particular. "He had just gone back to work."

Ketchum looked around the room awkwardly, noting the disrepair and obvious signs of poverty. "I'm sure there is some agency that will see you through. Perhaps Mr. Dalton will help."

She started to sob soundlessly, her flat chest moving pathetically with each sob.

Looking around, as if to make sure he was unobserved, Ketchum took something from his pocket and slipped it into the woman's listless hand. And then he left before she could look up, or protest.

The case had aroused Ketchum's professional curiosity. He sent for the latest medical dictionary and opened it to the *P*'s. There was a new listing for Pellagra. It covered Frazier's case and also seemed to explain four other cases in the Western Kentucky Asylum. The four, classified as mental problems, had recently been called to his attention after his success with young Davis.

Dr. Board, the asylum head, was one of the few local doctors with whom Ketchum was on a friendly basis. Not being in private practice, Board didn't think of Ketchum as a rival and indeed was rather amused by the young doctor's forwardness.

Ketchum had been thinking of calling Board when he ran into him on the street. They stopped to chat for a moment. Ketchum casually mentioned the Frazier case, and stressed its similarity to the four cases that had baffled Board and his staff. "All the symptoms are the same, even to the unexplained comatose state," he said.

Board's interest was immediately caught, as he had had no success in properly diagnosing the cases. "Tell me more."

"Why not drop in at the Frazier place with me?" Ketchum suggested. "You'll see the similarity right off."

Board was intrigued. "All right, I'll ride out with you."

Mrs. Frazier came languidly to the door. But her eyes brightened at once as they fell on Ketchum. She touched his sleeve diffidently. "I can't thank you enough," she said.

Ketchum cleared his throat noisily, trying not to look embarrassed. "This is Dr. Board," he said quickly. "He's a specialist. I've brought him for a consultation."

Board approached the bedside and bent over the comatose figure, as Mrs. Frazier backed out of the room. He checked the patient's respiration, his color, turned down his eyelids, and palpated his chest just as Ketchum had. "He looks just like the four I have in the hospital," he said. "Did you say you had a diagnosis for this case?"

Ketchum was not averse to mending a few fences medically. "Yes, Doctor, but I'm not going to lay it on you. You're an old practitioner, with thousands of patients behind you, and I'm just starting out."

"Never mind that," said Board, though obviously pleased by the flattery. "Where did you come by your diagnosis?"

"Just a second," said Ketchum. Then, as Board looked at him wonderingly, he ran out to his buggy and returned at once with the new dictionary he had brought along for just this purpose. He thumbed through the pages quickly, then came finally to the page he was looking for. He pointed with satisfaction to the word *Pellagra*.

Board took the book and read with fascination. "That sure covers Frazier and my four like an umbrella," he said at last. "You really got something, Yankee Boy."

He returned the book to its owner. "Now, you can be frank with me, Ketchum. What made you turn to that heading in the first place?"

Ketchum looked innocent. "I don't understand."

Board made a wry face. "You just didn't observe Frazier, then start going through a medical dictionary till you came to a disease that seemed to fit. You must have known what you were looking for."

Ketchum looked around uncomfortably at the dreary sickroom. "I'd be more at ease talking somewhere else."

Board nodded. "All right, let's ride out to the hospital, check the four cases I have there, then lunch in my office, if you have the time."

Ketchum accepted with alacrity. "I've got the time."

He had decided in that split second to take Board into his confidence. Board was influential and distinguished and could be of help, particularly if he could become sufficiently involved to treat his own cases as prescribed by Cayce.

As they sat at Board's massive desk and finished a light repast of tinned salmon and cottage cheese, washed down with unsweetened grape juice, Board sighed in contentment, then looked up inquiringly at his visitor.

"Well?" he said.

Ketchum took a direct approach. "Have you ever heard of a young man named Edgar Cayce?"

Dr. Board frowned. "I know the Cayce family. They're as numerous around here as dogwood."

"He's Leslie Cayce's son, the one they call the Squire."

Board looked up with a start. "You mean the boy they call the Freak."

Ketchum permitted himself a smile. "Exactly."

"Well, what about him?" Board's voice was edged with impatience. "Do you want to admit him?"

"Hardly," Ketchum said. He paused for dramatic

109

effect. "Particularly since he's the one who pegged Frazier's illness as pellagra."

Board's face was a study in bewilderment. "The hell you say! You mean that fellow diagnosed this case for you?"

Ketchum was secretly enjoying Board's confusion. "That's the cotton-picking truth, if you'll excuse a Southern expression from an unreformed Yankee."

Board sat back in his swivel armchair and grumpily contemplated the young man sitting so confidently across from him. "You sure got a lot of nerve, using a freak like that and then telling a doctor about it."

Ketchum's easy assurance was not shaken. "I am not wedded to any particular discipline of medicine," he said earnestly, "though I went to a school of homeopathy. I would use any form of therapy that would help a patient."

Board regarded his visitor with a jaundiced eye. "That's very admirable, but in the eyes of the public we'd be less than quacks to use a freak like Cayce." He laughed mirthlessly. "Not to mention what the gentlemen of the Kentucky Medical Society would have to say about it."

As one who lived dangerously close to the razor's edge, Ketchum was shrewdly able to take the other man's measure. He had once told Cayce: "I don't judge a man by what he says, or by what he does. All I ask myself is what he wants." And there was little doubt in Ketchum's mind what the doctor sitting opposite him wanted. He wanted to announce the diagnosis and cure of the four patients previously misdiagnosed by the best medical brains in Kentucky.

"Why," Ketchum asked, "need anybody know that Cayce had anything to do with it?"

Board coughed two or three times, then gave the younger doctor a probing look. Apparently satisfied, his manner turned briskly professional.

"Would you care to see the patients, Doctor?"

Ketchum smiled to himself. "Of course, Doctor."

The four inmates were confined in the same ward.

110

A nurse was in the room as the doctors walked in, and Board gave her an inquiring look.

"There seems to be no improvement," she said. "They're in a stupor most of the time."

As the door closed behind the nurse, Ketchum said, "That sounds optimistic."

Board frowned. "What do you mean?"

"They're apparently conscious at times. So we can give them the food that Cayce recommends for pellagra."

Board's manner turned bland. "Actually, Doctor, Cayce has nothing to do with this case. I have spoken only to you, and on the strength of what you've told me, pellagra is clearly indicated. And so we'll treat for pellagra."

Ketchum's head bobbed. "Exactly, Doctor. I can't help but agree with a man of your long experience."

The older doctor looked at him sharply, but was quickly reassured by Ketchum's respectful expression.

That day, as they came out of their stupor, the four men began receiving the vegetable greens, the beef and the fresh fruit suggested in the Frazier case. Soon they were staying awake for longer periods, their languor decreased, and they gained strength daily. In two or three weeks, they appeared well on the road to recovery.

Frazier was not so fortunate. His vital forces could not be rallied. He lingered for ten days, then expired without regaining consciousness. Ketchum had called on him daily.

Dalton, dropping in to inquire after his employee, had found Ketchum sitting by the patient. "You don't seem to be helping, Doctor," he said.

Ketchum shrugged. "There comes a time when nobody can get a man well."

Dalton's eyes narrowed. "In that case, Doctor, what are you doing here—running up the bill?"

Ketchum returned his gaze coolly, then allowed his eyes to travel around the dingy room with its few fragile sticks of furniture and faded oilcloth coverings for the floors. "There is no bill in this case," he said quietly. "The widow will need what little there is."

"Then what are you doing here?"

"I stop by every day, as I would with any other patient who can't get in to see me."

Dalton's face relaxed into a smile. "And how many other patients do you call on?"

"None. They're still fighting the Civil War down here."

Dalton let out a belly laugh. "And who's winning?"

Ketchum smiled thinly. "They are at present, sir. But you know how the war came out."

Dalton clapped him on the shoulder. "Yankee, if I ever need a doctor, I might just give you a chance."

This was hardly encouraging. Dalton had never known a day's illness. No more than forty years old, in the prime of life, he looked like the last man to require medical attention.

But that next week, as Dalton was supervising the construction of a new railroad depot, he slipped and lost his footing, and twisted his right leg under him, snapping the bone at the knee in his fall. In excruciating pain, Dalton was lifted gently into the back of a wagon, as Frazier had been, and carted off to his red-brick mansion.

Several doctors were summoned. They arrived hastily, as befitted Dalton's exalted financial position. After a quickly improvised conference, it was decided that Dalton was suffering from a multiple fracture. Two or three doctors expressed the fear that the millionaire might never walk normally again.

"It's just not a case of setting the bone and waiting for it to mend," said one physician. "The kneecap is pretty well shattered."

The four doctors were standing solemnly around Dalton's bedside, looking wise, when the injured man recalled his promise to Ketchum. "Before you gentlemen make a decision," he said, "I want to hear from young Ketchum."

Dr. Sanders, the apparent leader, reflected the physicians' disapproval. "Why call in a stranger when the best medical brains of the county are here, men you have known most of your life?"

Dalton gritted his teeth in pain. "It won't hurt to get another opinion, especially when I haven't heard one that I like. Now will somebody get on the phone and get Ketchum here?"

Within the hour the irrepressible Ketchum bounded into Dalton's chambers. He saluted the doctors cheerfully, but only one, a Dr. Williams, even bothered to acknowledge his greeting.

Undismayed, Ketchum turned to the patient. "Well, Mr. Dalton, our paths cross sooner than anticipated."

Dalton groaned. "Ketchum, take a look at this leg, and tell me what you think."

Ketchum gingerly lifted the blankets and saw the worst-looking break he had ever seen in his limited practice. The kneebone practically protruded out of the purplish skin. It was obviously a compound fracture. And it was understandable why, with the meager facilities available, reputable physicians would hesitate over the best procedure.

It was Ketchum's first fracture case, and he was able to say quite honestly, "This is as bad a fracture as I've ever been called upon to look at."

Save for Williams, a tall, middle-aged man with a kindly face, the other doctors ignored him throughout.

"Gentlemen," said Sanders, as if Ketchum weren't there, "this case carries a very heavy responsibility. Mr. Dalton must select the doctor who is to carry this responsibility, and it will be his case. The rest of us will consult."

Dalton painfully propped himself up on an elbow. "What do you say to that, Ketchum?"

Ketchum looked boldly around the room. "If I take the case, I take it alone, as I did with young Davis."

Dalton nodded approvingly, and turned to his wife, who had just walked into the room. "What do you say to that?"

Mrs. Dalton moved her shoulders slightly. "It's your leg, George."

Dalton coldly surveyed the roomful of doctors. "Gentlemen, I've never approved of committees. They don't get anything done. Ketchum is a Yankee, and on the brash side, but he's willing to take it on alone. And that's what I like in a man—confidence."

Mrs. Dalton looked up with a sardonic smile. "In other words, gentlemen, Mr. Dalton is willing to trust the Yankee boy over the rest of you."

Sanders' face tightened in anger, and without a word, he turned on his heel and walked out. Two of the other doctors followed, bowing curtly to the Daltons, and studiously avoiding Ketchum.

Only Dr. Williams stayed on for a moment, expressing his concern. "If there is anything I can do, Ketchum, call on me. You've got a very difficult case, and I don't envy you."

"Thank you," said Ketchum gratefully, wringing his hand. "I can use help."

As Williams left, Dalton and his new doctor were at last alone. "What do you mean, Ketchum, saying you need help?"

"We'll need some nurses in here around the clock, and I may have to call on Williams when I set the bone." Ketchum consulted his watch, which hung on a gold chain from his vest. "It's almost noon," he said. "I'll be back later and we'll get to work. Meanwhile, I'll get a nurse in here."

Dalton showed his annoyance. "Why can't you begin now?"

"I'll have to pick up some instruments, Mr. Dalton. But never fear, we'll get at it today, and you'll be as good as new before you know it. You couldn't do better in the finest hospital in Nashville."

Dalton grunted. "Just don't make any mistakes, Yankee, or I'll feed you to the Hoptown wolves."

"Have no fear, you're in capable hands."

Dalton fought back a wave of nausea. "Do you know why I hired you, Yankee?"

"I was the first local doctor to pass the State Medical examinations."

114

Dalton grimaced. "I don't give a damn about that."

Ketchum's interest was piqued. "Because of the Davis boy?"

Dalton guffawed. "I'm no mental case."

"Then why?"

"Because of what you did for the Fraziers."

"But Frazier died."

"His wife, you numbskull."

"And what did I do?"

"You gave her a hundred-dollar bill, Yankee. And I'll bet it was your last."

Ketchum turned pink. "Now don't go saying anything. You'll ruin my reputation."

"I won't, just get me walking again. And you'll get that hundred back a hundredfold."

From Dalton's mansion, which was approached by a circular driveway, Ketchum drove his buggy directly to Edgar Cayce's studio.

Cayce was in the middle of a sitting. He was patiently posing a rebellious ten-year-old boy, as a doting mother kept chiding, "Now Billy, sit still for the nice man."

Ketchum took the startled Cayce by the arm and led him into an adjacent office. "Cayce, it's my great chance, the opportunity you talked about. It's Dalton, the rich butter-and-brick man. His leg's smashed and I need your help."

Cayce looked at him questioningly. "Does he know about me?"

"Hell no."

"Then there's no request from him for the reading."

"Why not a third party, as it was with the Davis boy? I asked for him, just as I'm asking now."

Cayce frowned. "You know, Ketchum, I wish I had the feeling you cared about these people, apart from what it may do for you."

Ketchum returned his look evenly. "Doesn't that Bible you talk about tell you to judge not lest ye be judged?"

Cayce's face broke into a smile. *"Touché,* Doc. But suppose I'm wrong with Dalton? What then?"

Ketchum smiled wryly. "Unlike other doctors here, I can't bury my mistakes. I'll get out one step ahead of the tar-and-feather brigade. But if you're right, Cayce, there'll be no stopping this Yankee boy."

Cayce gave a sigh of resignation. "I really must owe you something from a past life, Doc, if there is such a thing."

Ketchum grinned. "One incarnation is about all I can handle."

The two men walked back into the studio, and Cayce apologetically advised Billy's mother that the sitting was over for the day. "I have an emergency," he explained.

Billy's mother, a woman of thirty-five or so, regarded Ketchum with dark suspicion. "I don't know what a Yankee has that's more important than my son's birthday picture."

"Come back tomorrow," said Cayce placatingly, "and I'll take Billy's picture as a birthday present."

The mother's attitude promptly changed. "If you put it that way," she said with a vinegary smile.

After mother and son had left, Ketchum quickly put Cayce in trance and suggested he describe the best way to repair Dalton's shattered leg. Cayce tuned in at once. As he spoke, Ketchum took voluminous notes. The recommended treatment was so radical that occasionally the pencil stopped its scrawl, as Ketchum scratched his head.

"No half-measures will help," said Cayce, "there is too much damage to the kneebone or patella, the kneecap, for the ordinary reset of bone and use of wooden splints. Drastic treatment is indicated, since there is a multiple transverse fracture. Take a steel surgical drill, and bore a hole in the kneecap, then set the kneecap and nail it together along the lines of the break."

Such a jointure of the flat movable bone was unprecedented, and Ketchum could hardly believe his

116

ears. "Please repeat the treatment indicated for Mr. Dalton's leg."

Almost word for word, Cayce repeated himself.

"What kind of nail would it be?" Ketchum asked.

"Like a roofing nail, with a large head on it, made out of iron. Tap this nail in, after the drilling, then put the leg in a cast and let it rest for eight to ten weeks, until the knee is strong enough to move of its own accord."

"Will he be able to stand and walk then?"

"No. Because of his excessive weight, it will be another two weeks before the knee will be strong enough to bear the full load. All in all, twelve weeks before the healing is complete."

"And the nail, when does that come out?"

"Keep the nail as is. Perhaps it would be wise to use two nails. It will do no harm. The body will carry the nails to his grave."

"To his grave?"

Cayce quickly reassured his questioner. "That will not be for another thirty years. The operation will be a success, done as indicated."

Ketchum, without practical experience in surgery, then asked a perfectly natural question. "Shall I have help with the surgery, or do it alone?"

"Take all the help you can get, making sure to administer the proper sedation so that the patient will be relaxed and comfortable at all times."

"And what would that be?"

"A general anesthetic on the order of liquid ether and the like."

"Should there be anything else in the way of preparation?"

"Yes, there should be X-rays, so that the full extent of the injury will be known, and it will be known precisely where to place the nails for the greater benefit of the patient."

Ketchum was well aware that his X-ray machine was securely moored to the floor of his clinic. "But how can there be X-rays when the only machine is in my office, and Dalton can't move?"

"If the mountain won't go to Mahomet, then Mahomet must go to the mountain."

"And what does that mean?" Ketchum's voice was the least impatient.

"Get some strong, husky men, and carry the body gently on its bed, into the street, and for whatever distance necessary, to the office where the X-rays will be taken."

At this point, Ketchum, dismayed as he was by this bizarre turn, had no choice but to go on. "How many men should carry the bed?"

"As many as is necessary. We have finished."

As Cayce lay back quietly, ready to be awakened, Ketchum's mind was already busily occupied with the task of getting his patient to his office. But there were a number of other things to be done as well. After leaving Cayce, Ketchum phoned Dr. Williams and arranged for his help with the surgery the following afternoon. Williams was most cooperative. With the nails still to consider, Ketchum then walked a few blocks to a blacksmith shop.

The smith, a brawny man with an Irish twinkle in his eye, was working at his forge, hammering a horseshoe into shape for a waiting horse. He eyed the well-groomed stranger curiously. "And what will ye be having here with your fine clothes?"

"A few nails, if you please."

"Try the hardware store," said the smith, pounding away.

Ketchum held up a hand. "This is something special, my dear sir, that only you can do."

Having with this device caught the smith's attention, Ketchum now described the iron nail he wanted with the broad head, just as Cayce had pictured it for him.

"How many of these would you be wanting?" the smith asked.

Mopping his brow, Ketchum moved back a step from the heat of the forge.

"Three or four, just in case one doesn't do it."

The smith eyed him wonderingly

"You're after being the new doctor?"

"That I am."

"And what would you be doing with a nail like that?"

The smith's warm brogue encouraged Ketchum to be his normally expansive self. "You're going to be after helping with a great job of surgery, Sir Smith," he said in good-natured mimicry.

The smith smeared a dirty hand across his grimy face.

"And what if that surgery should be after going wrong? No thank ye, Yankee, all the credit is rightly yours."

He picked out three large nails and held them to the fire, cutting them down to the desired size.

"All right," said Ketchum, "but you'll be sorry when this case is medical history."

"I don't after know what that means, Yankee, but I'm a stranger here, too, and I can't afford to be after making mistakes."

He took the glowing nails from his forge, slipped them into water to cool, and after they spat and sizzled a bit, handed them to the doctor with a stern injunction. "Don't be telling after where you got them."

Ketchum slipped the nails, which were about an inch and a half long, into his black suitcoat. "And what do I owe you, Master Smith?"

"Now it's Master Smith, is it? Nothing, thank ye. I wash my hands of the whole business."

"Okay, Pontius Pilate Smith, thanks for the nails, and the advice."

The smith stood in the doorway watching Ketchum as he jauntily strode off. "There goes either a very wise man or a fool," he told the patient steed whose shoeing had been so singularly interrupted.

Ketchum was now ready for the great experiment. Williams was bringing a surgical drill and he, Ketchum, had the hammer. A second nurse had been brought in to help with the anesthetic. All he needed was a little luck, and, of course, the X-rays.

In the cool of the evening, while it was still barely

119

light, the people of Hopkinsville were treated to a spectacle they would not soon forget. Down Main Street, clad in a robe and reading the afternoon paper as calmly as if he were alone in his living room, the community's leading citizen rode like Caesar on a narrow cot borne by four huskies. His bad leg was hoisted in the air, held securely by a pulley attached to the footboard.

With Boze at his side, eyes rolling in merry appreciation of the scene, Ketchum marched ahead of the litter as would a lictor of ancient Rome. Pedestrians, mouths agape, jockeyed for a better view of the remarkable procession.

Occasionally, a friendly voice called out in greeting, and Dalton returned the salute, peering over his newspaper and waving a hand.

Ketchum did not go unnoticed. But the friendliness offered Dalton was nowhere evident for his doctor. There were mutterings of "What's Dalton doing with that Yankee?" and "That Yankee doctor is putting on a circus, and making Dalton his clown."

As luck would have it, Dr. Sanders, stepping out of a drugstore at that moment, joined the crowd of spectators. His stage-whispered comment, as the litter slowly passed, was clearly audible not only to bystanders but to Dalton and Ketchum as well. "Add two more bearers, and there'll be just enough for pallbearers."

There were a few scattered laughs, but there was also an unexpected rebuttal. Mr. Dietrich, standing nearby, could not help overhearing the remark. "Ketchum will pull him through," said the school superintendent in an equally strong voice. "I have my money on him."

"You can afford to," Sanders came back. "It's not your leg."

This brought a new sally of laughter as the litter rounded a corner into Seventh Street and disappeared up the stairway to Ketchum's office.

In his clinic, alone except for Boze and the patient, Ketchum took several X-ray pictures of the shattered knee. Dalton, in pain, was unusually quiet. He seemed anxious to get back to his house. The return journey got under way in the darkness, without Ketchum. The doctor remained in his office to study the pictures and get his instruments together for the operation on the morrow.

That next morning, Ketchum kept checking his notes from Cayce's reading and studying the X-rays. Just before he started for Dalton's house he phoned Cayce for reassurance.

"You forget," said Cayce, "that I don't remember what I said."

At four o'clock promptly, everybody concerned had gathered in Dalton's bedchamber—the two doctors, Ketchum and Williams, the nurses, Rita and Bess. For the first time the patient showed signs of alarm, viewing the mysterious preparations going on about him. Ketchum had brought a collapsible, leather-topped table, which was quickly propped open. Bottles of liquid ether were produced, with paper cones to hold the anesthetic. The shades had been raised and the late afternoon sun streamed through the windows, helping to provide all the light that was necessary. The anxious patient, growing more anxious by the moment, was transferred from his bed to the surgical table, and strapped down firmly.

Ketchum, openly optimistic, was off in a corner of the room, giving Dr. Williams his first inkling of the plan to drill through the kneecap, and drive in a couple of nails to secure the shattered kneecap.

The older doctor recoiled in horror. "I never heard of anything like it," he stammered. "It sounds like madness to me."

But Ketchum was not to be put off by traditionalism at this point. "It's the coming thing," he said airily. "Guaranteed foolproof."

Williams' misgivings were not allayed. "I want a statement in writing, Doctor, that you take all the responsibility. Out of regard for the patient, I won't withdraw my assistance at this hour. But I will require an admission of liability by you."

Ketchum cheerfully agreed, signing the hastily drawn statement with a flourish.

Dalton had been viewing the discussion suspiciously from the other end of the room. "What is all this about?" he cried.

Ketchum quickly rejoined him. "Only doctor talk. Nothing for you to concern yourself. Just relax." He spoke soothingly.

Dalton's patience was wearing thin. "Relax? You must be mad."

The doctors' duties were duly divided. Williams was to supervise the administration of the anesthetic, with Ketchum handling the surgery itself, setting the bone, and hammering the nails in place.

No time was lost, as Williams efficiently went to work. A cone of liquid ether was held to the patient's nostrils, and in a few minutes he was completely out, his arms dangling off the table, his head lolling to one side. He was as peaceful as a sleeping child.

To avoid any sudden movement, nevertheless, one nurse held Dalton's thigh firmly; the other kept the lower leg, below the knee, securely in position.

Ketchum drew a deep breath. He took confidence in recalling what Cayce had said about thirty years more of comfort for Dalton, then sharply turned the drill into the triangular thickness of the kneecap. As planned, the drill cut through in two places. Ketchum carefully withdrew the drill. With a look at Williams, whose face was a blank, he picked up the hammer and with deft strokes tapped the nails through the widened openings, clipping off the protruding ends.

The broad head of each nail was planted firmly in the skin, and the kneecap seemed staunchly secure. Not much time had lapsed and the patient had slept comfortably through it all. But only time would now tell whether the operation was a success. Cayce had said it would take twelve weeks for a complete recovery and twelve weeks it would be.

Before the ether wore off, Dalton was carried back to his bed by the same huskies who had carted him through the streets of Hopkinsville. His leg was then put in a protective cast to give the breaks a chance to heal around the two nails. With all this done, it now remained to be seen whether the patient would walk normally again.

All of Hopkinsville knew of the operation and nearly all felt that their leading citizen had been cruelly exploited by a Yankee upstart and might very well be crippled for life. On all sides, Ketchum encountered dark, sinister looks. Mailed threats, invariably anonymous, came to his home and office. Typical of these was the scrawled warning:

"If anything goes wrong with Dalton, you'll pay with your life, Yankee."

One threat of a flogging was signed "The Night Riders," the sectional successors to the Ku Klux Klan, who seemed to be branching out from the tobacco war into any areas they found expedient.

As he sauntered through the streets, or into shops, Ketchum overheard the direct threats. Tar and feathers was one of the mildest.

He made out that he heard none of this. But he made sure he had his shotgun with him wherever he traveled. "They aren't going to scare me off," he told Cayce.

In Cayce, he had a sympathetic audience for a change. "I'm with you on this, Ketchum. I don't like injustice, whatever its polite name."

Ketchum peered at the psychic in surprise. "But, Edgar, you're a peaceable man."

Cayce's eyes glinted with amusement. "Jesus said peace was worth fighting for. I'm with Jesus on that."

Ketchum looked at Cayce with new appreciation. "You may have me believing in this friendly God of yours yet." He paused a moment. "That is, if Dalton gets well and I get a fat fee out of it."

The weeks passed, and Ketchum managed to hang on, with the modest help Dalton gave him.

Dalton was feeling better, but he had no idea how his leg would eventually react to the radical treatment.

"I'll let the state of my leg decide your fee, Ketchum," he announced one day.

"That's fair enough," said Ketchum. "Just remember those were handcrafted nails."

Dalton laughed. "You're incorrigible, Ketchum, but I can't help admiring your guts."

The two men had become friends. Ketchum stopped by to see Dalton twice daily. Meanwhile, his office calls had dropped off to nothing as the town watched and waited.

A crisis developed sooner than expected. One day, Dalton complained of sharp stabbing pains in his lower back. "You must have hit a sympathetic nerve with those nails," he told Ketchum accusingly.

The pain wouldn't subside after long hours, and a concerned Ketchum consulted Cayce once again. "Should I buy a train ticket," he asked, half-jestingly, "or let them ride me out of town?"

Cayce was mildly amused, and as usual involved in taking pictures. "Just keep your shirt on, Ketchum," he said soothingly. "Your work isn't finished here yet."

"I need another reading on Dalton," said Ketchum desperately.

After finishing his pictures, Cayce lay down on his black couch, and Ketchum, now becoming adept at it, conducted the reading.

As Ketchum hovered anxiously over him, Cayce began his tour of Dalton's interior.

"The trouble is not with the leg," he said, as Ketchum gave a sigh of relief, "but with the inactivity of this body which is accustomed to much in the way of everyday activity. As a result, the circulation, assimilation and elimination are not functioning normally, and the body has a problem with the kidneys, commonly known as a kidney stone. Ordinarily, if the body were not incapacitated, this would have dissolved and passed through the bladder and the urethra. There is a great need for exercise in this body, which cannot be realized because of the injury to the leg. However, by having the body drink considerable water, the stone, not too large in size, will be safely passed. Have the body drink as much water as possible to bring about this result."

"Is that all?" Ketchum asked.

"Do this, and all will be well."

"Suppose the body won't consume the water?"

The unconscious Cayce shook his head. "The stone will pass anyway, but not as quickly, and with greater pain."

That afternoon, having memorized Cayce's analysis, Ketchum made his diagnosis, much to the disbelief of his cantankerous patient.

"Now don't line me up for another operation," Dalton growled. "I've had it."

"It won't be necessary," Ketchum said lightly. "Just drink a lot of branch water—without the bourbon—and you'll pass that stone." He poured a tumbler full of water from a standing pitcher. "Drink this down," he commanded. "And follow it every half-hour with the same. I'll be back later tonight to check on you."

"I'm getting a little tired of this," Dalton said, motioning to the cast.

"Just a couple of more weeks," Ketchum said reassuringly, "and we'll have you up and around."

Dalton was not so easily mollified. "I suppose this kidney thing is extra." His expression suddenly turned sly. "You know, my wife wants me to bring Sanders back. He was over earlier today to say he didn't think I was being handled properly."

Ketchum felt the blood rush to his head. "That's a serious breach of medical ethics on his part, and of disloyalty on yours, Mr. Dalton," he said angrily. "To consult with anybody without notifying me is enough to turn me off this case."

Dalton became the appeaser. "Now, don't get your bowels in an uproar, Ketchum. I don't want Sanders around. I don't like his smell."

"That's more like it," said Ketchum. He reached for his soft, gray Stetson, planting it at a rakish angle. "I'll be back," he told Dalton. "Just be a good boy, and drink your water."

After dinner, he returned as promised to the Dalton home. Dalton had just downed a full glass of water.

"Good boy," said Ketchum. "I'm going to sit here until you pass that stone."

"You may be here till Christmas."

Just before midnight, as Ketchum was thinking of his own bed, Dalton bolted up in bed. "Hand me that bedpan, Ketchum," he ordered sharply.

Ketchum pulled a curtain around Dalton's bed, and then peeked in as Dalton let out a howl of agonized pain.

"I'm dying," Dalton gasped.

Stooping to the floor, Ketchum held up a pea-sized object which he had just scooped up from under the bed.

"You're already resurrected." Ketchum laughed. "Here's the kidney stone that's been giving you all that trouble."

6

The Miracle Worker

The near disaster at the Literary Club had not damp-
ened the Squire's enthusiasm. He was convinced there
was nothing his son couldn't do psychically. Edgar had
proved himself a hundred times over, and there were
new worlds to conquer. The Squire wished Edgar to
read not only for the ailing, but for people with all
kinds of problems—and opportunities.

Edgar was not sure himself where the boundaries
of his gift lay. If he could find oil for somebody who
then built a church or a college with it, wasn't this
a project the good Lord would smile upon? Spiritually,
motivation was all-important. For this reason, he
preferred his subjects to request help personally. They
were then obviously ready for that help.

He thought of himself as a psychic diagnostician,
for lack of a better term. He shrank for the appellation
of faith healer, for his transcripts not only recommended medical treatment—allopathic, homeopathic,
osteopathic, chiropractic—but often singled out the
name of the doctor to be consulted and gave the
formula for recommended drugs and herbs. Once he
recommended an obscure tonic, Clary Water, for a
Mr. A. P. Andrews in New York City. The product
could not be located anywhere. The ailing Andrews
had inquired at the principal drug houses and
advertised in the leading medical journals. Just as he
had given up the search, a young man in Paris saw

the advertisement and recalled that the compound had been manufactured by his father's company, which had long since gone out of business. The man in Paris dug up the required information at some trouble to himself and sent it on to Andrews. Meanwhile, in a second reading, Cayce had been asked to describe how the preparation should be made. In trance, he listed all the ingredients—garden sage, ambergris, grain alcohol, gin and cinnamon—and gave the exact amounts. His check reading, sent to Andrews, arrived the same day as the information from Paris. The ingredients tallied in every respect.

But these were not earthshaking developments, in keeping with the Squire's conception of the heights his son's gift should reach. Edgar, he felt, could be an important influence in the broad mainstream of human affairs, making a decisive impact on crime and punishment, mystery, intrigue, politics, finance. And so he wanted it known that here at last was a prophet with honor in his own land, a prophet ready and able to unveil the darkest secrets, as well as cure the incurables. There would be no charge for readings in the realm of public service, as Edgar would not have permitted it in any event. Moreover, the Squire was more concerned about his son's fame at this time. The money would come over the transoms when the world recognized the endless potential of his gift. The Morgans, Rockefellers, Dukes, Vanderbilts, the greats of the financial world, would beat a path to the simple door in Hopkinsville, Kentucky. For whether it was the market, the track, or miscellaneous information that was sought, the Squire had reason to believe that his son was infallible.

Edgar himself at first saw no reason why he shouldn't help people make money, or profit himself through the help he had given them, so long as the cause was worthy. But he had seen one man pyramid a small bankroll into a fortune, only to lose his wife as he was congratulating himself on his newfound riches. Another had generously offered to set up a fund for the psychic, with the money gained through Cayce's stock market forecasts, and then through an apparent mischance lost his own life. Still another beneficiary wound up in an asylum. Nobody had gained ultimately, but still the thing worked, and eventually, it seemed to his father, would redound to Edgar's own good.

In trance, he was infallibly guided by ethical considerations.

On one remarkable occasion, he had been hunting quail with his father on a farm several miles out of Hopkinsville. The owner, having heard of Edgar's peculiar gift, asked if he could locate some hidden treasure that had belonged in his family.

"I don't mind your shooting quail on my land," he pointedly told the two, "but I ought to get something in return." He was a tall, rawboned man, with a shifty grin and a sly eye. "And what's more I'll give you a percentage of what we turn up."

"How much of a percentage?" said the Squire quickly.

The terms were duly worked out, with handshakes all around.

The Squire looked around for a comfortable patch of grass. "How about stretching out here, son?" The Squire indicated a small glade in the shade of a tall elm.

"Great," said Edgar, "it beats quail shooting, when there aren't any quail." They had not bagged any birds as yet that day.

The Squire was elated, the hunt turning out better than he could have rightfully expected. Edgar, too, saw no harm in dredging up a fortune that would otherwise help nobody.

In the shade of the spreading elm, a little weary from miles of hiking, Edgar fell off to sleep even faster than usual.

As the farmer looked on expectantly, the Squire gave his sleeping son the suggestion that he locate the buried treasure with such precision that it could be promptly found.

"Plot the location with such detail," said he, "that we can draw a map from your instructions."

The sleeping Cayce first began to describe the treasure lode itself, mentioning family heirlooms and a wealth of gold trinkets, silver pieces and jewels. The farmer's eyes shone, and he leaned over with pencil poised to take down the directions that would make him a rich man.

But Cayce suddenly digressed from his description of the treasure. Instead of continuing on with the location, he addressed the subject directly, though still in trance, with his eyes closed. "This land and treasure does not really belong to you, and it would not be right to give you the information you seek. This land belongs to another"—he mentioned a name that made the farmer blanch—"and it would be right to give only him the proper location of the treasure. Send this other man to me."

When Edgar awakened, the farmer had gone, and the Squire was regarding him with open admiration. Edgar had made it obvious he could read for anyone, anywhere, anytime.

"What did I say," said Edgar, "that drove him off?"

The Squire laughed. "You practically told that man he was a thief, trying to take over somebody else's property."

Edgar yawned, reaching for a glass of milk, before he remembered where he was.

"And was I right?"

"I would say so, from the expression on his face, particularly when you mentioned the rightful owner. He seemed to know exactly who you meant, and took off like a tall bird."

The two men laughed together, and the son looked fondly at his father. "As long as you're conducting the readings, Pa, I have every confidence they won't be misused or capitalized on wrongly."

The Squire flushed with pleasure.

At the outset, it was often difficult to determine which requests were properly motivated, and which weren't. As the solution of crime appeared a laudable endeavor, it seemed for a time as if Edgar might become a psychic sleuth and concentrate on crime detection and missing persons.

Jefferson Pope, a young artist friend of Edgar's, who had once had a successful health reading, was as enchanted with the scope of Edgar's knowledge as was the Squire. In the field of unsolved mystery, particularly, he thought that Edgar Cayce's gift opened up all kinds of intriguing possibilities. Bursting with excitement, he dashed into Edgar's studio one day, holding a clipping from the classified advertising columns of a newspaper.

Young Pope excitedly displayed the ad. "You can do it, Edgar. Your dad says you can do anything, and I believe it. All you have to do is sleep on it, and we'll split the reward."

Edgar finally got a look at the paper. The advertisement sought information on the whereabouts of the wife of a prominent Pittsburgh steel magnate. His name was not mentioned. But there was a post-office box number, and the offer of a sizable reward. The magnate was obviously devoted to his wife, for the ad stressed that the woman must not be detained, arrested or otherwise molested, or the reward would be withdrawn.

Edgar scrutinized the ad, then turned to his father, who had just walked in. "What do you think, Pa?"

The Squire perused the clipping carefully. "I don't see how you could do anything but good, and"—he shrugged—"the reward figures to be substantial, with a steel tycoon involved."

A frown darkened Edgar's face. "I shouldn't take money for police work, Pa, not even indirectly."

The Squire shook his head. "I don't see any harm in it, Edgar, so long as the cause is good, but if that's the way you feel—" His face brightened. "But you wouldn't mind Jefferson here having the reward?"

"That would be all right," Edgar said slowly, still not quite easy about it, without knowing why. He laughed aloud, as a sudden stray thought crossed his mind.

"What's so funny?" the Squire inquired suspiciously.

Edgar's laughter subsided. "Here we are squabbling about the reward money, without the slightest notion of what I'll turn up, if anything."

The Squire and Jefferson Pope did not share his misgivings.

This particular reading presented a new dimension for both the Squire and his son.

The Squire pondered how he would phrase the questioning. After all, they had no subject making a direct appeal for assistance. In this case the information was sought by a third party, Jefferson Pope, who had no true involvement in the matter. But there was no question of the basic motivation. The ad clearly showed that the steelman loved his wife and would welcome her warmly, wherever she had gone off. If it was wrong for the man to tear asunder that which God has joined together, then it was equally praiseworthy to rejoin that which had been sundered.

In his own mind Edgar was sure Gertrude would have been totally sympathetic. And so he was ready for the reading, whenever the Squire was.

The Squire finally had figured out an expeditious way of getting into the problem. As Edgar fell into a trance, he said suggestively, "We have a request from Jefferson Pope of Hopkinsville, an interested citizen. He is seeking to locate the body of a woman who last week left her husband's bed and board in Pittsburgh, and is now being sought by this husband, who wants no harm or distress to come to her. Please locate the body, wherever it is at this time."

Such a request had never been made of Cayce before. But if he could visualize an inanimate mass such as the buried treasure and know its history, he should certainly be able to vibrate to a missing lady who was certainly more responsive than an inarticulate mass of metal.

As it proceeded, the reading was a revelation, clearly

132

demonstrating that Edgar was well within the outer boundaries of his gift, wherever these limits lay.

"This woman," he said, as his listeners followed him raptly, "is emotionally distraught and confused at the present time. She loves her husband, but developed the idea through her own feelings of insecurity that he did not return her love." Edgar's eyes were closed as usual, but he had nevertheless a description to offer. "I see this woman clearly. She has dark brown hair, piled up on the top of her head, hazel eyes set wide apart. She is forty or forty-one years of age."

Though pleased so far, Jefferson Pope and the Squire anxiously awaited more specific information.

"Where," bluntly asked the Squire, "is this woman at the present time?"

Cayce replied as desired. "In a hotel in Philadelphia." He mentioned the hotel and gave its address.

It was better than they had hoped for. The listeners exchanged happy congratulatory glances.

However, Cayce seemed more concerned with the nature of the woman than her whereabouts. His voice droned on. "Because of her time of life," he went on, "the woman had been suffering acute nervous symptoms, precipitated by a premature onset of the climacteric known as the change of life.

"There was a domestic quarrel over a trivial matter. I see her slamming a door, and walking out of the house, not even bothering to look back or pack a bag."

Thinking of the reward, Jefferson Pope suggested the Squire ask for any additional descriptive material that would impress the husband as to the authenticity of the information.

"She stands five feet six inches, without shoes," Cayce responded at once, "and weighed one hundred and thirty-five pounds at the time of her disappearance. Her hair is of a chestnut tone." He paused. "I see a birthmark, a round mole, on the right hip."

Jefferson Pope whistled under his breath. That could very well be the clincher. If Cayce was right about

133

the mole, he was presumably right about everything else. Jefferson Pope moved swiftly. Almost before Cayce was out of trance, he had gone to the telephone and sent a wire to the box number listed in the classified ad.

It was a telegram calculated to evoke a quick response from any husband: "Does your wife have a mole on her right hip?"

The reply came back by wire that same day: "Sending private detective first train. Please cooperate fullest. Reward stands."

Jefferson Pope was delighted. He counted the words in the terse wire, an even ten, the special-rated limit for a day message.

"You can tell he's a millionaire," he exulted, "the way he counts those words."

The detective arrived the next day. He was a hulking figure of a man, in a dark suit and bowler hat, with a gold watch fob and chain strung across his ample midsection. He stepped ponderously into Edgar's photographic studio, looked around curiously, while announcing himself, then asked for a Mr. Jefferson Pope.

The Squire had been awaiting the detective's arrival. "He'll be here in a few moments," he said, "but meanwhile you can ask whatever questions you like. My son got the information on the missing woman."

The detective took a folded telegram out of his suitcoat pocket and glanced through it briefly. "You mean you have this information as well?"

"Oh, yes, Old man came up with that, and a lot of other things besides."

The detective handed the Squire his card. His name was Hobbitt, Harrison Hobbitt, and he styled himself a private investigator. "And you may be?" he asked, trying not to stare down the Squire.

The Squire was enjoying the situation vastly. "I'm the father of the world's greatest living psychic."

The detective gulped this down, without digesting it, then gave the Squire a shrewd, appraising look. "Before we get into anything serious, my employer would like to know the source of information for"—he coughed discreetly—"the lady's birthmark."

The Squire ignored the tacit appeal to delicacy. "My son dug that up," he said with relish, "along with everything else."

"What do you mean everything else?"

"I thought your employer was primarily interested in finding his wife."

Harrison Hobbitt blinked incredulously. "You mean, you know where she is?"

The Squire nodded in delighted satisfaction. "We even know the train she took out of Pittsburgh, the time she arrived in Philadelphia and the hotel she checked into."

The investigator shook his head in disbelief. He looked at the Squire as if he had indeed departed his senses. "How could you know all that unless you had kidnaped her?"

The Squire hooked his thumbs in his vest. "I just happen to have the most amazing son in the world. There's nothing he doesn't know."

At this precise moment, the glorified subject of the discussion opened an inner door and poked his head into the room. "Pa," he called out in a high-pitched voice, "do you know when the minstrel show gets in town? Gertrude would like to know."

The Squire swallowed hard. "No, I don't Edgar, but I'd like you to meet Detective Hobbitt. He's come all the way from Pittsburgh about the missing wife you located."

Cayce stepped into the room and took the other man's hand. "Hope the information is helpful," he said. "I think she's sorry about running out, and would like to come back."

Hobbitt's jaw dropped. "He doesn't know about a simple show, but he knows all about another man's wife."

He was slated for still another surprise.

Jefferson Pope bounded in cheerfully. He acknowledged the detective with a friendly grin, then said, "Give us the lady's name, and we can check the Philadelphia hotel, and perhaps talk to her."

The detective shook his head hopelessly. "You have her described to a T, you know where she is, even the train she took, and you don't know her name. I don't understand. What kind of place is this?" He looked around the room uneasily, as if he were in a house of lunatics.

Jefferson Pope explained, with an apologetic laugh. "Nobody thought to ask that question. But we knew we'd be hearing from the husband, if there was anything at all to what Edgar said. And we were sure there was."

Harrison Hobbitt concentrated his gaze on the principal protagonist, the slim young man with the steel-blue eyes, now tinkering idly with a camera.

"We should take your picture, Mr. Hobbitt, in honor of this occasion," this young man said mildly.

Hobbitt held up his hands. "I don't want any pictures," said he gruffly. "I want to know how you found out what you did."

Jefferson Pope, with a wink at the Squire, put in sweetly, "I should think you'd be more concerned about where the lady is at present. Isn't that what the reward's for?"

The detective's calm was the least bit ruffled. "Yes, of course. Now what was the name of that hotel?"

The Squire beamed happily. "Why don't you go to that phone"—he pointed to the instrument hanging on the wall—"and call the hotel and ask for the little lady? That will effectively end the speculation about my son's abilities."

In something of a daze, the detective picked up the reciever and made his call. "I'll reimburse you for this," he said loftily.

The Squire made a grand gesture. "Don't bother with such trifles. Merely add it to the reward money."

They watched closely as the detective made a person-to-person call, giving the name of the missing woman to the telephone operator. Happily, it never occurred to them that the vanishing lady might have registered under a false name.

As they looked on intently, the detective's face brightened, then fell. He turned to them disconsolately. "She was there for several days, then checked out. She left no forwarding address."

If not for the disappointment, they would have laughed at the thought of a fugitive in flight leaving an address where she could be trailed and tracked down.

The detective relinquished the phone with a look of frustration. "We missed her by a day."

Jefferson Pope jumped to his feet. "Edgar can give us another reading and let us know where she is right now."

The Squire nodded an emphatic assent, as Harrison Hobbitt was freshly bewildered.

Edgar Cayce seemed strangely reticent. "Perhaps," he said softly, "this lady doesn't want to go back to her husband."

The detective was shaken out of his quandary. "What difference does that make?"

Cayce regarded him mildly. "Well, you don't know anything about what I do, sir. But it is necessary for me to be properly motivated to receive any useful information while I am asleep."

The detective gulped, then decided to rise above this last bit of insanity. "I should think the reward money would be motivation enough, sleep, or no sleep. What is this nonsense?"

Cayce returned his gaze thoughtfully. "That's what bothers me, the reward money."

His father, distressed at this new turn of events, fell back hopefully on logic. "It would be unkind to give this husband hope, then withhold it in almost the same breath."

Edgar Cayce sighed. "I suppose you're right, Pa. I shouldn't be playing God."

The Squire rubbed his hands together gleefully, and Jefferson Pope's face, strained for a moment, relaxed in a smile of expectation.

Without any more ado, Edgar slipped off his hard collar, his tie and shoes, loosened his belt, and lay down on the reception room couch, as the shaken detective watched with wide-eyed wonder.

The Squire held up an admonitory finger. "Don't say anything at all, sir, until Edgar has finished his reading. We are not yet sure how much he is open to suggestion or the influence of others during his sleeping state."

The investigator weakly shook his head. "Don't worry about me," he said. "I'm totally speechless."

His eyes bulged uncertainly as the Squire deftly put Edgar into the sleeping state and then asked, supplying the name of the lady but no address:

"Can you locate the body of this woman, which was in Pittsburgh, and then left for Philadelphia? Locate this body's whereabouts, and describe, if you can, where she is at this very instant. She is being sought by her husband, who loves her and is worried about her."

Cayce hesitated but a moment, then said in a clear voice, apparently tuning in to the subject's current movements, "I see her in a railroad station. She is leaving now and looking about for a hansom cab to take her to a hotel. She is carrying a small bag, with the overnight things she purchased during her travels. She is tired, very tired, her shoulders are drooping, and she wishes that she were back home in Pittsburgh with her husband."

Even the Squire, accustomed to Cayce's ingenuity, was taken aback by this running commentary. "What city is this?" he finally asked.

"New York City. A frightening city, so big, so strange, so impersonal, the heavy traffic on the street she finds very confusing."

"She has not yet checked into a hotel?"

"She is giving the name to a cabbie, the Astor House just around from the Pennsylvania Station in New York City. She is walking through the door of the hotel, approaching the desk to register." He seemed to be monitoring her with his voice.

138

The Squire darted a glance at the detective, who was truly speechless.

"Is she registering under her right name?" the Squire asked.

"Her right name," Edgar came back slowly.

The Squire looked triumphantly around the room. "We better give the little lady time to get to her room and perform a few of the necessary ablutions."

In the five minutes that ensued, with Edgar still in trance, a heavy silence hung over the room. Then, the Squire again nodded to the wall phone and suggested that Harrison Hobbitt make a new call.

The detective reached uncertainly for the phone.

"Just talk to the desk and make sure she's there," Jefferson Pope put in, concerned about startling the quarry before she settled down for the night.

"As a precautionary measure," said the Squire, "we'll keep Edgar under until Mr. Hobbitt ascertains whether she is there. We may need another reading."

The investigator put through his call to the room clerk of the New York hotel.

A minute later, he limply dropped the phone on the receiver. "She's there," he said dreamily, "checked in this minute."

He looked around the room with a curious expression. "I'm off to New York City on the first train, gentlemen. And I should be there in the morning. I don't know what to say, except that it has been a remarkable experience." He pointed to the slumbering figure on the couch. "That young man must talk to God," he said with a tone of reverent awe. "There's no other way that it's possible." He paused awkwardly. "May I have the privilege of shaking his hand? I may never meet his like again."

As Edgar came to, Jefferson Pope and the Squire also pumped his hand enthusiastically.

"You did it again, Edgar," cried Pope. "You're the greatest."

The psychic gave a wan smile. "You would do well, Jefferson," he said reprovingly, "to remember who is the greatest."

In this case, with the wife reunited with her doting husband, the ends apparently justified the means. But Edgar had an uncomfortable feeling that the reward money, even though he shared none of it, somehow blurred the motivation.

The Squire argued reasonably enough that doctors, even as they performed errands of mercy, exacted a fair fee, as did teachers, nobly educating the young, and ministers, preaching the word of the Lord.

"I guess," Edgar drawled in return, "that every man must march to the beat of his own drum. Somehow, in this case, the money part disturbs me, Pa."

After the announcement of the reunion, they heard no more from either the private detective or the steel magnate, and then ten days later there was a letter from Pittsburgh with a check in it. The envelope was addressed to Mr. Edgar Cayce, Psychic Extraordinary.

Edgar read the letter slowly, then turned to the Squire, who was bending over his shoulder. "He says his wife is happy to be back, and that they would like to come and visit me. They owe me so much." He put his head in his hands and prayed. "I wasn't sure, Pa, and now I am sure. The motivation was proper, for they are rejoined happily as man and wife, and beginning a new life together."

The Squire whistled at the size of the check. "You could buy a new house with that, Edgar."

Edgar slowly, impassively, tore the check in two. His father put out a hand to stop him but it was too late. "Send him a note with his check, Pa, and say their happiness is reward enough for me. I just can't put a price on happiness."

The Squire gave his son a long look, "All right, Old Man." He almost choked over the words. "Whatever you feel is right. But you're making a mistake. This man will never miss it, and he wants you to have it."

He was still grimacing unhappily when Jefferson Pope bounded in with a happy smile. He held up a check on a Pittsburgh bank. "Thanks to Edgar, I'm a rich man. How about that, Squire?"

The Squire eyed him glumly, then with a wink at Edgar, said largely in jest:

"It is easier for a camel to go through the eye of a needle than for a rich man to enter into the Kingdom of God."

Jefferson Pope didn't seem to mind.

The case of the missing woman, as the Squire thought of it, tended to further confuse Edgar Cayce's own thinking about the use of his gift. Did it matter that Jefferson Pope had profited financially, so long as a desired and worthwhile objective was accomplished? What harm for his friend or his father to share this money, so freely offered? And what harm was there in Cayce making it possible for him to have this money, so long as he, Cayce, had not profited in any way? The more he thought about it, the more confused he got.

Jefferson Pope was now certain that Edgar Cayce had found a secure niche for himself as psychic detective. He daily scoured the newspapers for unsolved crimes, urging Cayce to undertake random readings on them.

But Edgar only demurred with a smile. "Jeff," he said one day, "I can physically do only two readings a day, and I'd rather help people with their health problems. If they get better, at least I can see then the good that I'm doing."

But Jefferson Pope, flushed by that first success, was not easily put off. Shortly thereafter, he struck up a conversation at a bar with a traveling salesman which reawakened his interest in this phase of psychic work. The salesman had just come from the Midwest, where a major conversation piece revolved about the mysterious slaying of an elderly and eccentric recluse. The victim, shot through the heart, had lived with a younger sister in a palatial residence closely guarded by fierce dogs. Though wealthy, the spinster sisters had no servants, as they preferred their privacy. Tradesmen called weekly, leaving their supplies in a small gatehouse just outside the brick walls that enclosed the big house, which was further protected by a moat. The woman was apparently shot as she started down a second-floor staircase; her crumpled body was found at the foot of the stairs. Police theorized that the crime had been committed in the afternoon, while the sister was taking her customary nap in a remote wing of the mansion. But there was no tangible clue. The sister had been awakened, conceivably, by the opening and shutting of a window. One window, near the body, was unlocked. All other windows and doors were tightly secured from within. The sister said she had also heard the dogs, but thought nothing of this as they often barked for no apparent reason.

The sisters' aura of mystery, their background of wealth, the apparent lack of motive, all gave the case great public interest. The newspapers had a Roman holiday, running elaborate diagrams of the grounds, spotting the positions of the dogs, the gatehouse, and a drawbridge, lowered only when the sisters roamed the spacious gardens, tending their flowers and plants, and absorbing the fresh air and sunshine.

The surviving sister would normally have been a suspect. But there seemed no motive for a murder which deprived her of her lifetime companion. The sisters had lived together for sixty years. There were musty stories of a romance when hearts were young and gay, with a handsome suitor sadly turned away. But nobody now remembered which sister was involved, nor did it seem to matter greatly at this time.

As the traveling man went over the details of the mystery, Jefferson Pope's thoughts immediately turned to Cayce. "I know a man who can solve that murder," he said importantly.

The traveling man smiled indulgently.

"I guess there's no reward?" Pope said wistfully.

The traveling man frowned. "I think the sister offered one."

Pope brightened immediately. "Fine," said he, rubbing his hands together.

Edgar Cayce had agreed to the reading with mixed feelings.

"What could possibly be wrong about bringing a murderer to justice?" the Squire argued, visualizing the attention that such a feat would command.

Edgar had no definite answer. "I just don't feel right about interfering in affairs that don't properly concern me."

The Squire quickly saw the flaw in this argument. "How does the health of somebody you never saw concern you?"

The psychic grimaced unhappily. "That's what the lady of the vision saw me doing, helping the sick, and that's the way Gertrude sees it, too. And I have pretty much the same feeling."

The Squire shook his head wearily. "Edgar, you'll be performing a great public service, and maybe you'll know better about this type of thing once you solve this case."

The younger Cayce was not convinced. "I may not get anything," he observed pessimistically.

"You always get something. I've never known you to miss. You're the eighth wonder of the world."

Edgar was too distracted to inquire about the other seven. "All right, Pa," he said finally, with an air of resignation.

The traveling man, Moriarity by name, reacted much as Detective Hobbitt had when Cayce stretched out on his couch. He looked around the room suspiciously.

The Squire put his fingers to his lips, enjoining him to silence.

As Cayce's breathing became rhythmical, indicating a state of deep trance, the Squire mentioned the slain woman's name, gave her place of residence, and suggested Cayce tune in to the circumstances of her death. "How was she killed?" he asked.

Cayce replied at once. "Shot through the heart. Death was instant."

"Who committed this crime?"

Cayce shook his head, then mumbled a bit, inaudibly.

The Squire, sensing an unusual resistance, tried another approach. "Was she killed by a stranger?"

"No, somebody she knew."

Both Moriarity and Jefferson Pope perked up at this.

"And who was this person?"

Cayce sighed heavily.

"Who was it?" the Squire persisted.

"Somebody she knew," he repeated dully.

The Squire took another approach, as any investigator would on hitting a dead end. "Can you describe the murder weapon?"

The slumbering figure nodded slowly. "It was a gun known as the Single Action Army, manufactured by the Colt company, with six .45 caliber shells loaded from the side into the cylinder. The gun is known as the Peacemaker."

The Squire was firing his questions with the precision of a district attorney. "How many shots were fired?"

"One, all that was necessary. The hammer was cocked once, and fired from so close a distance that it left powder burns on the clothing."

Jefferson Pope looked questioningly at the traveling man. Moriarity shrugged his shoulders. "I don't know. The gun has never been found."

The Squire latched on to this clue. "What happened to the gun after the shooting?" he now asked.

Cayce replied promptly, "The gun was tossed out a second-story window, dropping into a gutter running along the roof. From there, the weapon slid down gradually until it reached a place where the gutter enters into a drain sewer. There it is now, gathering rust."

As the Squire peered down, frustrated, at his sleeping son, a way of indirectly evoking the killer's name came to him. "Who threw the gun out the window?" he demanded.

The oblique question was answered at once, succinctly and to the point. "The sister—it was her gun."

Moriarity gasped at the implication. Jefferson Pope's face lit up and then quickly clouded. The prospect of the sister passing out a reward for her own arrest and conviction was patently slim.

The aroused Squire was in hot pursuit of the killer. "Did she have anything against her older sister?"

"Yes, they argued about a man."

Moriarity smiled smugly, and even the Squire was incredulous at the thought of two spinsters in their eighties quarreling over a man. "Are you sure this was the cause of their ill feeling?"

"Very sure. It all began more than sixty years ago. Both loved the same man then, and he loved the younger sister. But the older practiced a deception when she found she couldn't have him for herself, telling the suitor that her sister loved another man."

"And this wasn't known at the time?"

"Not then. The younger sister only recently found a faded letter declaring his love. Her sister, long ago, had taken it from a messenger, read it, and somehow mislaid it."

The Squire kept firing away. "How did the younger sister learn about the letter?"

"Just cleaning out a drawer, she noticed the yellowed envelope with her name on it, and opened it out of curiosity."

"And then what happened?"

"On reading the letter, she realized that she had been cruelly duped. She thought of the love that could have been hers all these years. She demanded an explanation, and when her sister laughed at her, she lost her head and picked up a gun they had in the house. She fired once, then fainted. When she revived, she called the police."

Cayce's voice suddenly seemed tired.

"Is the body of Edgar Cayce all right?" the Squire asked anxiously, referring to Cayce specifically, as it was always necessary to differentiate between him and the subject of the reading.

There was no answer, and the Squire quickly proceeded to take his son out of his trance. "When

145

you wake, you will not remember anything you have said or experienced. It will be a pleasant awakening, and you will be refreshed. Wake up."

Cayce sat up slowly. He shook his head a few times, and then made an effort to speak. His voice had its normal tone, clear and high-pitched. The Squire gave a sigh of relief.

Edgar got up and stretched his legs. He looked at his father inquiringly. "I feel strange, Pa."

The traveling man was viewing him with wondering eyes. "If you're right in what you said, young fellow, you've got to be the greatest thing on this Godforsaken planet since you-know-who."

"What did I say?"

After Moriarity had repeated the gist of the reading, Edgar Cayce groaned. "Now I know why I feel funny. I don't like the thought of incriminating people."

Jefferson Pope took issue with this. "But you are bringing a murderer to justice."

Edgar looked disgusted. "Justice? Sending a poor creature, mourning a lost life, to the death chamber, that's justice? No, thank you, let the police do their job, and I'll do mine."

The Squire regarded his son uneasily. "Edgar we'll have to contact the police. We just can't suppress this information. If the gun isn't where you say it is," he added hopefully, "they'll forget it all."

"Do as you like," cried Edgar. "I wash my hands of it."

But he was not that easily out of it.

That evening, Moriarity phoned the Midwestern police investigating the murder and passed on Edgar's information. The following morning they found the gun where Edgar had said it was. The gun answered his description precisely. It was a Colt .45, a Peacemaker. It had been fired once.

Two days later, an out-of-town detective with a vigilant eye knocked at Edgar's door. With him was a member of the local police force.

Edgar was in the middle of photographing a four year-old boy. "I'll be a while," he told his visitors.

"We'll wait," they said grimly.

After the picture was finally taken, Cayce sat down, took out his pipe, and drew on it contentedly. "What can I do for you gentlemen?" he asked pleasantly.

The visiting detective, a sallow-faced man with darting eyes, assumed the leader's role. "Your name is Edgar Cayce?"

Cayce nodded, puffing away unconcernedly.

"You claim to be a psychic diagnostician?"

Cayce's trouble center, near the solar plexus, signaled a warning. "I don't claim anything," he said.

The detective's gaze held him closely. "Did you supply the information leading to the finding of the murder weapon in the case under police investigation."

"What case are you speaking of?"

"That in which an elderly recluse was foully shot to death."

Cayce was immediately relieved. "From what they tell me, I said where the gun was, and they found it." He laughed. "Beats me."

The detective's face sharpened. "This is a very serious matter."

"It had never occurred to me to think of murder otherwise."

The two detectives exchanged significant glances. "You realize, of course, that you are implicated."

Cayce's jaw dropped. "Me implicated? You must be out of your minds."

The detective's face hardened. "That attitude will get you nowhere."

Cayce's eyes traveled from the visitor to the local policeman. "What other attitude could I have?"

The Hopkinsville police officer, whom Cayce knew only by sight, interposed gravely, "The investigating police point out that only the murderer could have known where the murder gun had been thrown and lay concealed. That certainly seems reasonable."

Cayce's voice rose indignantly. "Are you gentlemen trying to suggest that I took that Single Action Colt and fired a bullet five hundred miles into the air, hitting

147

that poor old lady as she was coming down the stairs? Well, that's what I had to do, as I haven't been out of Hopkinsville in eight years."

The outburst had the effect of easing the tension.

"Then how," asked the investigator more reasonably, "could you have known about the gun?"

Cayce sighed. "Neither of you gentlemen will believe me. But let me call a neighbor, a doctor of some prominence in this town, and he can perhaps explain it to you. He is only down the street, and he can be here in a couple of minutes. I assure you I won't run away in the meantime."

Edgar went to the phone, and as the policemen looked on curiously, he called Wesley Ketchum. His tone was urgent. "Ketchum, I'd like you to come over right away."

Ketchum was amused. "Well, that's a switch, Edgar, you calling me for something."

In a few minutes his steps echoed sharply on the stairs, and Ketchum came bounding into the room. His quick glance took in the local detective, recognizing him as a patient, and then traveled to the second policeman. "Who have you killed, Edgar?" he asked humorously.

Edgar groaned. "That's about the worst thing you could have said, Ketchum."

As Edgar explained the situation, Ketchum broke into a wave of uncontrollable laughter, the tears streaming down his face. "It serves you right, Cayce, for not signing with me. Then nobody would bother you but me."

Ketchum then proceeded to explain patiently the strange power that was Edgar Cayce's. "When he's asleep, gentlemen, this man knows exactly what's going on in your body, your house, or the world around you. He's a freak." He told them about Dietrich and Dalton. "He can even pick the horses, though he's never done it for me."

The detective looked at him skepticallly, but the Hopkinsville man had been impressed by the doctor's credibility. "The doctor must know what he's talking about," he whispered. "I can't make this arrest."

Ketchum gave Cayce a look of amused triumph. Then, turning to the visiting detective, he said loftily, "Haven't you arrested anybody for the crime yet, my good man?"

The detective masked his irritation. "I wouldn't be here if we had."

"But why haven't you arrested the sister, since Mr. Cayce supplied the motive?"

The detective shrugged his disbelief. "How do we know there's anything to it?"

"How did you know there was anything to the gun information?"

"We found the gun."

"Right, so why not pursue this line of inquiry with the sister?"

The detective gave him a grudging look. "She is being questioned," he admitted reluctantly.

"And how long has this questioning been going on?"

"Since yesterday."

Ketchum indicated the phone on the wall. "Call your headquarters. I happen to know that Edgar Cayce is always right. As a doctor, I also know that no guilty octogenarian can stand up to hours of grilling without acknowledging her guilt."

In a few minutes, the detective was conversing with his superiors in the Midwestern city. As they watched, his face underwent several changes of expression, and the phone slid limply out of his fingers.

"The sister has confessed. It was all like Mr. Cayce said."

7

Help Begins at Home

Something soon happened to change Dr. House's opinion of Edgar Cayce. House's wife, Carrie Salter, Gertrude's favorite aunt, had become ill, and the doctors had urged an early operation for an abdominal tumor.

Gertrude thought otherwise. Sitting on the House verandah, enjoying the cool breeze on a sultry summer day, Gertrude urged her aunt to turn to Edgar Cayce.

Although fond of Edgar, Carrie was less than enthusiastic. "How could all those doctors be wrong?" she asked.

"Doctors! Look at that Dr. Ketchum, sniveling around Edgar in the dark, then taking all the credit." Gertrude gave her youthful aunt a fond glance. "Before you let them cut you open, Carrie, promise you'll have a reading from Edgar."

Carrie did not find the prospect of surgery particularly enticing. "If Dr. House has no objections," she consented, as usual giving her husband his full title. "After all, what harm can it do?"

Dr. House made a wry face, but agreed on one stipulation: secrecy. "What would my patients say if they knew my wife was consulting a freak?"

The session was arranged, and the Cayces came over to the Houses' after dinner. There was nobody else in the house, and House, taking no chances,

150

Dr. Wesley Ketchum, *circa* 1905. This photograph presented
to the Edgar Cayce Foundation by Dr. Ketchum's son,
Alton Ketchum.

Edgar's parents: Carrie Major Cayce and the Squire,
Leslie B. Cayce (*facing page*). Photographed in Hopkinsville,
Kentucky, about 1900.

Gertrude Evans and Edgar Cayce, engaged at the time, gave
each other these portrait photographs for Christmas presents.
(Bowles Studio, Hopkinsville, Kentucky)

(*Opposite page*) Photograph by Edgar Cayce of a mother and
child in Hopkinsville, Kentucky, September, 1904.

Carrie Salter House (Mrs. Thomas B.), Hopkinsville, Kentucky, about 1906.

Family portrait. Sitting: Edgar's parents, Carrie Major and Leslie B. Cayce. Standing: Edgar holding son Hugh Lynn Cayce; Gertrude Evans Cayce; and Annie Cayce, Edgar's oldest sister. Cayce Studio, Hopkinsville, Kentucky, 1909.

Edgar Cayce, *circa* 1910. (Tresslar's Studio,
Montgomery, Alabama)

carefully drew the shades. Gertrude, as was becoming her practice, quickly put Edgar in trance and gave the suggestion that in this state he go over her aunt's body. There was no mention of a tumor or any other ailment.

"Do you have the body?" she asked the sleeping figure.

He hesitated but a second. "It is in this very house," he replied.

Dr. House and his wife sat within a foot or two of the sofa on which Cayce was comfortably reclining, while Gertrude, sitting near his head, jotted down notes as he spoke. Dr. House's expression was noncommittal, as Cayce, in a strong voice, mentioned that the subject was in good health generally.

"The body is in excellent condition, but should be more careful of her diet, especially at this time as so much is dependent on her."

A faint smile played on Dr. House's lips, but his wife's face wore a puzzled frown. "What is that all about?" she whispered to her niece.

Gertrude promptly asked, "Why should Aunt Carrie—the body—watch her food intake at this time more than any other? Please answer this question."

"The body," said Cayce, "is expecting that crowning achievment of woman, motherhood, and should consider at all times the heavy responsibility she has toward this new life within her."

There was an embarrassed silence. Gertrude, herself pregnant with her first child, assumed that Edgar must somehow have mistakenly tuned in to her condition. Dr. House was openly scornful. "Why, even the Freak—I mean Edgar—should know that Carrie can't have children. That's been a well-known family secret for years. Every doctor in town has confirmed that diagnosis."

Aunt Carrie, a gentle soul, sympathetically reached out and pressed Gertrude's hand. "Don't worry, dear. I do appreciate that you and Edgar have tried to help."

Gertrude's eyes were pleading now. "Let me put

it to Edgar a little more directly, please. He may have confused our conditions. I understand that can sometimes happen when there are several people in a room with the subject."

Dr. House, with a shrug, got up and poured himself a bourbon and branch water.

Carrie was more polite. "Certainly, my dear, whatever you say."

Gertrude made her words as deliberate as she could. "Are you trying to say that this body is pregnant with child?"

Cayce's lips moved. "Not only trying to say it, but have said it. And the body is again cautioned to be very careful as the child may be delivered before its time, and sickly for a while after birth."

"Is there anything like a tumor?" Gertrude quickly asked, before Cayce could conclude the reading.

"The body is in good health; there is no tumor, and the nausea from the stomach and the like is a form of what is commonly known as morning sickness."

To the disbelieving Houses, it seemed for a moment that a smile was playing on the lips of the slumbering figure.

"Is there anything else?" Gertrude threw in.

"We have finished. There is no more to add. The body knows what it should do."

Before Cayce could be brought out of his trance, Dr. House, normally not renowned for his humor, said sardonically, "The body knows darn well what it should do; it should let one of our fine surgeons operate on her."

"And what do you think?" Carrie turned to her niece.

Gertrude held on loyally. "I think Edgar meant you should do what your own feminine intuition tells you."

"My own feeling," said Carrie, "is that I don't have a tumor. So the body"—she looked sharply at her husband—"is going to have some tests made for pregnancy."

152

"It's time," responded House, "for me to get to sleep."

Cayce awoke, refreshed as usual, then took on a puzzled expression as his eyes traveled over the room without finding his host.

"Where's Dr. House?" he asked.

"He was tired," said Aunt Carrie, "and went off to bed."

Cayce looked apologetic. "I guess I didn't say anything much."

Gertrude playfully touched her fingers to his lips. "No, dear, only that Aunt Carrie, who's never supposed to have children, is pregnant and expecting one."

"I'll be darned," Cayce said. "No wonder Dr. House walked out. I don't blame him."

Carrie leaned over and kissed Edgar affectionately on the brow. "Edgar, there's only one like you, thank the Lord."

That was the last the couples saw of one another for a week, and then one morning Aunt Carrie called. She was jubilant: "Gertrude, Gertrude," she cried, "I have the most wonderful news. I'm going to have a baby."

Gertrude's voice gave no inkling of surprise. "But, dear, isn't that exactly what Edgar told you?"

In a few months, Carrie's baby was born prematurely, at seven months, and was sickly from birth. They despaired of its life. Convulsions racked its tiny body. Dr. House had no idea what was wrong. Several doctors were called in, without being able to relieve the infant. Finally the Houses decided to ask Edgar Cayce for help.

"It's our only chance," the mother pleaded.

House reluctantly called in the three doctors attending and announced his decision.

Dr. Sanders was one of the doctors. "If you call in that faker," said he, "it's on your own head."

"I have to consider my wife's wishes," House said lamely. "After all, Cayce was right about Mrs. House being pregnant."

Sanders, followed by a Dr. Hackett, a medium-sized man with a solemn face, strode stiff-legged out of the house.

Only Dr. Janson, the long-time family physician, remained. "As long as your minds are made up, I can't budge you," said he. "But before you do whatever Cayce says, I think you owe it to the child to let the family physician know."

Dr. House took his hand, gratefully. "I promise you that."

Again, a reading took place at the Houses', this time for an infant who could neither speak nor understand, but only cry heartbreakingly with each new convulsion.

The reading was brief. Cayce described the convulsions and said they would vanish almost at once if the proper relaxing agent were given. That agent was the pupil-dilating drug, belladonna, a form of the deadly nightshade. It was, illogically, to be administered in more than the normal dosage.

Dr. House was chagrined. "That might be a fatal dose. I never have heard of anything like that." He remembered his promise to Janson.

Janson listened in disbelief. "If you give that child what Cayce says," he told Carrie, "you'll be giving your child deadly poison."

The convulsive cries of the baby could be heard from another room. Carrie's mind was made up. "You're one of the doctors that wanted to operate on me for a tumor," she recalled. "I'll do as Edgar Cayce says. He was right before and I pray he is right now."

"The responsibility is yours."

"So be it," said Carrie.

She turned to her undecided husband. "Measure out the dose, Dr. House," said she with determination. "I'll give it to the child if you won't."

House's face was solemn. "Actually, it is an overdose of an already dangerous drug."

"Yes," rejoined Carrie, "but Edgar also prescribed

an antidote if the baby didn't react favorably, and he said we would know right away."

House was noticeably agitated. "It is a terrible chance we are taking, Carrie, and my own professional reputation is at stake."

"And your child's life is at stake; what of that?" There was a desperate note in her voice. "If they only prescribed a course of treatment. But they do nothing, and expect us to watch our baby die without lifting a finger."

Her voice rang out. "Let us trust in God, Dr. House, and Edgar's medicine. Measure out the dose."

The Houses went into the baby's room together, as Edgar and Gertrude waited anxiously. They were gone no more than five minutes. When they returned, Carrie was carrying the child in her arms, only its tiny head showing in its swaddling clothes.

There had been a miracle. The baby was relaxed and no longer sobbing convulsively. "Look," cried Carrie, as the baby smiled and then with a yawn closed its eyes. "That's its first sleep in forty-eight hours."

Edgar Cayce had stepped out onto the porch to hide his emotion. Dr. House followed him out and saw him standing against the rail, his eyes raised to the stars.

House touched him lightly on the shoulder and took his hand. "Forgive me for ever doubting you," said he. "You saved Carrie, and now you have saved our son. Whatever you are doing, I believe in you. God's hand is on you, and our hearts are yours. Whatever you ask, may God make yours."

Now more than ever, Gertrude was convinced that Edgar's future lay in helping the sick. "That is why God has given you this gift," she said.

Cayce was not so sure. "If God wanted me to heal the sick, why didn't he fix it so I would become a doctor?"

She smiled. "You would have been a doctor like everyone else, bound by the same orthodoxy they are bound by."

"I like taking pictures." He laughed. "If something goes wrong, I can always take another shot."

The prophet still lacked recognition of his gift, and without this realization he was not ready yet to be a full-fledged instrument of life and death.

But God worked in wondrous ways, as Edgar Cayce was to know. He was to remember what his mother had once said: "We ask for strength, and God gives us difficulties which make us strong. We plead for courage, and God gives us danger to overcome. We ask favors, and God gives us opportunities. We pray for happiness, and God gives us challenges to test our faith."

The faith of Edgar Cayce was soon to receive a supreme test. Gertrude's baby had been born not long after Carrie's child, and, like Carrie's, it was ailing almost from birth. Milton Porter Cayce, at three weeks, developed whooping cough and then colitis. Daily, the child grew weaker, without the doctors being able to help. Although he had read successfully for Carrie's child, Cayce didn't feel confident enough to read for his own child. His father spoke to him; so did Ketchum and others. But he only shook his head.

Only Gertrude did nothing to influence him. "Edgar has to make this decision himself," she said. "If he doesn't feel it wise to read for his own flesh and blood, then it wouldn't work."

Ketchum's professional advice was not sought.

"What can he do?" she told the Squire. "Without Edgar, he is no different from any other doctor in town, except that he's a Yankee."

The Squire was admittedly baffled. "Edgar has helped so many others, why does he feel that he can't help his own?"

"He's too emotionally involved," Gertrude replied patiently. "He said it was like a doctor operating on his own wife or child, or treating himself, for that matter."

The Squire nodded. "Doctors are always saying that a man who treats himself has a fool for a doctor and an idiot for a patient."

Listening to his baby's racking cough, Cayce prayed for guidance. But pray as he would, no message came through. One night, as their baby appeared to be failing, Edgar turned to his wife. "Gertrude," he implored, "tell me what to do."

She shook her head, thinking of what it might do to her husband if the baby died anyway. "When you ask me, Edgar, you have already decided in your own mind."

"You're right, Gertrude," he almost sobbed. "I don't have the confidence. For all I know, I may be the fake they say I am."

"You're no fake, Edgar," she said gently. "You're just not sure now what you can do, and what you can't. But you will be."

That night the infant passed away.

Edgar was inconsolable. "What could have been lost," he said bitterly, "if I had read for that poor thing? I helped Carrie and her son, Dalton and the Dietrich child, and I did nothing for our darling son."

For once, Gertrude had no word of comfort. She was desolated by the child's death. Her face was drawn and her eyes hollow from the sleepless vigil at the child's side. She sat silently, holding the baby's tiny hand in hers, caressing the tiny face that was at last at peace.

"At least, he isn't suffering any more," said Edgar, with a catch in his voice. "God has seen to that."

"Yes, God must have needed him more than we did," she said wearily.

From that day, Gertrude's decline became increasingly noticeable. She had never been robust, and now she developed a cold with a hacking cough. She took to her bed, rising only to prepare Edgar's breakfast or greet him in the evening. They were able to afford a maid now, which made it possible for her to rest during the day.

As she showed no sign of getting well, Dr. Janson began to show concern. Janson suspected that Gertrude's will to live had received a traumatic blow with her baby's death. But how did a doctor treat a mental condition? He could talk to Gertrude till he was blue but he could not lift her depression. Looking at his wife fade before his eyes, Edgar Cayce was in the greatest quandary of his life. He had no confidence in the doctors, yet where could he turn? All the doctors could say was that she was suffering from an infection. But what it was, and what brought it on, that was conjecture. Icy fingers of fear clutched at Cayce's heart. Suppose that he should lose her, as he had the baby. He couldn't bear the thought of it. He got down on his knees, and then remembered he had prayed in the same way for his child. Prayer wasn't enough. God needed some manifestation of man's desire to help himself. Yet he was still afraid to rest Gertrude's life on the fragile thread of a psychic reading. Perhaps he could do a test reading, one that would not commit her to any treatment, but might give the doctors a clue.

He turned to his father. The Squire, as usual, was eager to put Edgar to sleep. Where once he thought his son a dunce, he now considered him a genius, who could do no wrong.

"Of course, Edgar, you're the one who can do it. And you should. After all, she's your wife."

Young Cayce groaned inwardly.

"All right, Pa, let's see if I can come up with anything."

He stretched out on his comfortable black couch in a deserted studio.

After the suggestion for help was given, the slumbering Cayce reacted as he would have to anybody else's name. The words that poured out were totally impersonal. "We have the body. It is not in good condition, and has been affected by a depressed mental attitude brought on by excessive grief. There has been a serious loss of appetite. And even when food is consumed, because of an emotional imbalance, there has been a corresponding imbalance of the glands, preventing the body from assimilating properly that food which it has taken. Thus, when there is an illness,

158

the body has become impoverished by lack of nutriment in the blood to supply the rebuilding forces in the body. The seat of the present difficulty is in the left side, at the lower extremity of the lung, what some might call pleurisy."

When Cayce came to, his father told him exactly what he had said. "You mentioned it was pleurisy, but you also said that it had something to do with Gertrude's attitude, and I don't know what any doctor can do about that."

Cayce gave the Squire a bleak look. "What more can I do? Tell me, and I will."

"You can tell Dr. Janson about this reading. And if that isn't enough, you can give Gertrude a reading in depth, not only telling what is wrong, but how it can be made right."

"Speak to Janson first," said Cayce. "I can't read for Gertrude unless she asks me to. I need to know she has confidence in me. Otherwise, I don't know what will happen."

"Gertrude always has had confidence in you."

"It's one thing to be told, another to be shown. I have to be shown."

Dr. Janson was notified of the pleurisy diagnosis, and it checked with other symptoms that had been noted. Complete rest was the best treatment, along with quinine to quiet the fever. But Gertrude's condition appeared only to worsen.

Dr. Janson, a kindly man, asked Cayce to drop by his office. He didn't waste any words. "Edgar, I've known you both since you were children, and I have to be frank with you. Gertrude is a very sick girl. She seemed to lose her zest for life after the baby went, and she has become increasingly vulnerable to an ailment that runs in the family."

Cayce had imagined the worst, and now it seemed to have materialized. "What disease are you talking about?"

"The same that took the life of her younger brother—tuberculosis."

Cayce broke into a cold sweat. He managed to say, "Exactly what are you trying to tell me?"

Janson crossed to the window and looked out sadly on the shaded elms and the bright green expanse of lawn. "I sometimes wonder, Edgar, whether there is any sense to anything we do. We are all so helpless, when God has decided what he wants for us."

Edgar Cayce stood up with a stark look. "And what has God decided, Doctor?"

Janson shook his head. "Bitterness doesn't help, Edgar. Gertrude wouldn't want that."

The young husband reached forward and shook the doctor by the lapels of his suitcoat. "Gertrude is not going to die. I won't let her die."

Janson sighed, making no effort to remove Edgar's hands, and said in a tired voice:

"Unless there is a miracle, Edgar, she has a week, maybe two weeks to live. The disease has gradually sapped her strength and eroded her will to live."

Cayce said with a ringing voice, "I tell you she won't die."

"It's in God's hands, Edgar."

In that instant, as with a drowning man, the whole kaleidoscope of his life passed in review—the mysterious lady who had disclosed his mission to help the sick and the afflicted, the admonition of the great evangelist at the brook that God would help him find his purpose, Gertrude's smile as she told him there was no limit to what he could do, and the memory of his helpless baby racked with a cough that choked the life from its tiny frame.

Dr. Janson was watching him curiously.

"I have given others a reading," said Cayce, "and they have been helped. Now is the time to find out whether I really have any power, or whether it is all imagination."

The doctor nodded. "You are going to give her a reading?"

"Tonight, but she must ask for it. Only in that way can I do it."

"But your baby, how could he ask?"

"He couldn't," Edgar said savagely, "and that's why he's dead, and Gertrude"—his voice faltered—"is at home helpless, because I didn't ask for him."

"Then ask for Gertrude," Janson said. "You're her husband."

"I must know that she trusts me. Then I cannot fail."

He ran most of the way home.

Gertrude smiled feebly as he walked into her room and approached the bed. Her wax-like fingers groped for and found his. She looked up at him tenderly. "Edgar," she said softly, "you are everything a husband should be. I want you to know that, always."

He slipped his arms around her as she tried to sit up.

"I can manage," she said with a touch of her old pertness. "I'm not all that bad." She managed a smile. "You look so serious, Edgar. Don't frown. I will never leave you, really."

"You do want to stay with me then?"

"Always, Edgar, into eternity."

"Then you do want to get well?"

She smiled as she brought a hand to his lips. "You are so solemn."

His heart ached as he noted the thinness of her voice and the haggard features. "You once told me that I could be anything I wanted to be, with faith."

"The moment I first saw you in the bookstore, I knew you were no ordinary man, Edgar. You had greatness written all over you."

He laughed. "I seem to have kept my secret well."

"Oh, you're so modest, that's one of your charms."

Wearily her head fell back on the pillow. The conversation had taken her last bit of strength.

He took her hand in his. "I need you, Gertrude, more than the baby needs you. You must see that. You must." His voice had a rare urgency.

She squeezed his hand. "I know that, Edgar."

"Will you do something for me?"

"Anything, Edgar, that I can."

161

His eyes implored hers. "Will you ask for a reading?"

She gave him a look of infinite tenderness. "Of course, Edgar," and then she closed her eyes, and fell off to sleep, exhausted, a faint smile giving her face a look of extraordinary repose.

After Edgar had left, Dr. Janson summoned Gertrude's mother and her Aunt Carrie. They arrived out of breath from hurrying up the stairs.

Janson was equally candid with them.

Mrs. Evans slumped into a chair. "It's not fair," she cried. "She's so young."

Janson gestured helplessly. "The rain falls on the innocent and wicked alike."

Mrs. Evans' anxious eyes, shadowed by other encounters with tragedy, equally inexplicable in her concept of a righteous God, tried now to search the doctor's face for some expression of hope. "There is no chance?" she asked, as Carrie sat silently next to her, trying with her own mental force to give her sister the strength she needed.

Janson pursed his lips. "There is one chance, but I wouldn't count on it."

Mrs. Evans looked up hopefully. "And what is that?"

"Edgar."

She frowned in her perplexity. "And what of Edgar?"

"He is giving her a reading."

Mrs. Evans' face dropped. "And you, Dr. Janson, call that a chance?" Her voice was heavy with reproach.

Dr. Janson had the grace to blush. "We have nothing better."

Carrie Salter House spoke up. "He helped my little boy, and I will never forget him. Have faith, Lizzie. God works in wondrous ways." Softly, she intoned from Edgar Cayce's favorite book:

" 'And when he saw her, he said, 'Daughter, be of good comfort; thy faith hath made thee whole. And the woman was made whole from that hour.' "

162

Gertrude's mother said dryly, "Carrie, are you comparing Edgar Cayce to Jesus Christ?"

A gleam come into Carrie House's dark gray eyes. "Lizzie Evans, I am ashamed of you. What was said two thousand years ago is as true as it was then. With faith in the Father, others can perform the same healings and more."

"But Edgar Cayce doesn't even pretend to be a healer."

As a practical man, Dr. Janson intervened. "Ladies," said he, "the reading is to be conducted here in my office in the next hour. The Squire will do the questioning, and several of my colleagues will be here, including a lung specialist from Louisville. I have also invited a druggist, in case there is any urgent demand for special drugs."

Mrs. Evans looked up startled. "You're not bringing Gertrude here in her condition?"

Janson laughed rather wryly. "Edgar seems to be able to tune in anywhere, and since the other doctors are curious about his gift, I thought I would have the reading here."

He checked his watch, and the ladies rose from their chairs with the hint. Just as they were leaving, there was a rattle on Janson's door. He opened it, and a serious-miened Cayce walked in, with his father and Dr. Ketchum closely behind.

Mrs. Evans, her eyes brimming with tears, kissed Edgar on the forehead. "May God be with you, Edgar."

Carrie Salter House squeezed his hand, and whispered for him alone. "Every day, I thank God for you, Edgar. God will bless you as he has me."

Cayce watched the two sisters move down the hall, their arms interlaced. He wanted to tell them not to fear, but his mind was too preoccupied to frame the words.

"Come along, Old Man," his father said. "Everybody is waiting."

Dr. Janson had summoned two doctors, both bearded and distinguished-looking, and the druggist, a nondescript type, from an adjacent room. He pointed to an overstuffed couch. "Will this do?"

Edgar slipped off his tie and shoes, loosened his collar. He stretched out on the couch, nodding briefly to the men in the room.

"I am ready, Pa."

His father drew a chair to the couch.

It was a litany Ketchum had heard now dozens of times, but to the other doctors it was an entirely new phenomenon. From their expressions, it was obvious they thought it mumbo jumbo.

As Cayce's eyes closed, and his breathing took on the rhythm of sleep, his father proceeded in an incongruously dull monotone:

"Now the body of Edgar Cayce is assuming its normal forces, and will give such information as is desired of it at the present time."

The Squire now turned his focus on the subject of the reading. "You have before you the body of Gertrude Evans Cayce, who is located at South Main Street, Hopkinsville, Kentucky. You will go over this body carefully, examine it thoroughly, and discuss the conditions you find at the present time, giving the cause of the existing condition, also suggestions for help and relief for this body. You will speak distinctly, at a normal rate of speech. You will answer the questions I will ask."

As though she were anybody else, Cayce's voice, as usual, betrayed no emotion in trance. He spoke in his normal voice, clear and resonant. "We have the body," he said slowly, as if visualizing the form of his absent wife. "We have here inflammation, or congestion, in the lower part of the lung, close to the diaphragm, and an abrasion or irritation on the diaphragm and the pleura below. There is a great deal of congestion in the bronchials and the sinuses, and in the nasal passages. And also a good deal of soreness in the throat and across the diaphragm from coughing. The cough is produced by an insufficiency of blood circulation to remove those products of inflammation and infection from the body through the proper

164

channels. Hence, as we see, the impoverishment of the blood makes it easy for the body to take cold, and further add to the congestion in the upper respiratory regions, aggravating the condition that is already serious and causing hemorrhages."

The faces of the doctors were a cold mask; nothing had been said so far by Cayce that was not already apparent to Dr. Janson and the other men of medicine.

"We know there is congestion if there is tuberculosis," observed the specialist from Louisville.

The faces of the professional observers took on a sardonic look as the Squire, unaffected by their skepticism, came to the crux of the reading: "Give any suggestions for help and relief for this body that will make it well." He paused a long moment. "Speak distinctly and answer this question."

The words gushed out of Cayce. "To relieve this body immediately of the congestion in the lungs, which threatens to extinguish the life force of this body, char the inside of a keg, leaving the interior akin in substance and texture to the material known as charcoal. Into this keg put an ample quantity of apple brandy—repeat apple brandy"—there was no humor in his voice—"and let the body inhale the fumes freely through the day, as if she were breathing of the atmosphere. It can do the body no harm, and the fumes thereof will have a beneficial effect also on the bronchials and the nasal ducts and the entire upper respiratory tract. If this is done, at the same time making a liquid compound of heroin, which will relieve the hemorrhaging which has been weakening the body, then the body will gradually recover and resume its normal forces."

As Cayce's voice lumbered to a halt, the two visiting specialists turned up their noses disdainfully.

"I'll take some of that brandy myself," said the man from Louisville.

"But not in a charred keg," volunteered an equally erudite colleague from Nashville.

165

"And I'll take vanilla," said the druggist with a sigh.

Dr. Janson looked silently from one to the other, then said gravely, "I see no harm in giving her brandy fumes to smell. But I can't see myself prescribing heroin."

The Squire made a sign of protest. "Unless you doctors do everything that Edgar said in trance, she will not get well."

Dr. Janson was adamant. "I will not write out a prescription for the heroin," he said doggedly. "I never heard of such a thing."

"If you had," the Squire pointed out, "there wouldn't have been any need for my son's reading."

"The brandy keg yes, the heroin no."

"Good brandy never hurt a body," the doctor from Louisville wheezed, seeming to regard the entire proceedings as one vast joke.

With Cayce slumbering on through this discussion, the Squire turned a pleading face to Dr. Ketchum, who had been scribbling down Cayce's remarks in trance. "If the druggist will fill the prescription for the heroin compound, I'll write it out," he said with a careless glance at the three older doctors.

He was met with cold stares.

"Who is this man?" demanded the specialist from Louisville.

Janson made a face. "He's from the wrong side of the river, a Yankee."

The Louisville doctor ostentatiously looked Ketchum up and down. "If anything goes wrong," he snapped, "you'll hear about this."

The Squire was now aroused. "Dr. Janson said Gertrude only had a week to live anyway, so that's rubbing it in when a man is only trying to help."

The visiting doctors nodded shortly to Janson, and without another word started for the door.

The doctor from Nashville halted for a moment, his gray beard quivering, and said in baleful tones, "This is the worst miscarriage of medicine I have ever witnessed. And nobody in this room can absolve himself of participation in this unholy farce."

Dr. Janson seemed startled to be included, but quickly recovered his aplomb. "Sickness makes strange bedfellows," he said with a smile.

Dr. Ketchum turned to the still slumbering figure. "Squire, you better get your son up before he develops a case of sleeping sickness."

It was not a very good joke, but they all laughed, relieving the tension.

The Squire now put the suggestion that would bring a refreshed Cayce comfortably out of trance without any vestige of remembrance. "The body will be so equalized as to overcome all those things that might hinder or prevent it from being its best mental, spiritual and physical self. The body will create within the system those properties necessary to cause the eliminations to be so increased as to bring the best conditions for the body. The mental will so give that impression to the system as to build the best moral, mental and physical forces. The circulation will be so equalized as to remove strain from all centers of the nervous system, as to allow the organs to assimilate and secrete properly for normal conditions of his body."

It was a classic example of hypnosis at its best.

"The nerve supplies of the whole body will assume their normal forces; the vitality will be stored in them, through the application of the physical being, as well as of the spiritual elements in the physical forces of the body."

His voice suddenly sharpened.

"Now, perfectly normal, and perfectly balanced, you will wake up."

As usual, when giving no more than two readings a day, Cayce sat up refreshed and eager, craving something to eat. But as his eyes wandered around the room, recognizing the familiar faces, he remembered what he was waking up from, and anxiously turned to his father.

167

"Pa"—his voice quavered—"Pa, did I say she would get well?"

His father's head bobbed. "You sure did, Old Man, and so she shall. You are never wrong."

They told him what he had said, and he shook his head, marveling. "I don't know where it comes from. I only pray it is right."

The Squire laughed. "I don't know if Gertrude will appreciate the remedy. She's so set against alcohol."

"She only has to smell it," said Ketchum. "I'll take care of any excess."

Cayce had already slipped on his shoes and tie, and put on his suitcoat.

"If you get that prescription ready, Doc," he said to Ketchum, "I'll bring it over to Gertrude." He shook his head in mock bewilderment. "Heroin and booze, all in one reading for my own wife. The ways of the Lord are truly wondrous to behold."

Shaking his head all the way, the druggist went back to the store and filled the prescription and Cayce brought it home with him. The charred keg, with the apple brandy, would be ready the next day.

"What is this medicine, Edgar?" she asked, as she swallowed the heroin mixture he gave her.

"Get-well medicine," said he.

She could barely raise her head from the pillow, then sank back exhausted from the exertion. But a few hours after she took the first potion, the hemorrhages draining her strength suddenly stopped.

The next day she managed a languid smile as Edgar rolled a small barrel, its charred interior steeped in brandy, over to her four-poster bed.

As directed, she breathed deeply of the brandy. "Edgar," she said, "you'll be the death of me yet."

Cayce looked up startled.

"I was only joking," she reassured him.

That night with the congestion in her lungs already somewhat relieved, Edgar sat by Gertrude's bedside, reading to her from the Bible.

She slipped her hand into his. "Edgar," she said, "you saved me from myself."

168

"The readings did it, Gertrude."

She shook her head. "It was more than that. Lying there, watching you fret over me with that old charred keg of brandy, making yourself sick smelling it, I realized where I belonged, and where I really wanted to stay."

He remembered now the vision of the lady who had told him that he would some day heal the sick and the lame, and that other vision of a soul mate who would one day end his loneliness. He got down on his knees and prayed.

"Forgive me, O Lord, for ever having doubted you and thank you for permitting me to be your servant. And may I ever serve you in the way that your messenger Jesus Christ made so clear: 'For the Father loveth the Son, and sheweth him all things that himself doeth: and he will shew him greater works than these, that ye may marvel . . . Verily, verily, I say unto you, Whatsoever ye shall ask the Father in my name . . . ask and ye shall receive, that your joy may be full.'"

8

Ketchum Marches On

After Dalton staged a complete recovery, to the consternation of the Hoptown medical fraternity, the Yankee doctor from the wrong side of the Ohio River began to truly blossom out. Dalton, with his leg as good as new, rewarded him handsomely, with a check that made even Ketchum whistle. The following week, the Yankee doctor saw the proud owner of Hopkinsville's first automobile, a two-cylinder Brush, with rubber tires, and a horn that made the horses rear up and roll their eyes. He took the wide-eyed Boze for the first spin, and they managed to rattle along at the tremendous speed of thirty miles an hour.

Boze, sitting next to the doctor, held on for dear life as they hit the country roads, leaving a trail of dust and outraged horsemen in their wake.

"What kind of critter is this?" asked Boze, between noisily chattering teeth.

"It's a gasoline-eater," Ketchum rejoiced.

"And what is gasoline?"

"It's like hay for horses."

"This ain't no hay-burner," said Boze. "I stake my life on that."

"You're not just saying that," chuckled his jubilant employer.

Conscious of the stir he was evoking in Hopkinsville's streets, Ketchum dressed impressively for every outing. Behind his steering wheel, he was a picture of sartorial splendor, fashionably equipped with huge goggles and a long buff-colored coat that hung below his knees.

Boze regarded him as if he were just arrived from Mars.

"Don't put anything like that on me," he said apprehensively. "Somebody will done shoot me."

On one excursion with the faithful Boze, Ketchum suddenly branched off into a narrow dirt track that ran between two watermelon patches, and rocked along for about a quarter of a mile, well out of sight of the highway, before he brought the car to a screeching halt.

Boze viewed him with alarm. "Now, Dr. Wesley, you don't expects me to go after any of those watermelons after all the noise this hay-burner is makin'? That old Farmer Jones will be waiting for Boze with a double-barreled shotgun."

Ketchum removed his cap in the hot sun, and said reassuringly, "Now go along, Boze, you know nobody has watermelons like Trancas Jones, and nobody can pick them better than you. You got a formula that can't be beaten."

Boze scratched his head, somewhat mollified by the praise.

"I dunno about this formula business. All I do is rap 'em good with my fingers and if they go Plink, they're green. An' if they go Plunk, why"—his eyes rolled with pleasant anticipation—"they're how we like 'em."

Ketchum opened the car door and watched Boze disappear into the patch. Five minutes later, grinning from ear to ear, he returned with a huge watermelon under each arm. "These is both plunkers"—Boze chuckled—"one for you and one for me."

Ketchum looked over the melons appreciatively. "Boze, I got to hand it to you and Farmer Jones. You're an unbeatable team. He grows the best watermelons and you pick them best."

Boze wagged his head. "Don't forget yourself, Dr. Wesley. You masterminded the whole business."

He plopped himself on the running board of the

Brush and howled, slapping his thighs, until the tears streamed down his face.

"We better cut out," said Ketchum, "before old Jones turns up and spoils our fun."

As they rode back, Boze shot a quizzical glance at his employer. "It ain't rightly my business, Dr. Wesley, and you know I would never say anything, but how's a quality man like you go after watermelons this way?"

Ketchum turned his head from the road for a moment and lowered his voice, forcing Boze to bend toward him. "Boze, ever since I was a boy, I liked to take from the rich and give to the poor, especially myself."

Boze's face wrinkled in dark perplexity.

"But you is poor no more, not with what that Mr. Dalton done for ya."

Ketchum gave his aide an affectionate glance. "I'll always be poor, Boze, until I'm the biggest, richest doctor in Kentucky, and then we'll march over to Farmer Jones's front door and buy his whole watermelon patch from him. And do you know what, Boze?"

"What?" said Boze, still perplexed.

"Then I'll turn over the whole patch to you, and it won't be fun anymore."

"Why is that, Dr. Wesley?"

"Because then we'd have to steal from ourselves." His laugh, rising above the angry sputter of the laboring automobile, reassured the worried Boze. The ever-ready smile once more replaced the frown. Boze again felt the security of knowing he was with quality.

As most of the city, Cayce had heard of Ketchum's acquisition, but he couldn't credit the reports until he was almost run down by the Brush at a downtown intersection in broad daylight. He jumped to a curb in the nick of time as Ketchum blazed around a corner, horn honking noisily, and he bellowing at the top of his lungs, "Watch out, watch out."

Finally he managed to bring the runaway vehicle to a standstill, directly in front of Cayce's studio.

Muttering darkly, he was pulling all kinds of levers and buttons as Cayce and several other onlookers gathered curiously on the sidewalk. To nobody in particular, the perspiring Ketchum announced that the clutch had failed, along with the brake pedal, and then the emergency hand brake had stuck. "It wouldn't all happen together in a million years."

Edgar could hardly restrain a smile, noting the doctor's unaccustomed discomfiture, and the smoke issuing in dense clouds from the machine. Getting Ketchum's eye, he said dryly, "That's the price you pay for being a trail-blazer, Doc."

Ketchum's scowl lifted as he recognized the psychic. "I'm sorry about coming so close," he cried.

Cayce laughed. "Better luck next time."

"I didn't mean it that way," said Ketchum, not appreciating the humor. "I was coming over to see you."

"All right," said Cayce, "but park the Red Hornet downstairs. I've got a lot of fragile equipment in my studio."

As the crowd continued to grow, Ketchum removed his long coat, his cap, and his goggles, deposited them in a special compartment, and followed Cayce up the stairs.

Cayce showed him into his inner office. "Now that you're an up and coming doctor," Cayce said, "I hardly thought I'd be seeing you."

Ketchum appeared a little embarrassed. "Edgar, you don't mind my not telling people about your part in the Dalton case?"

"Nope," said Cayce, lighting up a pipe, and angling his legs up on his desk, "nor about Davis case, either. It's all the same to me." He puffed contentedly on his pipe. "Nobody would believe you anyway, not anymore than you believed Dietrich or Al Layne."

The color slowly came to Ketchum's face. "I want to make it right, Edgar. I'll offer you a deal you can't refuse."

Cayce continued to puff away serenely. "You sound like a horse trader, Doc."

Ketchum started. "That's my father's business." His manner turned persuasive. "I have it all worked out, and your father can be in the deal, too, in an advisory capacity, to give you greater confidence."

Cayce nodded slowly. "Give me another twenty-four hours, Doc; I want to feel comfortable about this."

Ketchum made no effort to hide his disappointment. "I'll wait for your call," he said.

Edgar had not quite made up his mind. Not sure himself about what use he should make of his gift, he was still very much concerned about the gift becoming a tool of the materialistic and the money-minded. "I have the fear," he told Gertrude, after dinner that evening, "that my subconscious mind, or whatever's doing it, is subject to the influence and suggestion of others. Otherwise, it wouldn't be amenable to requests for help."

It sounded logical, and also left him dangerously vulnerable. But Gertrude still encouraged him, even with her reservations about Ketchum, recognizing now that the doctor's medical background would tend to make Edgar's work more effective. "Your father and I will make sure that nobody abuses your power." She gave him a tender glance. "When I think of all the people you have helped, Carrie and her baby, myself, the Davis boy, Mr. Dalton, it seems plain that you have been chosen specifically for this work."

Aware of the enormous responsibility, dwelling on his own ineffectualities and imperfections, he still was uncertain of his course. Taking pictures was so simple in contrast.

He stared up at the sky that night, feeling tremendously alone in his self-doubts, not knowing which way to go, hoping for a sign. A star blinked in the sky, and he laughed, thinking it a sign of his own indecision.

As he walked into the house, still searching for an answer, his eye lighted on the Bible. It was open, though he could not remember opening it. He picked it up and looked at the passage. It was Psalm Forty-six.

"God is our refuge and strength, a very present help in trouble.

"Therefore will not we fear, though the earth be removed, and though the mountains be carried into the midst of the sea."

His mind was made up. Banishing his misgivings, he called Ketchum at his office the next day, asking him to drop over at his convenience.

Ketchum was there in five minutes. He was openly enthusiastic. "Edgar," he said grandly, "you are making medical history."

Cayce quietly offered him a chair. "You tell me about your offer, and I'll tell you about my conditions," he said gravely.

Ketchum, now very businesslike, took out a legal sheet listing the crux of an agreement.

Cayce held up an admonitory finger. "I want to stipulate that the readings have to be reasonably priced, and we can't refuse anybody with a problem because they don't have the money."

Ketchum nodded almost too quickly. "Yes, yes, I understand."

He passed the paper across the desk.

As Cayce studied the document, Ketchum stood up and walked around the spacious room, examining the blowups of photographs that Cayce had hung on his walls. In spite of his view of Cayce as a freakish accident, the doctor was impressed by Cayce's originality as a photographer. There were no stiff daguerreotype-like poses so current at the time. The pictures all had motion, charm and individuality. There were no stereotypes. No two babies looked alike, or were posed similarly. Where mother and child had been portrayed, the love between the two was reflected not only in the features but in the posing, the turning of the head or the drop of a hand. There were shadowy silhouettes, and misty studies of beauties, and family groups, posed naturally, without everybody staring directly at the camera. It was a gallery that not only reflected how the people of Hopkinsville looked, but how the photographer saw them.

175

"Some of those aren't bad, Edgar."

Cayce, frowning over the agreement, didn't look up.

"I think I'll engage you to take Katy's picture with me when we tie the knot."

Cayce looked up quickly. "You getting married?"

"Eventually, when I get around to it."

"Who's the lucky lady?"

Ketchum gave him a sharp look. "Miss Katherine deTuncq—the *q* is silent. She teaches at Bethel College, and I intend to end her days of servitude."

Cayce had gone back to the paper. "A Yankee, I suppose?"

Ketchum's voice had a trace of acerbity. "Why must she be a Yankee?"

"Isn't she?"

"Are you suggesting your local belles wouldn't have me?"

Cayce put down the paper with a smile. "Anybody would be happy to have a man with a fire-eater on wheels."

Ketchum scowled. "Well, you're right, the little lady is from St. Paul, Minnesota. There's only one drawback."

"What's that?"

"She hasn't agreed to the proposition yet."

Cayce laughed. "Why don't you get it all down on a piece of paper, Doc, so she knows what she's getting?"

"That's not funny, Edgar." He picked up the paper and resumed his seat. "Well, what do you say, Old Man, will you sign it?" As he did occasionally, he used the Squire's intimate address.

Cayce didn't appear to notice. He looked closely at Ketchum, then spoke slowly as if trying to emphasize that he meant precisely what he said. "On certain conditions, I will accept your offer. It will be understood that my father, whenever possible, will act as conductor of the readings, and that a stenographic account of all that is said be taken down. At least two copies will be made, one for the patient and one for our files. No readings are to be given except for sick people who make the request themselves. I will give two readings a day, in a special office, separate from my studio. I want nothing from these readings, for I do not consider this a profession or a means of livelihood."

He reached for the paper, and frowned over a clause that had puzzled him. "You say here that you will set me up in a new photographic studio, getting me the most expensive equipment."

Ketchum's head nodded. "You can have whatever you want, new office furniture, new cameras, new stationery, you name it."

"If you can spend five hundred dollars that will satisfy my wants."

Ketchum took out a thick roll of bills, and peeled off five $100-bills. "That should do for a starter. Get whatever you need."

Cayce sighed. "You still don't understand. Whatever I have must not be abused. The power was given me without explanation. I've tried to discover what to do with it, and Gertrude has helped. But so far it's been hit and miss."

"Yes?" said Ketchum, shrugging a little.

"When you flash your money like that, I get the impression you think you're buying me. Nobody can buy what God has given freely."

Ketchum felt constrained to hide his annoyance at this simple fellow who was forever preaching at him. The old feeling came over him that perhaps Cayce was still only a mentalist with a limited gift. How did he know he would ever be right again?

"Would you fall asleep for me now, and let me ask a couple of questions?"

"What kind of questions?"

"The questions a professor would expect a senior in medical school to know."

"What would I know about anything like that?"

"Not any more than you would about House, Davis, Dalton and the rest."

Cayce's old suspicion of experimenting physicians

reasserted itself. "I don't want any more tests." But suddenly, looking at Ketchum, he understood. "You've got buck fever, Ketchum. At the last minute you want assurance that you're not getting a pig in the poke."

Ketchum's face broke into a roguish grin. "You don't blame me, do you?"

"All right," Cayce said, "I just hope I don't get anything, and that's the end of it."

He stretched out on the couch, and Ketchum quickly put him under. Unusually, Cayce was to be asked for specific information which had no relation to an individual's problem. Would he be able to give it?

As Cayce's rhythmical breathing showed him in trance, Ketchum had his question ready. "What is the longest muscle in the body?"

Cayce replied without hesitation. "The sartorius, the long muscle of the thigh."

Now for the jaw-breaker. "What is the shortest muscle in the body?"

The answer was a tongue-twister, the bane of every medical student, and Ketchum could hardly remember it himself.

Cayce hesitated a moment. "It's in the upper lip." He drew a deep breath, then said slowly, pausing between each word:

"Levator labii superioris alaeque nasi."

Ketchum clapped his hands in excitement. "My God," he said, "what this boy could do with the stock market or the racetrack."

With a simple suggestion, he brought Cayce out of his trance.

"Well," said Cayce, rubbing his eyes, "did I pass the medical examination?"

Ketchum wrote down what he had said.

Cayce shook his head. "Beats me, I have a hard time spelling camera."

The Squire sat in at the signing. The agreement provided that Edgar was to be used only in cases where the diagnosis was difficult and the prognosis hopeless and would read no more than twice a day. He could have anything in the way of equipment for his

178

photographic studio. He was to have a separate office for his psychic work and a special couch, high from the floor, so that the person giving the suggestion had to stand to talk to him. An office, leased adjacent to his studio, resembled a doctor's quarters. In the reception room there were two large rocking chairs, with cushions for the seat and back, a center table with the current magazines, and carpeting wall to wall.

The Squire was enthusiastic. He occupied a massive desk in the reception room, fixed the appointments, and waved the visitors in. "Edgar," he said enthusiastically, "you have arrived."

His son winced. "Thanks, Pa."

Cayce made it clear that he was not a faith healer. He did not require prayers or music, or emotional fervor of any nature. He responded to need, but actually read better when he had a feeling of well-being and his stomach was empty. He could not read with a full stomach, nor could he read more than twice a day without feeling depleted. As a rule, he awakened refreshed and hungry. But a glass of milk and a cracker would appease him.

As he began to read for Ketchum with some regularity, he made a practice of going over the stenographic transcripts. He had thought this might help his conscious mind understand what his subconscious mind did. But the language was so technical that he was generally confused.

One day, he looked up at Ketchum baffled. "'A weakness or degenerate condition of the nerve tissues resulting in a lack of correlation between the sympathetic or autonomic and the cerebrospinal or motor nervous systems.' What is that?"

Ketchum couldn't help laughing. "You're the greatest fount of medical knowledge the world has ever seen, and you haven't the slightest idea what you're saying. It's the damnedest thing I ever heard."

The Sunday School teacher in Cayce objected. "Doc, please stop your swearing."

"Anything you say, Edgar, anything at all."

Ketchum's practice had prospered. He was taking the cream from many of the local doctors, and if looks could kill, he would have been long dead. There were mutterings about his doing the work of the devil, but as long as people were getting well, he was bowing and taking the credit. He had joined several fraternal orders, and with pretty Katy deTuncq, who constantly decorated his arm, he was becoming a conspicuous figure in the local social scene. But many eyes followed him darkly as he drove through the city streets, making calls or pleasure riding, in the horseless carriage that had become his trademark. He had no illusions about his popularity. "If I miss just once in a big case," he told Cayce, "those doctors would have me out of here faster than a darky at a Klu Klux Klan rally."

Cayce was all too aware of local sentiment. "If I were you," he observed seriously, "I'd tone it down a bit."

Ketchum gave him an inquiring look. "What does that mean?"

"It's bad enough to jump over people when you're an outsider, but to flaunt it in their faces, that's asking for trouble."

"What would you suggest?"

"I'd try being a little more subdued and inconspicuous."

"Like what, for instance?"

"Getting rid of that Red Terror, for instance. You don't let anybody forget you're around."

Ketchum smiled bleakly. "I don't give a hoot about Sanders and that crowd of phonies. They'd use you, too, if they dared."

"Just remember what I told you. I know this town, they're good haters, and they've got long memories."

Cayce had developed a certain fondness for the brash doctor, though he never quite trusted him. He enjoyed his ready wit and respected his dedication as a physician. He didn't want anything to happen to him.

He was disposed to help in any way he could. And Ketchum was not reticent about asking favors. One day he announced, "I would like Katy to sit in on a reading, if you have no objection." He laughed. "She's a little leery of me because of my association with you."

"I understand that, Doc," said Cayce with a straight face. "Gertrude feels that way about you."

Ketchum grinned. "That's a *touché* for you, Edgar."

Being curious as well as critical, Katy didn't have to be invited twice, though her own orthodoxy made her doubt anything smacking of the mystical.

For the demonstration, wanting to impress her, Ketchum selected a case by a doctor friend in Cleveland. "All we have," Ketchum explained, "is the name and address of the patient, and Edgar will get the rest."

Katy was incredulous. "You mean he'll tell us what's wrong with the patient?"

"Yes," said Ketchum rather smugly, "and then go on to say how he can be helped or cured."

"I'll believe it when I see it."

"And so you shall," he promised.

That evening, after closing his photographic studio, Cayce lay down on the couch for an extra and third reading of the day. The first two had been impromptu, one for a sick friend of his father, the other an emergency of Ketchum's. Edgar was frankly tired, and he was going against his own judgment, but Ketchum had promised Katy and he, Edgar, had promised Ketchum. So there was no alternative.

With a sigh he closed his eyes and prepared for the suggestion that would put him under. When tired, he often became nervous and fretful, and he was glad now that his father was conducting the reading. It gave him a stronger feeling of security. He had not as yet got over his early mistrust of Ketchum.

The Squire checked his watch against the studio clock. It was exactly 8 P.M., the appointed time for the reading. The patient, by prearrangement, was to be in his Cleveland home.

Cayce routinely fell off to sleep and was breathing rhythmically as the Squire completed his suggestion.

Katy's eyes widened, and she giggled.

"Why, he's snoring," she exclaimed.

The Squire gave her a dark look.

"Don't interrupt," Ketchum whispered.

"You now have the body," said the Squire in a studied monotone. "It is at Euclid Avenue, in the city of Cleveland, in the state of Ohio. Now you have the body. Signal when you see the body."

Cayce repeated the suggestion almost inaudibly, then said: "The body is not at that address. There is no body there. It has moved."

Ketchum groaned, and his heart sank as he saw the impish smile on Katy's face.

"No body means nobody," she hummed blithely, impervious to the Squire's baleful glance.

"This is nothing to joke about, young lady."

"I'm just being sympathetic," said she.

The Squire kept repeating his question, with no result. Katy's smile had become one almost of scorn. Twenty minutes had now elapsed, and absolutely nothing had come out of Cayce.

The Squire was beginning to show his concern. "He's never been like this before." He gave Ketchum an anxious look. "You don't think his vocal cords have gone back on him again?"

Ketchum shook his head. "No, it's something else." He bent over Edgar, rolled back his eyelids, checked his pulse and breathing. "He's normal," he said, with unconscious humor, "that is, for him."

Suddenly, as they all stood around uncertainly, the man on the couch began to speak in his usual dull monotone. "He's gone," he said. "Gone." He paused. "We have finished with this body."

The Squire rested his hand on Edgar's brow and stroked his head soothingly. "Now be calm and recover normal use of your senses," he said in a crisp tone, "and awaken feeling refreshed and vigorous, not remembering anything and feeling no worse for the reading you have just given."

Cayce took longer than usual to regain consciousness.

The Squire repeated, "Awaken feeling refreshed, and vigorous, none the worse for your experience. Wake up!"

At this command, Edgar slowly sat up and began rubbing his eyes. "What was that all about?" he demanded. "I feel as if I lived through a lifetime."

The Squire's face still showed his concern. "We don't know, Old Man. You didn't get anything."

"Nothing? Why, that's strange; that never happened before."

Katy yawned, and offered her hand. "Well, it was very nice to meet you, Edgar, even if you did sleep through most of our acquaintanceship. I'll see you in church. I must say I liked your Sunday School performance more."

Ketchum lagged behind for a second or two. "I'll be in touch with you tomorrow, Edgar, I've got to find out what happened back there in Cleveland."

It was Edgar's turn to yawn. "Pa, I think I'd like a glass of milk."

The next day, shortly before noon, the telephone in Cayce's studio rang insistently. It was Ketchum. "Edgar," he cried into the phone, "even when it appears you made a slipup, you're greater than ever. There's nobody like you."

Cayce was in no mood for pleasantries. "I'm in the middle of taking a picture. What's the problem now?"

"Why, last night, you couldn't get anything, not even the body, and you said the man was gone. Well, I checked with my doctor friend today. His patient had forgotten the appointment, and had gone to the Lake Erie docks to take the night boat for Detroit. That's why you couldn't pick him up at that address. He wasn't there."

Cayce listened impatiently, waving a hand to reassure the young couple sitting for a wedding picture that he would soon be with them.

"And that's not all," Ketchum went on. "At eight

twenty P.M., the exact time that you repeated he was gone, this man died on the boat of a heart attack. Edgar, you're out of this world."

Cayce hung up the receiver, shaking his head wearily.

"What was all that about?" the bridegroom asked.

"Nothing important," said Cayce, "just an excitable friend calling to tell me a story. You wouldn't believe it."

As for Ketchum's bride-to-be, she still had her misgivings. "You can talk about the man dying all you like, Wesley Ketchum," said she, "but it still didn't happen in front of me."

"I'll call the doctor in Cleveland," said Ketchum. "He'll verify it."

"All I know," she said, "is that the poor man didn't say a word for twenty minutes, and then all he could say was, 'He's gone.' What kind of nonsense is that?"

She leveled her gray-eyed gaze on her protesting suitor.

"I would suggest to you, Doctor, provided, of course you still want to marry me, that you observe the practice of medicine in the usual way. You have been to a good undergraduate college, you have taught school, you have been to an orthodox medical college, even though the specialty is homeopathy, and I would think that with your intelligence, you could very easily apply the knowledge you have picked up in years of study to the furtherance of this most noble profession and your patients' health."

Boze had come into the doctor's office just as she was completing her remarks.

"Amen," said he, rolling his eyes. "That sure was some mouthful."

"Now, don't you agree with me, Boze?" she said, not intending the question seriously.

Boze fidgeted uncertainly from one foot to the other. "I can't rightfully say, Miss Katy. That Mr. Cayce is sure a powerful sikkic man."

Katy threw up her arms. "I just don't understand grown-up men going in for this twaddle, when we females are supposed to be the impractical, flighty, superstitious ones."

She gave the doctor a mock curtsy, and her eyes flashed. "When you settle down to serious business, Dr. Ketchum, you will know where to find me."

She twirled her parasol airily, tickling Boze lightly under the chin with it in passing, as she tripped daintily out of the office.

Boze looked at his employer expectantly.

"What ya gonna do, Dr. Wesley?"

Ketchum moved his shoulders slightly. "I'm going out and get me a shave and a haircut, that's what I'm gonna do."

Boze's eyes followed the receding figure down the stairs. "Those white folks," said he aloud. "They makes as much trouble for themselves as black folks."

For the next two or three weeks, Ketchum managed very well without Cayce. The weather had turned cold, with autumn fading into an early winter, and there had been a rash of pneumonia, influenza, diphtheria, and bronchial complaints, all readily identifiable to a perceptive physician. Through Cayce, Ketchum had reached people that couldn't otherwise be helped, but he was willing to rock along with Katy as long as it didn't interfere with help for the so-called incurable cases. By now, his practice was so extensive, and his experience so broad, that he was gaining a new poise

But there were cases still that defied medical and insight.

knowledge. He groaned one day over an open lesion on the leg of a ten-year-old boy. Thick yellowish pus drained out of the sore, and the flesh appeared to be turning dangerously green.

"What is it, Doctor?" the anxious mother wailed. "I have been to four doctors already, tried all kinds of salves and ointments, and nothing has helped. I can't send the boy to school; they won't permit him in class, and it keeps getting worse."

Ketchum didn't like the look of it. It was the ugliest

wound he had ever seen, extending across the delicate inner flesh of the calf.

The boy looked at him with frightened eyes.

"What have they said it was?" Ketchum asked, gently dapping at flaky scales and pus.

"Well, Dr. Sanders thought it might be a carbuncle."

There was that blasted horse doctor again.

"And Dr. Benson thought it might be an infection from a rusty nail, septicemia, I believe he called it. But"—her face contorted in her anxiety—"it just kept getting worse, no matter what they prescribed. I heard what you had done for Mr. Dalton, so I came here with the boy." She was near tears.

He patted her shoulder lightly. "There, there, we'll have Junior fixed up in no time at all."

He examined the wound carefully through a magnifying glass. All that did was make it look worse than before, without providing any additional clue. It wasn't the ordinary abscess, or a conventional carbuncle or boil. He also knew from the mother that about every ointment in the medical armory had already been used.

He sighed, thinking of Katy and her endearing young charms.

"Bring the boy back this afternoon, about five o'clock, and I'll have another go at it. And don't worry."

The mother seized his hand gratefully. "Thank you, Doctor, thank you."

"Don't thank me until I've done something. Now relax, I'm sure it will be all right."

Ketchum immediately got Cayce on the phone.

"Where have you been, Doc?" Cayce said with a laugh. "I've missed you. You must have found another psychic."

Quickly Ketchum mentioned the dilemma, without getting into details. "I'll need a reading right away."

Cayce quickly assented. "I'll cancel my next sitting. If I can't help kids, then I shouldn't be helping anybody."

Ketchum left Boze in charge of a crowded office, saying he'd be back in a half-hour, and walked down the block to Cayce's studio.

Cayce's warmth pleasantly surprised Ketchum. "I guess absence makes the heart grow fonder," he quipped.

"Jesus loved children and suffered them to come unto him, above all others. When we are helping children, Ketchum, we can be sure whose work we are doing."

The Squire was out somewhere, and Ketchum, now equally adept, quickly put the psychic to sleep. Cayce, at Ketchum's suggestion, promptly found the body. He went right to the leg, which Ketchum had deliberately not mentioned previously, so as not in any way to influence the reading.

It was as serious as Ketchum had thought.

"The right leg has a prolonged infection, which could go into gangrene if it is not treated properly. Originally, it was caused by a scratch, which became infected from dirt, from the boy not washing carefully with soap. This was then aggravated by the medicines, the ointments, unguents and the like, which have been poured into the infection, affecting the body's power to heal itself, and so irritating the tissue that the mildest of emollients is now required. It must be that which will heal, ridding the body of the infection, but at the same time not eat away or erode the tissue."

"And what kind of preparation would that be?" asked Ketchum.

"Oil of Smoke."

He thought he had not heard properly; the two names seemed contradictory. He repeated his question.

"Oil of Smoke, as before," said the sleeping Cayce.

"And where would I find this preparation?"

"It is very rare, and is not made any more. But there is some in this drugstore in Louisville, Kentucky." He gave the name and address of the store. "Write and it will be sent. Do not be deterred."

It was almost as if the unconscious man was aware of the next step in the drama. Instead of writing, Ketchum got on the telephone, as soon as he got back to his office, and called Louisville. The clerk had never heard of Oil of Smoke. He consulted the owner, who vaguely remembered the preparation, but said it had been discontinued long before.

"Will you look for it?" Ketchum pleaded.

He waited on the phone for ten minutes, while they combed through their crowded shelves.

"No luck, Doctor," the clerk finally reported back.

Ketchum checked his watch. It was three o'clock; the mother would be back in two hours with the boy. He looked around his busy office and announced another emergency. There were groans and growls, but Ketchum held firm. "I'm sorry, but a boy needs help desperately. Come back tomorrow, and I won't charge you."

He was soon back with Cayce, explaining what had happened. "How about a reading, to see if you can locate that bottle?"

"I'll try," said Edgar, "just as quickly as it takes to cancel my present sitting."

This time, Ketchum simply asked the sleeping Cayce, "Please locate the Oil of Smoke, in the drugstore in Louisville, so they will find it at once and so help the boy with the sore leg."

Cayce hesitated just briefly, as if his eyes were searching every shelf in that store with an X-ray stare. He then spoke up clearly. "In the back of the drugstore, back of where the pharmacist normally compounds his prescriptions, is this small bottle hidden behind several preparations of Oil of Turpentine, at the extreme rear of the shelf, against the wall. Have them look there, and they will find it, and it will be good."

Even after his many experiences with Cayce, Ketchum was still skeptical. To make sure there was no misunderstanding over the telephone, with the bad connections then prevalent at distances, he sent a telegram to the manager of the Louisville drugstore;

explicitly directing where the Oil of Smoke could be found.

An hour and a half later the answer had not yet arrived when the mother returned with her son. "Come back in two days," he said with considerably less confidence than he felt, "and I will have the medicine that will cure your boy."

The next morning, a messenger brought a telegram which he hurriedly tore open. It was from the druggist in Lousiville:

"Found it—mailing Special Delivery."

In his elation, Ketchum ran down the street to show Cayce the wire.

He was surprised to see Cayce's eyes brim with tears. "God be prasied," he said softly.

The two-ounce bottle arrived on the second day. It was old and the label was faded. The manufacturer had long before gone out of business. The label could barely be read. But there it was, "Oil of Smoke."

Ketchum gave the bottle to the mother, with instructions that she apply it to the wound twice a day. Better too little than too much, in view of the boy's history of overtreatment. He heard no more for a week and then she brought him in. The boy was smiling broadly. His leg was completely healed, and only the slightest redness remained where the sore had been.

"God bless you, Dr. Ketchum," the grateful mother cried. "You are the greatest man in the state of Kentucky, even if you are a Yankee."

Because of his discretion, as he thought of it, Ketchum's romance with Miss Katy prospered. He saw no harm in letting her think he was through with Cayce. Why wave a red flag at a bull?

"You see, Dr. Ketchum," she told him one day, "you are a very good doctor. You don't need any spooks."

"Yes, dear," agreed Ketchum, kissing her lightly.

Katy, as a Northerner, sympathized with Ketchum's problems as an outsider and constantly recommended him as the finest doctor in Hopkinsville. One morning, as the Christmas season approached, she telephoned that she would like to send somebody very special in to see him. "She's a lovely woman, Dr. Ketchum, and a very dear friend. She's terribly worried about her daughter right now."

He was rather confused. "Who's the patient?"

"Oh, it's the daughter. She's been away to school and she'll just be getting home for the holidays. She's been feeling poorly."

"It doesn't sound like a complicated case," said Ketchum cheerfully.

The following day a tall, distinguished woman, with graying hair, walked in alone and introduced herself as Katy's friend. There were several patients in the waiting room, and others in treatment rooms, the mark of the young doctor's rising popularity.

Ketchum showed her exceptional deference, but suggested she make an appointment for another time. "You can see that you would have to wait quite a while, and there wouldn't be much point to it without your daughter being here."

The mother acquiesced readily, obviously finding Ketchum's manner to her liking. "Very well, when may I have an appointment?"

Ketchum looked through his book. "Tomorrow morning at nine; would that be convenient?"

"Fine," she said, "I'll be in with my daughter."

He hesitated a moment. "How old is your daughter, madam?"

The lady gave him an imperious look. "Twenty years old. What difference does that make?"

"And she has been away to school?"

"Yes," she answered coolly.

"Well," said Ketchum, appraising the smartly tailored figure, "isn't she old enough to see a doctor by herself?"

The mother's tone held a certain hauteur. "My daughter would not come in here by herself."

"But if she is ill?"

"She hasn't seemed well lately. I visited her at college. She seemed pale and listless, with no energy. But she won't admit that anything is wrong." She drew herself to her full height. "Now if there is still any question, Dr. Ketchum . . . ?"

"No," said Ketchum reassuringly, "I was just trying to get the picture."

That evening, after the last patient had left, Ketchum turned wearily to his chief cook and bottle-washer. "Boze, I have a sneaking feeling that I have a tough one at nine A.M. tomorrow. I better give Brother Cayce a call."

Boze's eyes lighted up, as usual, at the mention of Edgar's name.

"You can't go wrong with him, Mr. Boss."

As he picked up the phone, Ketchum regarded Boze curiously. "So I'm not Dr. Wesley any more?"

"When you consult Mr. Cayce, like Miss Katy say, then you Mr. Boss."

Ketchum sighed. "You're about as unpredictable as Miss Katy."

Cayce was bustling about the darkroom, waiting for Ketchum when he arrived a few hours later.

"Sorry to bust up any dinner plans," the doctor apologized.

Cayce was friendly and relaxed. "Oh, that's all right, I'm stuck tonight anyway."

"How's business?" Ketchum looked around the studio, noting the many improvements.

"I couldn't handle any more. How's yours?"

"With your help, fine."

"Good, shall we get to it? I couldn't turn up the Squire, so you'll have to do the honors."

Cayce stretched out luxuriously on the high couch.

"I haven't seen this patient," said Ketchum. "She won't be in until tomorrow."

"That's all right, Doc; I don't see them, either."

Cayce had no trouble falling off to sleep.

Ketchum supplied the girl's name and her address over the Christmas holiday.

Cayce lay quietly for a while, as Ketchum hovered over him anxiously. "Yes," he said finally, "we have the body here."

As usual during a reading, Cayce's face showed

no expression and in even this dramatic situation his voice incongruously retained an even tone.

"The trouble with this body began with her own beauty. The trouble is in the lower part, in the pelvic area. But it does not have to be a trouble."

It didn't add up to Ketchum, listening closely. "Please elaborate," said he.

"In the pelvis area, right now, there is new life developing. That is the problem."

Ketchum groaned out loud. What a case! he thought grimly. And Katy had sent it to him.

"As a result," Cayce went on smoothly, "we now have this body nausea, vomiting and the like, commonly known as 'morning sickness.' "

Ketchum shook his head wearily.

The daughter, of course, had been keeping the complete symptoms from her mother, as they might have been a giveaway. She was obviously unmarried.

Ketchum scratched his head in perplexity. "What do I do in a case like this? Would you suggest any treatment?"

"No treatment at all," came the rejoinder. "The problem is wholly psychological. Nature takes care of those things."

"I don't mean about having the baby," said the befuddled Ketchum, "but about not having it perhaps."

"The mother will deliver a bouncing boy, and all will be well. It will be no great problem if approached tactfully, and the proper person informed as soon as possible."

"You mean he doesn't know?" Ketchum said incredulously.

"That is true." He paused a moment. "You can handle it, through the mother. We are through."

Sharply at nine, the mother arrived with her daughter. She was a flaxen-haired, blue-eyed beauty with dimpled cheeks and a worried expression lurking in her eyes.

The mother looked at her daughter fondly. "This," said she, "is my pride and joy."

Ketchum now understood the daughter's trepidation, provided that Cayce was right.

With a look at the mother, Ketchum said, "May I talk to your daughter alone in my private room?"

The mother looked at him in surprise. "Is that necessary? There have never been any secrets between us."

Ketchum thought to himself with a smile, That's what you think. "Yes, I think it essential," he said aloud. "It makes it easier for me."

The mother, obviously protective of her daughter, regarded the youthful doctor suspiciously. "You are not going to examine her intimately?" she asked, almost accusingly.

"It will hardly be necessary at this time," said Ketchum.

The daughter's embarrassment went unnoticed by the mother.

In his office, Ketchum gave the girl an easy smile, which seemed to say, "I am your friend. You can tell me everything."

He brought his fingers together in a steeple, and he looked as wise and profound as his twenty-seven years would permit. "If my diagnosis is correct," said he, "you need a counselor more than a doctor."

She gave a noticeable start. "And what would you counsel?"

"I would counsel that you tell your mother all about it, and then I would counsel an early marriage."

At this, the girl bowed her head and began crying unashamedly. "I'm sorry, but I've kept it to myself for so long."

"How long?" asked Ketchum, always practical.

She looked up through her tears. "I've already missed two months."

Ketchum nodded sympathetically and then laughed reassuringly. "You're not the first girl to be in this situation. Who is the lucky man, and where is he?"

Hesitatingly, she gave his name. He was a student at a college near her own college. "We're both in our last year."

193

"You haven't told him about it?"

She flushed and hung her head. "I love him. I wouldn't want to cause him any trouble."

Ketchum's eyes twinkled. "You seem to be the one in trouble."

She began crying all over again.

"Here, here." He put his arm comfortingly around her shoulder. "Does this man love you?"

She held up her head, dabbing at her eyes with a tiny kerchief. "He says he does."

Ketchum stood up. "Then that settles it. You've got to let him know, so that he can share this thing with you. It will be a great awakening for both of you."

As Ketchum interpreted the Cayce reading, the prospective father was the proper person to be informed.

"Now, we will let your mother know, and enlist her support."

The girl looked at him apprehensively. "What will she say?"

"If she loves you as I think, I know what she will say. She is, after all, a mature woman and knows about these things. They occur in the best of families."

He summoned the mother. She had been sitting on the edge of her seat.

In the office, the mother glanced suspiciously from the smiling doctor to her weeping daughter. "What is wrong?" she demanded.

"Nothing that can't be readily mended." He motioned to the daughter. "Tell her what the problem is. She loves you and will understand." That last, with a silent amen, for the mother's benefit.

For the next two minutes, the daughter sobbed out her story, while the mother, in disbelief at first, tried to control her shock.

"This is no time for reproaches," said Ketchum, invoking the psychological approach of Cayce. "This is the time for love to prove itself."

The mother gave him a penetrating glance. "I guess you're right," she said with a sigh. She turned to her

194

daughter, and asked in a subdued voice, "Is this the young man you've been seeing for a year and a half?"

The girl nodded silently, searching her mother's face for a sign of recrimination or acceptance.

Ketchum, feeling in complete command of the situation, was even more expansive than normally. He addressed the mother, who was obviously looking to him for guidance, remembering that she was a Southern lady of distinction:

"General Lee made the statement once that any fool general could take an army into battle, but it took a very wise leader to get it out again. If you will take my advice, you will contact this young man at once and have a nice little chat with him."

He turned to the girl, who had now brightened up considerably. "I wouldn't expect any man to marry a girl unless she is the only one in the world for him. But I have a feeling he is dying to marry you. And if you feel the same way about him, the best thing to do would be to slip across the state line, get married, and have it spread across every paper in town. Give it all the publicity you can, and people will never think there was anything to it."

The girl stood up, radiant now, and, leaning forward, impulsively kissed the young doctor on the cheek.

Her mother drew back startled. "Daughter," she cried in a reproving tone.

But at the door, she, too, thanked the doctor in her own way, slipping a check into his outstretched hand. "I have only one question, Doctor."

"Yes?"

"You said you weren't going to examine my daughter."

"That's right. And I didn't."

"Then how did you know she was pregnant?"

Ketchum pocketed the check after a quick, appreciative glance. "That's my secret," he said, smiling wisely.

9

Civil War

The tobacco war swirled in and out of Hoptown and affected the Cayces as it did nearly everyone else in this tobacco metropolis. An atmosphere of fear and foreboding had replaced the peace and serenity of both the black and white community after the turn of the century. Edgar Cayce had uneasily witnessed this change. As the independent tobacco growers of Christian County, the Black Patch country, marshaled their forces against the tobacco trust dominated by James and Washington Duke and their American Tobacco Company, Cayce had seen the bitterness develop to where friends and relatives were divided into two irreconcilable camps. For southwest Kentucky, a border state, it was almost like the Civil War reborn. In this predominantly tobacco area, where the welfare of each citizen inevitably depended on the price per hundredweight of dark-fired tobacco leaf, even the tobacco growers were ranged on opposing sides, those who would sell to the Trust and those who wouldn't, in an effort to gain a fairer price for their crop.

Once there had been fifty competing buyers of tobacco, and the price had been a profitable eight cents a pound. But now there was only one buyer, the American Tobacco Company, and the price had dropped to a bankrupting four cents. The growers struck back, organizing a boycott, and the Trust countered by upping its prices to growers who stayed out of the boycott. The seeds of a full-scale war were sown.

Originally, Cayce's sympathies had been with the protesting growers, who were his friends and neighbors. Everywhere he looked he could see their fields and their barns, and the pungent hickory-smoked aroma of curing tobacco had been in his nostrils ever since he could remember. He had taken to smoking a pipe and cigarettes, becoming a chain-smoker, almost in defense against the trenchant odor which pervaded even homes and business establishments.

Like others not directly involved in the tobacco fight, the youthful mystic deplored the rising crescendo of violence that marked the burgeoning tobacco war. The growers had formed an association, and any grower—or commission merchant—who was not with them was against them. They quoted Scripture in this connection, and enlisted the moral support of the local ministry in their behalf.

The Dark-fired Tobacco District Planters' Protective Association of Kentucky, with twelve thousand members, was drawn from the best elements of Southern society. Most newspapers, politicians, and public opinion stood solidly behind the Association in the beginning. They began simply enough, as other vigilante groups have begun, meaning to right injustice as they saw it. But with resistance, they began to change their tune. They had slogans such as "Down with the Trust or We Niggers Bust," aimed at enlisting black support. They waylaid farmers who wouldn't join their association on lonely roads and beat them up. They drove others out of the tobacco country with terror tactics, burning their houses and destroying their crops. They made examples of farmers who wouldn't join, forcing them with the lash of whips and branches to scrape their own plant beds, destroying their crops before they had a chance to get started.

Already, as in the Reconstruction period following the Civil War, or the War for Liberation, as it was more commonly known, hooded Night Riders were foraging through the countryside after dark, intimidating Association holdouts with threats, beatings, floggings, even shootings. No one had yet been killed in the quickening combat, but it seemed only a matter of time as the Trust invoked the forces of the law.

To Ketchum, a Northerner in an alien land, the conflict seemed a childish waste of energy, time and money. When he heard of giant warehouses storing millions of dollars' worth of finished tobacco being burned to the ground, he shook his head incredulously. "No wonder the South lost the war," he told Cayce. "These people act emotionally without regard for their self-interest."

Cayce patiently explained the role of tobacco in southwest Kentucky. They even marked the seasons by the tobacco crop. In the autumn the dark premium tobacco was fired in the barns; great logs were rolled together and kept burning slowly while the smoke rose to the eaves where the tobacco hung. In May and early June the tobacco was put in, nurtured carefully in special plant beds, as the budding plants were particularly vulnerable to climatic changes in these early stages. By then the woods were full of dogwood and redbud, hickory and red and white oak trees, hazelnut bushes, violets and skunk cabbages, pawpaws and May apples.

But the tobacco plant was clearly the most beautiful.

"If the growers can't get their price for their tobacco," said Cayce, "we have hard times. The ladies can't get their new dresses, and the men stay in overalls. It affects us all, but particularly the farmers. Without eight cents a pound for their tobacco, they may as well store it or burn it, economically. But, still," he added dryly, "they are only burning Trust-owned tobacco, already purchased from growers outside the Association."

Ketchum smiled slyly. "So they're not as dumb as I thought."

"Nobody has ever accused Dr. Sanders of being backward mentally."

"And what does he have to do with it?"

"He's supposed to have thought up the boycott."

The discussion was taking place in Ketchum's office on Seventh Street, where Cayce had just concluded a reading for a woman with an abdominal and respiratory indisposition, counseling that she go on a purifying and cleansing diet and that above all she think constructively. "Instead of snuffing, blow. Instead of resentment, love."

As usual, Ketchum's interest was piqued by mention of Sanders, whose path appeared to be continually crossing his. "But he's not a tobacco grower."

"No, just concerned about the welfare of his patients."

Ketchum grinned. "If they don't get their tobacco money, the doctor doesn't get his fee."

"It's not just that. He's truly concerned with people." He added, "His people, Kentucky people."

Ketchum's grin broadened. "And I'm not?"

Cayce gave him a speculative look. "Actually, Ketchum, I think you're a lot more part of this country than you think."

Ketchum glanced up from a ledger. "How do you figure that?" he frowned.

"You could have stayed up in Ohio and had things pretty much your own way. Instead, you chose to come down here and do it the hard way."

"That's because I'm obstreperous."

Cayce laughed. "But you could have been more profitably obstreperous across the river."

"But there wouldn't have been any Edgar Cayce there."

"You didn't know that."

Ketchum gave Cayce a shrewd glance from under bristling eyebrows. "I'm not so sure. There must have been some reason for my coming here, even if it was only to present you to the world."

"But you had never heard of me."

"Not consciously. But since I met you, I've been thinking a lot of the subconscious mind and its almost unlimited potential. Maybe my subconscious mind directed me here to be instrumental in legitimizing your work for mankind."

Cayce gave Ketchum a sharp look, as though seeing another side of him for the first time. "In a way," he said thoughtfully, "I suppose we are all instruments for one another, just as my meeting Reverend Moody helped point the way."

"Or Layne, for that matter. He got you ready for me, in a sense."

This was the first time that even obliquely Ketchum had given the osteopath any credit for Cayce.

Cayce shook his head in mock wonderment. "You're a real Dr. Jekyll and Mr. Hyde. There's two sides to you, diametrically opposed."

With a chuckle, Ketchum altered the serious tone of the conversation. "I haven't got to that book by Robert Louis Stevenson yet, but wouldn't Dr. Ketchum and Mr. Hyde be more like it?"

When the two got together, there was often a rapid-fire exchange of ideas, unusual this time only because Ketchum gave as much as he got.

"You know," said he, still breezing through his accounts, "I have at least one thing in common with Sanders."

"And what is that?"

"A lot of tobacco growers on my books, and the load gets heavier every day."

"They'll pay one day, and if they don't, why, Doc, then you've moved that much closer to heaven on the arms of those you have served."

"You're very charitable with my services," said Ketchum.

"And with my own."

"Touché."

Cayce looked up inquiringly. "Oh, that's my concession," said Ketchum, "for you getting the best of that argument."

Although his sympathies weren't involved, Ketchum's interest in the tobacco war was that of any other innocent bystander who might be drawn into the line of fire. "Have you heard rumors of a Night Rider march of massive proportions on Hopkinsville."

Cayce nodded. "Yep, the stories are all over town."

"What do they propose to do?"

"The two biggest warehouses are here," said Cayce, "and they're crammed with choice tobacco waiting to be shipped to the factories."

"They wouldn't dare fire those buildings, not in a law-abiding community of eight thousand people."

Cayce shrugged. "When people start taking the law in their own hands because of a cause, the law becomes an inconvenience they find it increasingly easy to overlook."

Ketchum gave his psychic diagnostician a keen glance. "You know, Cayce, sometimes you make sense even when you're awake."

"Thanks, Doc," Cayce said wryly, getting up to leave. As he stood up, the outer door to Ketchum's office opened, and a tall, rawboned young man in a rough shirt and trousers came in. He was no more than twenty-one or twenty-two, with a sure stride and the confidence of youth that had never known a bridle. His left hand was bandaged, and from its appearance, the bandage was possibly a week or two old.

"Hi, Doc," he said, with a questioning glance at Cayce.

Ketchum regarded the newcomer imperturbably. "I have no secrets from this man—actually, he's my secret partner."

The young man's eyes brushed coldly over Cayce. "All right," said he grudgingly. "I've trusted you this far."

Cayce's steps lagged as he studied the youth's countenance.

Ketchum looked up in surprise to see the psychic still standing there, watching. "This is Gordon McCool," said he, "from Caldwell County. He says he shot himself. Now," to McCool, "let's have that arm."

McCool held out his left hand, and Ketchum deftly removed the bandage, revealing an angry wound showing signs of healing.

Ketchum gave the hand a careful scrutiny. "Not

bad, but don't go shooting yourself again." His lips curled sardonically. "McCool says his gun went off accidentally. I don't have to report this type of case, not if I'm satisfied they're accidents."

Cayce looked at the two curiously. "Is he right-handed?"

"Left-handed," said Ketchum. "That's what makes it a curious case, and you know how I like curiosities, Cayce."

He dabbed the wound with iodine as McCool winced, then skillfully applied a new and smaller bandage. "That ought to fix you for a while, provided you stay out of trouble."

"Thanks, Doc, you're not all bad, for a Yankee."

Ketchum threw up his hands in mock dismay. "Why do you Rebs keep coming to a Yankee, if that's the way you feel?"

McCool laughed, pulling down his sleeve. "Only a Yankee wouldn't care how this happened, and if I'm going to get anybody in trouble over treating this, it might better be a damn Yankee."

Cayce laughed at the consternation on Ketchum's face. It was one of the few times he had ever seen the brash young doctor discomfited.

McCool was now calmly sizing up the taller of the two men. "Cayce," he intoned, knitting his brows, "you wouldn't be the one they call the Freak?"

"He's the Freak, all right," Ketchum said, as Cayce moved to get his black felt hat and scramble into his coat.

"The darkies say you have second sight."

Cayce returned the other man's glance evenly. "I don't claim anything."

McCool's lips drooped in amusement. "What do you see for me?"

Ketchum interposed quickly. "Cayce doesn't work that way; he goes into trance and comes up with whatever he sees, sleeping."

"No wonder they call him the Freak," said McCool with an insolent stare.

A metamorphosis appeared to have come over

Cayce. The color had left his face. He gave the young man a look of commiseration.

As McCool was speaking, Cayce had suddenly experienced a blinding flash. He saw the man on horseback firing guns, others returning their fire, and a man slipping lifeless from his horse.

His eyes closed momentarily and when they opened he turned to McCool and said in a solemn voice, "Don't do what you are planning to do tonight. Do not ride with the rest."

The young man's face went pale. His hands trembled despite a visible effort to control them. Through lips which had suddenly gone dry, he said hoarsely, "Who have you been talking to?"

Ketchum was watching the unexpected drama with his jaw hanging. "McCool," he said, "I don't know what Cayce's talking about, but I'd do as he says. I've never known him to be wrong."

"It sounds like a put-up job to me," McCool almost snarled. "I should have known I couldn't trust a Yankee, especially one who uses a freak."

Scornfully, he tossed a bill on a table, then turned on his heel and strode out of the office.

Through a window, they watched him get astride his horse and ride off with his rifle plainly showing in his sidepack.

Ketchum turned eagerly to his friend. "Did you really see anything, Cayce?"

Cayce groaned, shaking his head. "I try to hold these things off, but sometimes they come in on me when I least expect it."

Ketchum's eyes gleamed. "So you're psychic in the waking state, too. That's great, Edgar. Think of the possibilities."

Cayce regarded him severely. "You just don't understand, Ketchum. You just don't understand."

Before Ketchum could respond, Cayce ran out of the office and quickly disappeared down the street, headed for home and the one person who did understand.

As always, with a look, Gertrude knew when

203

something had gone wrong. She quietly poured him a glass of red wine, not showing her concern, then served the tenderly fried chicken and greens he liked so well.

Cayce poked at his dinner desultorily, as Gertrude tried not to notice anything unusual in his behavior. Suddenly, with a start, he recalled that they had planned to visit at Aunt Carrie's after dinner. "I don't feel much like going out tonight."

"Aunt Carrie looks forward so much to seeing you, Edgar," said Gertrude, thinking it might get him out of himself.

He shook his head. "Some other night will do as well."

She leaned across her corner of the table and touched her lips to his forehead. "As you say, Edgar dear. Maybe I'll just run over to the library; there's a book I've been wanting to pick up for some time."

"No," said Cayce, so vehemently that she found herself staring at him. "I'd feel better with you here tonight."

His arms around her waist took the harshness out of his words. He walked into the hall, where the phone hung from the wall, and telephoned Aunt Carrie. Although his voice was low, Gertrude couldn't help overhearing snatches of conversation. "Tell the doctor to stay at home tonight. It won't be healthy out in the street."

She looked at him inquiringly when he returned to the room, but all he said, with an air of lightness, was, "Same time, same day, next week, with the same people. They didn't mind at all."

Gertrude went to the front window and peered out into the dusk. The day had been unseasonably warm for December, almost balmy. As it grew dark, a breeze blew up, but the night was still moderately warm.

"You wouldn't care for a little walk around the block," she suggested, remembering the conversation.

"No," said Cayce, "let's stay home and turn in early tonight, Gertrude."

"Is there anything wrong?"

"I'm not sure," he said, "so I'd rather not say at this time. If I told anybody, they would only laugh."

She smiled. "You're always right, Edgar. That's why I married you."

Normally, Hopkinsville went off to sleep an hour or so after the evening meal. There were no children in the streets after dark, and even the downtown area, with its general store, bookstore, drugstore, shoe store, and clothing shops, was deserted after nine. A stray individual, stopping by a saloon for a beer or a bourbon, the pride of Kentucky, might occasionally loiter past ten, but by eleven the town was invariably shut tight.

There had been so many rumors of Night Rider raids, without the raids materializing, that the town had shrugged off the new rumors, even though sentiment was shifting against the raiders because of the growing terror. But the raid was more imminent than the town thought. Taking advantage of the clement weather, Sanders had summoned an army of raiders from the surrounding counties for a march that would dramatically stress the power of the Association in its massive struggle against the Trust.

Earlier that day, as the main force was gathering in a secret glade, raider scouts had sifted inconspicuously into Hoptown, making a close surveillance of two major warehouses, storing tons of tobacco waiting to be shipped, and of a cigarette-processing plant, all closely situated. Other scouts had instructions to be on the alert for patrols of state militia, aid for extra sheriff's posses or police details. Sanders wanted no violence if it could be avoided.

"If we kill anybody in Hopkinsville," he warned his men, "public opinion will go heavily against us."

Cayce was not entirely in the dark about the coming showdown. It had been predicted regularly in the weekly *Kentuckian* by one of the Association's most outspoken foes, Mayor Charlie Meacham, who was also the proprietor of this prophetic journal. He called for a standing army, impressed from the ranks of loyal citizens by the Sheriff, but none took him seriously at this time. He had cried wolf once too often.

Twice now at his insistence, two hundred men had assumed battle stations in the outlying woods and fields, digging trenches and bulwarks and mustering all the firearms they could for the town's defense. All night, they had drunk bourbon and branch water against the cold watch, and then in the morning, feeling rather foolish when the enemy didn't show up, slunk off sleepily for their homes to the good-natured taunts of citizens making their morning rounds. But what they didn't know was that Meacham had been right, and the preparations had forestalled the raids, Sanders not wishing to risk the bloodshed. Now, Sanders' scouts advised that the militia had been withdrawn, the buildings were lightly guarded, and the police and fire departments undermanned and unready.

Meacham's warnings fell on deaf ears that day, even as he lashed out at the men who had taken the law in their hands. "We've had our stomachful of outlaws, hiding their faces behind masks and cowardly intimidating peaceful citizens with their burning torches and blacksnake whips."

Only Sanders—and Cayce—knew this was H-Day for Hopkinsville. Alerts had been sent out to Association sympathizers that December morning, couriers racing through the countryside ordering riders to gather at a fork ten miles outside of Hopkinsville. But even as they poured in for the rendezvous they had no clue as to their target for the night.

Even in the glory days of the Klan, there had not been such an assemblage of riders. They gathered in a great glade, out of sight of the main highway to Hopkinsville, as the skies were beginning to darken. Sanders, with his lieutenant, Clyde Duncan, at his side, stood up to greet them. Their response was so deafening he could hardly be heard.

He held up a hand for silence. "Tonight," he cried, "we march on Hopkinsville."

Even the horses, which had carried their riders so

206

swiftly, snorted loudly as new cheers exploded on all sides.

"Our job," continued Sanders, "is to burn the Trust warehouses and the Trust tobacco, and then to get the hell out of Hoptown as quick as we can."

In the front ranks, none cheered more lustily than a rawboned young man who had ridden in a few minutes before at the head of a platoon. He was carrying a rifle in his right arm, and the left was freshly bandaged. There was a wild look in his eyes, and he was mounted appropriately on a spirited black stallion, whose eyes seemed to have the same fierce look. The platoon leader had been in Ketchum's office only a few hours before. His name was Gordon McCool.

His voice rose over the others. "Give 'em hell," he shouted, brandishing his rifle over his head.

The doctor smiled and held up a hand. "We will move in quietly, depending on surprise. We will not fire unless fired upon."

There were groans from the riders, but their captain's voice carried over the protest. "We will show our strength in other ways. We will disarm the law and take over the town, and set fire to the barn and warehouses. We will let them know that the riders are in complete control."

This salvo was greeted with a giant uproar.

By this time, there were more than five hundred riders gathered in the glade, with hoods and masks dangling.

Cries of "Let's go" rose above the neighing of the horses, but again the captain held up a hand. "Before we take off for Hoptown, we will have a little blessing from the preacher."

A red-faced man, with a solemn mien, stood up on the knoll next to Sanders, and with his eyes raised to the sky gravely intoned, "May the good Lord bless this mission, and guide us in Jesus' name. Amen."

There was a respectful silence, and then a series of hurrahs.

The captain waved an arm. "Get all that out of your system, boys. I don't want to hear a word all the way into Hopkinsville. Every detail has its orders. The main body moves on to the warehouses with me. Rogers and his boys move on to police headquarters, and pin them down. Duncan blocks off the firehouse and ties down the firemen, and Jones moves on to the telephone office and will disrupt communication within the city. Our advance patrols will cut the wires on all telephone poles, cutting the city off from the rest of the state. Every man will do his job quietly and efficiently. And no shooting, unless we are shot at."

His voice rose. "So good luck to you all. Remember, you ride in the tradition of Lee, Stonewall, and that great cavalry leader, Jeb Stuart."

The body of horsemen moved into the dirt road toward Hopkinsville ten miles away. They rode at ease, in long columns, with masks and guns ready. The night was clear, and the odor of smoke-cured tobacco filled the star-filled night. Dr. Sanders and Duncan rode at the head of the columns, McCool and his men not far behind.

As they passed through a town called Gracie advance men climbed poles and cut the telephone lines. This was a relay station, and no calls would now filter out beyond this point. Shortly before 11 P.M., traveling as quietly as five hundred men on horseback could, they reached a schoolhouse two miles west of Hopkinsville and there dismounted while they fed their horses from nosebags and waited for the advance guard which had moved singly and stealthily into Hopkinsville to report back on any late activity there.

As the men lounged around, Sanders looked anxiously down the main road to town, watching for his scouts. Just before midnight they returned, their faces wreathed in smiles.

"Not a soul is stirring," one reported. "All we do is move in and take over."

"How about the warehouses?" Sanders asked.

"Two or three guards in front of each warehouse," a scout reported.

"What about the police, any extra details?"

"We'll catch them in the station; they'll only be a handful."

"And the firemen?"

A scout laughed. "Sleeping, as usual."

Sanders turned to an aide. "Go on ahead and cut off the telephone office, so they can't get a call in to the police."

To assure surprise, and complete freedom on foot, most of the horses were tied down at this point, a group grudgingly remaining behind to have them ready when the men came storming back from the raid.

The other raiders, except for a flying squadron that kept their horses, then swung down the highway at a brisk pace, with a last order from Sanders to "put on your masks and hoods and do what you have been told."

In less than an hour, their footfalls deadened by rubber-soled shoes, the men reached the outskirts of the city. They halted at the railroad tracks, near a clutter of Negro shacks, then split off into two separate columns. One column walked the ties into town, the other angled off onto a dirt road and crossed over a narrow wooden bridge at Little River to converge on the downtown area. It was 2 A.M., and the city was deserted when they finally joined forces. They moved quietly and efficiently. Operating closely under platoon leaders, the various squads separated to carry out their assignments. A dozen men marched into downtown telephone headquarters and pulled out the telephone lines before three startled women operators, dozing in nightclothes on cots, and a lone girl reading from a magazine, were aware of the intrusion.

Another detail broke into the Armory, confiscated weapons stored there, and stood guard to prevent deputies and militia from arming in the event of a premature alarm.

Other masked raiders stormed into the police station and caught three officers sleepily playing cards. They looked up, stunned, into the muzzles of assorted shotguns, pistols and rifles.

"One move and you're dead," the platoon leader warned.

At that moment, the telephone rang, and the policeman nearest the phone reached for it.

As he leaned over, he caught a shotgun blast in the back and fell over in pain. Fellow officers moved to help him, then stopped suddenly as a fusillade of bullets passed dangerously past their heads.

The shots rang out in the darkness, echoing through the downtown area. Sanders, hearing the shots, sent reinforcements to the police station. They arrived to find the situation under control.

Down from the police station, another platoon smashed into the firebarn, crashing through windows and doors. They backed six firemen, who had been playing checkers, against the wall, covering them with their guns. Other firemen were rousted from an upstairs dormitory and brought down in their nightclothes.

"We got orders," the squadron leader warned, "to shoot anything trying to leave this building."

The firemen were unceremoniously shoved into a storage room, which was locked after them.

"Scream all you like, as long as you don't try to get out." The leader laughed.

Charlie Meacham was not forgotten. The captain had kept one small cavalry detail to sweep in after the foot soldiers, and these, led by young McCool, swooped down on the newspaper plant, hurling bricks through the front windows, then plunging through the gaping holes with their horses, dismounting long enough to hack the presses with axes, smash the linotype machines, smear the walls and furniture with printer's ink, and light a torch to the plant.

Meacham had hastily arrived on the scene and was angrily viewing the havoc from the sidewalk. As the vandals rode past, he shook his fist at them and they responded by cheerfully clubbing him down.

"That's for calling us hoodlums," shouted one rider.

Aside from the shots, the operation had proceeded smoothly, according to plan.

The main force, led by the doctor and reinforced by McCool's raiders, split into two groups and moved against two giant warehouses, quickly overpowering a handful of guards. Smashing down doors, they broke into the huge building and applied kerosene-steeped torches to the great masses of tobacco awaiting shipment to processing plants.

The pine planks and the tarred paper of the warehouses caught fire instantly. And where the brick partitions appeared to withstand the blazes, sticks of dynamite were thrown in, razing the walls and sending bright flames shooting high into the orange sky.

McCool's riders moved on to a manufacturing plant next to the railroad station, attacking a freight train which had been loading tobacco at a siding. Two men climbed into the cab of the locomotive and hauled down the engineer, who had been trying to move out of the freight yard with his precious cargo. Flaming torches were flung into the cars, and tons of hickory-smoked tobacco were soon adding to the flames and smoke.

Giving a Rebel battle cry, McCool's riders, slashing away with whips at the citizens beginning to collect around the burning buildings, crashed their way into the factory, dashing cans of kerosene over bales of tobacco and backing off as the leaping flames cast the hooded marauders in grotesque silhouettes.

In a few minutes, a tobacco crop worth a million dollars had been destroyed, and the mission had been accomplished. By this time, startled citizens were poking their heads out of windows. Some had drawn guns, aiming them at the hooded riders, who rode past headed for the rendezvous with the main marching force on the outskirts of the city. Shots were fired from the windows, and the riders fired back, in an atmosphere that was now as bright as daylight.

The night wind, catching the sparks from the burning warehouses, had scattered them onto neighboring rooftops for blocks around, threatening a general conflagration. Men who had rushed out of their houses to resist the riders turned instead to the more immediate task of saving their own homes and the town. Wesley Ketchum, listening to Cayce's prediction, had believed the raid was coming and had stayed indoors, retiring early. He was a jumpy sleeper and the shots echoing from the downtown area, together with the unusual commotion of men and horses, had awakened him shortly after 2 A.M. He had gone to the windows, seen the fires in the sky, and quickly donned his clothes. It was just as well.

His home, at Campbell and Seventh, was but a few blocks from the downtown sector, and the flying sparks, as he saw, had ignited the roof of his livery stable in the rear and threatened the house itself. Ketchum was not the man to sit around and wring his hands. He clambered up on the stable roof with a garden hose and began playing water on the mushrooming flames, damping down his house at the same time.

As he fought the flames, he recalled Cayce's warning to McCool, wondering ruefully why he hadn't also predicted that Ketchum's home would be a target. "That's the trouble with that man," he growled to himself. "He doesn't give a hoot about his friends."

By this time, the town firemen had broken out of their involuntary confinement and were racing with all the horse-drawn equipment they had to the blazing downtown area. Hundreds of citizens had quickly assembled and they formed a bucket brigade to subdue the spreading flames. The Night Riders were able to retreat without any pursuit in force.

It was beginning to appear that Sanders' plan had been perfectly brought off. Though there had been some shooting, nobody had been hurt except one indiscreet policeman, and he not critically. Not one rider had been scathed, and none of the citizenry had been hurt, save from the blow to Charlie Meacham and his pride. In his home, Cayce had been awakened by the sound of guns and the clamor of men and horses. Gertrude had joined him as he peered out the window at the orange sky.

She looked at him in wonderment, and whispered, "You knew, Edgar, you knew?"

He nodded sadly. "Yes, I knew. But knowing doesn't always help."

His thoughts turned to the young man who had scoffed earlier that day at the warning from the man he called the Freak.

At that moment, McCool, bringing up the rear, was riding safely out of the battle area, when a shot from a window passed by his head.

Angered by the fire, the irrepressible young man turned in his saddle for a final blast from his rifle.

As he did so, one of the warehouse guards, who had been clubbed down, fired his rifle from one knee at the rider who now lagged behind his men. The distance was some one hundred yards and the angle was bad, and the flames cast flickering shadows. But somehow, amazingly, the bullet found its mark. McCool felt a searing pain in his chest, a wave of nausea, and then funnels of darkness as consciousness ebbed. The rein loosened in his hands. Instinctively, he fell forward, his arms circling his horse's neck. Blood spurted from his wound, welling into his clothing and dripping to the ground. The masterless horse, his ears flared, trailed mindlessly after the others and pulled up wheezing at the schoolhouse, where some riders were already welcoming the marchers coming in at a trot behind them.

As McCool slid off his horse, more dead than alive, eager hands carefully lifted him and placed him on a blanket, cut away his shirt and jacket and inspected the wound by the light of a match. He was unconscious, and his breath came in labored gasps. His face was like chalk.

As the wound was exposed, the men shook their heads. The main artery to the heart had been severed by the bullet. McCool was rapidly bleeding to death.

At this point, Sanders arrived with Duncan, and the other riders respectfully cleared a circle around the dying man. Sanders needed only one look. "Even if we could get him to a hospital, he's a goner." He turned to an aide. "Let's get him on a horse, and take him with us. At least, we can give him Christian burial."

As the doctor spoke, the dying man gave a last convulsive twitch, and his head wobbled back and stayed there.

Another Edgar Cayce prediction had strangely come true.

10

Cayce Reincarnates

Ketchum would have referred the case to a psychiatrist if he had known of one. He couldn't even begin to figure out what was wrong with the five-year-old boy. He looked healthy enough, with rosy cheeks and a chunky little body, but he was a nervous wreck. according to his worried mother, a normally placid woman who didn't seem prone to exaggeration. The child did appear inordinately restless. He couldn't sit still in his chair for a moment. Even the doctor's scrutiny had no subduing effect. He was, as the doctor noted, an extremely high-strung child with an excess of nervous energy. But it hardly seemed cause for concern, until the mother gave him the rest of the picture.

"He has nightmares in the daytime." the mother reported. "Sometimes, after napping in the afternoon, he wakes distraught, wrings his hands like an old woman in agony, and cries ceaselessly. It's almost as if it were a seizure of some sort." She would try soothing the child, and in a half hour the wailing would subside, without the boy having the faintest recollection of what had troubled him.

She sent him to a special school for problem children, thinking that a disciplined routine would have a beneficial influence, but the boy only grew more restive. The crying fits were merely postponed, until he got home and fell off to sleep and dream.

Ketchum was in a quandary. The mother was a patient, so was her husband, and his parents. He had to do something—but what?

"The problem is obviously with the nervous system," he told the mother, "but I'll need to see him again."

Deferred treatment was invariably a prelude to a Cayce reading. And as usual, Edgar could find time for a child, even with a loaded schedule.

It was another of the increasing number of emergency readings, conducted by Ketchum in the absence of the Squire, the record of the proceedings dependent on notes taken by Ketchum and given a stenographer for transcription.

The reading began, as usual, with Ketchum giving the child's name and address and asking for diagnosis.

Cayce, as usual, announced he had the body.

Ketchum sat back, with pencil and pad at hand, ready to jot down whatever he thought significant.

Cayce made a long pause, as if trying to concentrate deeply. When he finally spoke, he referred to the subject in terms Ketchum had never heard before. He spoke of entity. And instead of dealing right off with the child's condition, which Ketchum had grown to expect, he got into a world of confusing fantasy. Ketchum could hardly credit what he heard.

"With this entity, we have had a return from a previous experience fraught with great fear. And with the entity, remembering this fear, special influences are now required into the experiences of this mind—so that it may be kept from fear, from loud and discordant noises, from darkness, the scream of shells in the night, the shouts of individuals, anything that caused the entity to experience fear in the past."

Ketchum's pencil poised indecisively, and then he put it down with a sigh. Cayce was obviously tuned out, a new departure, but he supposed it had to happen sooner or later. Nobody was perfect, not even the man he had come to think of as the human X-ray.

But Cayce was not through. His voice droned on, in that flat monotone so curiously devoid of expression.

"The entity, when cut off before, was just coming to awareness of the beauty of associations, of friendships, of the great outdoors, nature, flowers, birds, of God's manifestation to man, of the oneness of purpose with nature." He paused. "And then the tramping of feet, the shouts of arms, the artillery shells bursting nearby, brought destructive forces. The entity then was only two or three years older than in the present experience, and now again, the rattling sabers, of those in this experience called the Night Riders, the burning of barns, the tramp of marching feet, the thunder of horses' hooves, the shots in the night, all these awaken the old memories and fears."

Ketchum tried to get the reading back on track. "What is wrong with this child? Can he be helped? Tell what will help him."

Cayce's theme did not change. "This entity lived once in the country known as Poland, and was subjected to the horrors of war and its devastation. It needs to be reassured in this lifetime. The mother should be patient with this boy. Do not scold. Do not speak harshly. Do not fret or condemn the body-mind. But tell it daily of the love that Jesus had for little children, of peace and harmony. Never stories about the witch or the hobgoblin, never those as of fearfulness of any great punishment. But stress love and patience. This will not be found in a school, from others, but in a mother's constant love."

Ketchum's jaw dropped. Whew, he thought. Cayce has finally flipped his lid. The reference to the school he considered pure coincidence.

He tried still again. "What is to be done for the child in this life?" asked Ketchum. "How will it recover from its present nervous strain and be a normal happy child?"

Cayce replied promptly. "All will be well, with the proper assurances, and with time. As with other children, these experiences from the past are pushed back into the background, until they are happily forgotten. Then, as the child's personality unfolds, the entity will gradually become better adjusted until, alas, there will be another war in ten years or so of worldwide proportions."

Ketchum groaned. Instead of making it any better, his questioning only seemed to deepen the aberration that Cayce was apparently experiencing, even to a fanciful prediction of a world war in 1915 or 1916. There seemed no point to continuing. He quickly brought Cayce back to consciousness, and, as usual, Cayce reached for a cracker and a glass of milk.

Looking over at the silent Ketchum, he sensed an absence of the enthusiasm which normally followed a reading. "What's wrong?" asked Edgar, munching on his cracker.

Ketchum held up a blank pad. "That's what's wrong. You didn't say a thing that was relevant to the case."

"That's odd," said Cayce, finishing his snack. "I generally get something."

Ketchum snorted. "You got something all right, but it was out of this world, and even out of this time. You were talking about reincarnation, as if it was the most logical thing in the world, and made it responsible for this poor lad's condition."

"That's strange," Cayce mused aloud. "I don't believe in reincarnation. It's against my religion."

"Anyway, that was the reading, and I don't see how it can help any."

Edgar had pulled out his pipe, a sign of particular concentration, and drew on it reflectively. "Wasn't there anything that could be applied to the current problem?"

"Well," Ketchum said grudgingly, "you did say the boy needed constant reassurance and love, and should be withdrawn from his particular school and disagreeable situations, but that could be said about any five-year-old child."

Cayce regarded the doctor quizzically. "Just because the advice could be applied to many doesn't necessarily mean that it doesn't fit one."

Ketchum threw up his arms. "Edgar, I can't tell that young mother that her child is a nervous wreck because he got scared stiff in a war that ended long before he was born. She would have me committed."

Never before in their association had a reading been inaccurate, and it was hard to face the awesome possibility that the information was fallible.

"If it is wrong once," said Cayce, putting his finger on Ketchum's thinking as well, "then it can be wrong at any time." He gave Ketchum a penetrating look. "I don't have much confidence in myself, Doc, but I have trusted the information, even with the life of my wife."

Ketchum nodded appreciatively.

"Why not get the reading typed off from your recall," Cayce went on, "and let me look at it? Meanwhile, tell the mother to do as suggested. It's sound advice, in any case, and can do no harm." He laughed. "You remember the pregnant girl, and how well that worked out?"

Ketchum's head wagged. "That's right, but you didn't blame that on some event of years before, in another lifetime; you put it right on the proper person."

After dinner that evening, Edgar Cayce sat in his favorite easy chair, reading and rereading with a puzzled frown the transcript Ketchum had put together.

Gertrude studied her husband covertly, from time to time, then gave him an inquiring look. "What is it, Edgar?"

He welcomed the opportunity to discuss this new troubling thought. "I said something today that changes the concept of life as I have always understood it."

She waited for him to go on. "In doing a health reading," he said solemnly, "I casually mentioned a past life as having an effect on a condition in this life. And gave this boy I was reading for an identity in that life, saying he had come back to work out things in this life."

After being married to Edgar for several years, there was very little that could surprise Gertrude. "You were obviously talking about reincarnation," she observed matter-of-factly.

"But why?" He shook his head anxiously. "Could my gift be leaving me?"

Gertrude's faith never wavered. "Perhaps there is reincarnation. Half the world believes in it—India, China, Malaya, and all those places." She dismissed most of Asia with a vague wave of her hand.

"But they are not Christians, and Christianity does not accept the concept of rebirth on earth."

Gertrude was enjoying the role of devil's advocate. "Emerson and Thoreau were good Christians, and they believed in reincarnation."

Not well-read, except for the Bible, Edgar took pride in Gertrude's extensive knowledge. "That may be," said he, "but they don't speak for the Christian Church. The Catholics and Protestants, including our own persuasion, don't even consider it."

"Didn't Christ say you didn't live until you were reborn?"

"He was speaking of rebirth in the Kingdom of Heaven, not here on earth."

She gave him a quick smile. "Edgar, haven't you ever felt you knew somebody before?"

He frowned, as if trying to determine what she was leading up to. "Why, yes, I always felt as if I had known you."

He suddenly recalled with a thrill of insight the cloth-of-gold dream, and his mother saying he had known his soul mate before, and would know her again. He hadn't understood this at the time, as he thought only in terms of one life on earth.

Gertrude was excited now, having long ago formed the belief from her own reading, and her feelings of complete soul rapport with Edgar, that a continuous life cycle was a distinct possibility. There was a mischievous twinkle in her eye as she suggested that Edgar use his own special gift to resolve this problem of reincarnation. "Why not give a reading on the subject?"

He looked at her dubiously. "How would I go about it?"

She was growing more enthusiastic. "We could ask

220

any number of questions. Why do certain members of the opposite sex become attracted and get married? The scientist explains it as a biological urge, but why do the least likely so often gravitate toward each other? In some families, one is born a genius, the other an idiot, one is born blind or deformed, or with other weaknesses. Why?"

Cayce picked up the second question. "Through some family or genetic disposition, I suppose."

She laughed. "How would that account for Mozart composing serious music at three, and Josef Hofmann playing the piano well at the same age? That wasn't handed down."

Edgar showed his surprise, not having ever surmised that she thought this way.

She kissed him playfully. "There are many hidden facets about a woman, Edgar. We can't let our man take us for granted."

"But, Gertrude, I never knew you even thought about reincarnation."

"You weren't ready, Edgar."

"And now I am?"

"Oh, yes." She was supreme, confident. "Or your subconscious mind wouldn't have turned it up in a reading." She quoted loosely. "When the time is ripe for an idea, not all the armies in the world can stop it."

He got to his feet, and stood looking down at her with a gleam of friendly banter. "It seems to me that I have a lot to learn from you."

She turned to him seriously. "We learn from each other, Edgar. That is the wonderful thing about our marriage."

He chuckled. "Well, I'm ready to lie down, whenever you're ready."

Some time had passed since dinner, and Edgar's stomach was sufficiently empty for the reading.

"I hope my head's not quite as empty," he said, as he loosened his collar and took off his shoes. "Anyway," he added cheerfully, "I won't have to put these back on again tonight."

221

He had closed his eyes now, and was soon thoroughly relaxed, secure in the knowledge that Gertrude was conducting the reading.

Gertrude had carefully framed the first question. "If there is such a thing as reincarnation, how does it express itself in our daily lives?"

Cayce drew a deep breath, then spoke in his usual trance tone, as if discussing rheumatism or a cold in the head:

"The body is the vehicle of that spirit and soul that wafts through all time and ever remains the same, except for those changes and modifications that come with the choices one makes in a life experience, thereby affecting the situation with which the individual begins another experience. The Bible says as one sows so shall he reap. This was not said of one life, but of continuous lives in which names and parents may change, as well as the sex of the entity, his color, creed and station in life. But his soul-mind is essentially the same, subject to those changes that some call karma."

Gertrude listened raptly, rejoicing at the directness of the reply, and struck by Edgar's use of the word *karma,* an expression quite new to him, which she only vaguely recalled herself from Thoreau's description of the credit-and-debit ledger carried from one life to another in the Hindu concept of reincarnation.

She proceeded with a second question:

"If we do remember anything, as expressed by instant feelings of familiarity with strangers or by special aptitudes or inclinations, in what way is this remembrance transmitted from one life to the next?"

Again, in a casual monotone:

"The subconscious mind is the storehouse of all our experiences and thoughts, for all our lives, here and elsewhere. To the degree that these experiences and thoughts have been in the right direction, a man is civilized, cultured, humane and so forth. So does his past record shine through his conscious mind and present body, forming the pattern of the body and the character of the person."

Edgar droned on, happily oblivious of what he was saying.

"Nothing is forgotten by the subconscious. Therefore, if you in one or more past lives, or in studies in other planes, learned this wisdom which comes through you, it is not surprising that the subconscious is full of the same wisdom, provided that the individual is allied with the forces of good. That's where the importance of morality comes into our daily lives, 'As man thinketh in his heart, so is he.'"

"Why," asked Gertrude, "don't we consciously remember?"

"Some do," the slumbering Cayce replied. "However, it is not beneficial to consciously remember. If the body, from its material and mental development, were to be wholly conscious of that through which it passes in its soul activity, the strain would be too great. Material activity could be unbalanced and the body become demented. Imagine the remorse of the murderer if he remembered his crimes for eternity in their horrible detail. Better that he have a lingering impression of guilt in the subconscious, which makes him atone for this killing by striving for excellence in his present relations with his fellow man. But woe to the man who kills. For, as Jesus sayeth, 'They that take the sword shall perish with the sword,' and this was not said of this life alone, in which the wicked so often prosper without retribution."

Gertrude, intrigued by the steady flow of information, had been jotting it down in abbreviated hand as rapidly as she could. She had shared Edgar's eagerness to know the origin of his gift, and thought this might be the time to explore this area as well.

"In what way," she asked, "did the psychic knowledge of Edgar Cayce develop from the past?"

In trance, Cayce's mind apparently took on many dimensions. Even while discoursing in the sleep state on a certain subject, none of which he remembered after a while on awakening, he also had recurring dreams which he did remember. One of these dreams,

223

which had baffled him for years, pictured, without explanation, a desert oasis with three palms and a well.

Cayce, in trance, for the first time now spoke of the three palms and a well. "The entity was then called by the name Uhjltd." The sleeping Cayce spelled out the name. "This entity was one of power, prestige and royalty in what is known as the Arabian land and the leader in many wars upon the surrounding peoples, tribes or nations. In a battle against the neighboring Persian King this Uhjltd was defeated and his forces scattered to the winds. He was left to die, mortally wounded, in the barren desert. As he looked up in despair, barely able to crawl, he saw in the distance an oasis surrounded by three palm tress. He tried pulling himself along by the arms, dragging his wounded legs, toward the well, suffering from hunger and thirst, as well as infection and loss of blood. As his strength waned, the realization came that only a superhuman effort of the will would ease his death throes.

"The entity," Cayce droned on, "drew himself into the subconscious recesses of the mind, closing himself off from the agony of the sweltering sun and the festering sores of the body, and found serenity in this deeper consciousness. He willed that he would suffer no longer, hoping to die as he had lived, a valiant soldier without a murmur of complaint."

Gertrude was so fascinated by this dramatic narrative that her pencil remained motionless for a few moments.

"Hours later," Cayce continued, "the entity known as Uhjltd regained consciousness in the cool evening, and discovered to his amazement that his wounds and fever had disappeared. Even his tongue, swollen from lack of water, had regained its normal texture. He was able to walk, without difficulty, the four hundred yards to the well of the three palms, and there quenched his thirst. By the innate psychic powers in all of us, this entity had saved himself on the brink of death, and developed that force which stayed in the soul consciousness. This ability to submerge the body

224

to the mind had become part of the personality, and used properly, could raise him to spiritual grandeur, or failing, being material, reduce him to new depths."

Gertrude, moving from the sublime past to the mundane present, saw an opportunity now to fix the correctness of Cayce's calling once and for all. "Should Edgar Cayce properly work in a bookstore, or as a photographer, or a clairvoyant?"

Cayce promptly responded. "As to the vocation, this in the present plane may be directed in any channel through will. The better condition would be toward those of the psychic and occult, or teaching or developing along the lines of such plane to give the manifestation of such forces to the populace."

Gertrude was delighted, as it only confirmed what she had always believed, that Edgar Cayce's psychic gift belonged to the world.

He showed signs of restlessness—a tiring voice—and she quickly gave the suggestion that brought him out of his long sleep.

He sat up, rubbing his eyes, and said with a smile, "Well, was I a king, or somebody equally important?"

She leaned over impetuously, and touched her lips to his forehead. "You were never more important than you are now, Edgar."

The next day being Sunday, Edgar took advantage of the day to pore over his Bible, as Gertrude busied herself preparing the transcription on reincarnation. He had puzzled over many Biblical passages dealing with the apparent continuity of life, and now he searched with new eyes.

Chapter Nine of John had always baffled him. "And his disciples asked him, saying, Master, who did sin, this man, or his parents, that he was born blind?"

"Since he was born blind," Edgar observed aloud with a frown, "how could his own sin have caused his blindness, unless it was committed in another life? Doesn't that indicate the disciples were familiar with reincarnation and the law of karma?"

She smiled, as she went on with her transcribing. "It would seem so, dear."

He had turned now to Matthew, seventeenth chapter, and read aloud as before:

" 'And his disciples asked him, saying, Why then say the scribes that Elias must first come?

" 'And Jesus answered and said unto them, Elias truly shall first come, and restore all things [as a prelude to the Messiah's coming and resurrection.]

" 'But I say unto you, that Elias is come already, and they knew him not, but have done unto him whatsoever they listed. Likewise shall also the Son of Man suffer of them.

" 'Then the disciples understood that he spoke unto them of John the Baptist.' "

In ostensibly addressing Gertrude, Cayce's voice had now taken on a querulous note. "Nobody ever explained that one to me properly before. How else did they understand that he was speaking of John the Baptist unless they recognized that John the Baptist was the incarnation of Elias?"

She said without looking up, "Edgar, you're the Bible authority. You know more about the Gospels than anybody in Hopkinsville. Even the minister says that."

Such praise, even in the intimacy of his home, made Edgar self-conscious. "I'm not trying to blow my own horn, Gertrude, just trying to understand what they were trying to tell us long ago."

He had now thumbed his way to Revelation, thirteenth chapter, tenth verse, again knowing exactly what he was looking for. "Here's another passage that always intrigued me: 'He that leadeth into captivity shall go into captivity; he that killeth with the sword must be killed with the sword. Here is the patience and the faith of the saints.' "

Gertrude gave him a curious glance. "And what does that mean to you now, Edgar?"

He looked at her sharply. "I'm not becoming a convert to reincarnation after one reading. These are things I've always wondered about and never had any explanation for. And neither has anybody else, without reincarnation."

Her laugh tinkled like a bell across the room. "You don't have to apologize to me, Edgar Cayce. You convinced me yesterday. Just wait until I'm finished."

He looked startled for a moment, not knowing precisely what she meant, then went ahead with a new interpretation of that now controversial passage.

"Jesus certainly wasn't speaking of this life alone. Every man who killed another with the sword was not killed by a sword himself—not in the same life. And what is the patience of the saints but an understanding that surpasses man's understanding, and leaves justice to God's law."

She clapped her hands in excitement. "Edgar, you say things so beautifully. And do you know that you said pretty much the same thing yesterday in response to my question? So you're really in agreement with the information."

"That's good," he rejoined dryly. "I don't know very much by myself."

She sighed. "Always belittling yourself." She handed him several sheets of paper with a triumphant smile. "All finished, and all yours."

Cayce sat back in his chair and began to read slowly from the transcription, his eyes widening in astonishment as they came upon his own incarnation as Uhjltd. "How did I ever say a name like that?" he exclaimed.

"You spelled it out," Gertrude replied as she poked around the bookshelves for a favorite volume.

He came to the episode of his being wounded and left for dead near the site of the well and three palms. He stood up in his excitement. "I can't believe this," he cried. "It beats everything." His voice was incredulous, and he was obviously deeply moved.

She gave him a look of silent inquiry.

"Why, I've dreamed of that well and those three palms since childhood, without knowing what it meant. And here I am talking about it in my sleep, as realistically as if it had been the scene of some unforgettable event in my past. What can it possibly mean?"

As she had listened to her husband the day before, and later reconstructed what he had said, she remembered reading about the new psychiatrist, Doctor Freud, who maintained that dreams were a vehicle by which the subconscious mind cleared up the mysteries of the past. She could hardly contain her excitement. "Edgar," she said in a quavering voice, "you must have been dreaming about your past life in the desert."

He thought back now on the dreams and visions he had had as a child and adolescent. Could he have known Gertrude in a past life, she being the hidden face in the cloth-of-gold dream? And the lady of the vision, could that have been a carry-over from a previous experience? And the little children he played with as a child, who had receded with the years, until he no longer saw them? Could they have been scattered images or entities lurking in his subconscious past, until they finally submerged in deference to his conscious mind?

He excitedly paced the floor. He felt much as Columbus must have when he first sighted land. His eyes moistened with the depth of his emotion. "How lonely the good Lord must be with only Jesus to share his knowledge of Creation."

Gertrude's eyes were also glistening. "We can strive to penetrate those mysteries."

Then, abruptly as it had come, his mood passed. His eyes lost their gleam. "Suppose it's all a figment of my imagination?"

She had found the book she was looking for. "You are in good company, Edgar," she announced. "Listen to what Longfellow, the greatest of the Yankess poets, has to say:

"Life is real! Life is earnest!
And the grave is not its goal;
Dust thou art, to dust returnest,
Was not spoken of the soul."

228

Without waiting for any response, she turned to another page with the same sureness her husband had shown with the Bible.

"From John Burroughs, the great naturalist. Another Yankee," she added, regretfully:

"I stay my haste, I make delays—
For what avails this eager pace?
I stand amid the eternal ways
And what is mine shall know my face."

Her raised eyes caught his tender look. "You read so beautifully, Gertrude."

"It's the poetry, Edgar."

She turned to Wordsworth's "Ode on Intimations of Immortality." "This is so beautiful, Edgar, I do love it dearly, as I know you shall." With the clearness of a bell, she read the immortal verse:

"Our birth is but a sleep and a forgetting:
The Soul that rises with us, our life's Star,
Hath had elsewhere its setting,
And cometh from afar:

Not in entire forgetfulness,
And not in utter nakedness,
But trailing clouds of glory do we come
From God, who is our home."

Edgar's face lit up. "Why, Gertrude, he said exactly what I did in my reading, only better and shorter."

She put the book down lovingly. "He's a great poet, Edgar."

"Is he a Yankee, too?"

She laughed. "No, silly, he was an Englishman, the poet laureate of England, as a matter of fact."

His mind digressed for a moment. "Don't we have any poets in the South?"

"Sidney Lanier is from Georgia, and you might stretch Edgar Allan Poe—he lived in Richmond—and

I suppose Stephen Foster, though he put his poems in music."

He gazed at her in admiration. "Gertrude," he said fervidly, "the day I laid eyes on you was the luckiest of my life."

She slipped her arms around his shoulders, and looked deep into his eyes. "We didn't do it, Edgar. God made us soul mates."

After a weekend of fantasy, Cayce was confronted Monday by a very practical Ketchum, who had no more acceptance of reincarnation than he had of a personal God.

"Edgar," he demanded testily, "what am I to tell my patient about her child?"

More sure of himself now, Edgar replied calmly, "Have her do as the reading said, love and comfort the child, keep it from discordant influences."

"How can I go into past lives?" Ketchum's tone was edgy.

"You don't. The mother would no more accept this basis for the child's nervousness than you do. Just give the recommendation." He smiled humorously. "As you have said many times, you are the doctor. Well, Doctor!"

"And that's your last word?"

Edgar got up from his desk and peered into his studio. "Art calls, Doc, and the artist must go."

Ketchum slammed the door in his frustration. But a week later he called in a tone of conciliation. "Edgar, I passed on your recommendation, and the mother started paying special attention to her little boy. She called this morning to say that, unless it's a case of wishful thinking, she can already see results. The boy appears calmer, and hasn't had a nightmare in two days."

As a thoroughgoing pragmatist, Ketchum showed an interest in anything that worked. "Reincarnation," he conceded, "is no stranger than the rest of what you're doing. And if the one is right, why should the other be wrong?"

With this remarkably open attitude, Ketchum,

together with the Squire, arranged to pursue the subject of reincarnation.

The Squire was even more responsive. "Whatever comes through Edgar is directly from on high, of that I am convinced."

In the meantime, obsessed by the new concept, Cayce was examining the apparent incongruities of life, the obvious injustices, more and more in terms of the karmic pattern of reincarnation. Reincarnation seemed to make sense; it gave a certain inherent order to man's place in a developing universe. As for the Bible, he was discovering ever more references suggesting that not only Christ but the older prophets and the singers of psalms accepted reincarnation.

To friends who disputed his new look at the Bible, he replied equably enough. "Well, I read it in, and you read it out."

He was pleased at his father's and Ketchum's interest in a nonmaterial area that groped for comprehension of God's ultimate purpose.

He willingly acceded to an extra reading. Ketchum had finished with his patients, and the last camera study had left the photographic studio.

The Squire was waiting in the adjacent chambers, poised importantly behind his immense desk. "Gentleman," he said, "I feel we are on the verge of great revelations."

"Don't over-suggest me, Pa," cautioned Edgar. "You know how impressionable I can be."

The Squire was totally confident. "Don't worry, Old Man, you'll come through as usual." His eyes gleamed. "And what this will do to revamp the history of philosophy and religion! You will revolutionize these subjects, just as you have medicine."

Edgar laughed dryly. "I don't see any medical revolutions taking place, aside from Doc Ketchum, and he really isn't sure what's happening."

Ketchum rubbed his hands gleefully. "That's right, Edgar. I'm a revolution of one. Those Southern doctors would like to use you but they don't dare, and they hate me because I've been successful with you. Some revolution."

Very little could dampen the Squire's ardor where his son and favorite was concerned. "Edgar," he said in a dramatic tone, "whenever you're ready."

The question floating about in Ketchum's mind were of immediate interest to almost anybody. Why are we here, where are we going, is there life after death, and of what is it constituted? These were the broader areas of interest, shared by the Squire, and there were a number of smaller ones.

Ketchum, with his native inquisitiveness, was curious as usual, about the source of the psychic diagnostician's gift, this time in terms of reincarnation.

Cayce repeated his metaphysical experience at the well, and then added:

"Around this desert oasis, near the three palms, Uhjltd in his gratitude and foresight built a new community known as the City in the Hills and Plains, since it was situated between the last of the sloping hills and the beginning of the flat plains leading to the desert. Protection was given to travelers and caravans, and because of the spiritual awakening fostered by the regenerated Uhjltd, the place became a haven for the persecuted people of other lands. For the first time, the brotherhood of man and the fatherhood of God were taught, and the city, called Toaz by some and Is-Shalan-doen by others, not only became a center of commerce but of philosophy and religion. Hospitals were built for the sick, and new methods of healing introduced. At the instigation of Uhjltd, something of a seer himself, a school was set up for prophets, where they could develop their gifts on the highest spiritual levels."

Uhjltd had two sons, Ujndt, which Cayce carefully spelled out, and Zend, and they in turn became spiritual counselors to the populace.

Even Ketchum marveled where it all came from. Surely, so much could not come out of nothing or nowhere. And if Cayce was right about everything else, in his sleep state, why should he now be wrong?

Except, there was no way of proving any of this out, or was there?

At Ketchum's whispered urging, the Squire put the next question:

"What happened to this Toaz, this city in the hills and the plains?"

Cayce was prompt to reply. "As with other cities over the centuries, there came a change of fortune. The old leaders died out, the aging Uhjltd was slain, new conquerors came and brought new values. Decay set in, as it has so often with other civilizations. The population moved off and dwindled, the buildings were covered with the swirling sands of the desert. But under the sand, not more than seven or eight miles from the ancient city of Shushtar, in the land of Persia, lies buried the remains of this civilization. And in the years to come, before the turn of the century, in perhaps another sixty or seventy years, archaeologists will dig up the remnants of this old, spiritual culture founded by a man who established a monument to his benevolence and altruism in his own time."

With all their questioning, the Squire and Ketchum hadn't related Edgar Cayce's gift in this lifetime to his past-life experience. "In what way," asked the Squire, "did this power carry over after so many years?"

"In the usual karmic way," was the answer. "Used properly, as it was, this gift of Uhjltd's set up a predisposition which could raise the entity to new spiritual grandeur. Or, should he fail in the next experience through an excess of materiality, plunge him to new depths."

There was apparently some explanation for this lapse.

"And did the man known in this lifetime as Edgar Cayce at any time succumb to snares or temptations which affected his psychic abilities?"

"In the physical plane just before this, the entity was a soldier of fortune, serving with the British forces in this country, by the name of John Bainbridge. He was among those sent from English prisons to fight

233

in Canada, during that known as the French-Indian Wars. He escaped with others and landed on Virginia shores, near the resort now known as Virginia Beach, *an area to which he will always be drawn.* He was a ne'er-do-well, a gambler and was never wed in that physical plane, though he was in many escapades that have to do with those of the nature of the relations with the opposite sex. He traveled all along the East Coast and into Kentucky, Ohio and Illinois, joining in the fray at the fort which later became known as Fort Dearborn. He served as a scout with the Colonial forces, redeeming himself somewhat. He was trapped during an Indian raid, with others, and was seeking to make his escape on a raft down the Ohio River, with Indians in warm pursuit. The small band was trapped on a raft for several days, running out of food, and the entity was weak from hunger when a younger companion, more enduring because of his youth, offered some of his ration to the entity, though hungry himself. He refused the food, though grateful, as he wanted nothing of somebody else's in this situation."

The food problem soon became academic, as the Indian party overtook the scout and his charges, massacring the entire group. It was all very inconclusive.

The Squire, a Bible student in his own right, now had a few questions on a metaphysical level. "All agree on one God, the need of morality, the efficacy of prayer, the brotherhood of love, but beyond that the landmarks are vague and confused. Why are we here on this planet and where are we going? What happens after death?"

Ketchum's expression showed that he was primarily concerned with this earth plane. But Cayce replied promptly:

"When the material body is laid aside, that which is called the soul becomes the form of the entity. And that which is known as the subconscious forms the mind or intellect of the entity in space. The entity on passing from the earth has the ability to manifest that which is merited in its previous lifetime. Just as

234

the flesh body clothes a finer physical body constantly being reshaped according to the mental patterns, so the mental or spiritual body or energy pattern after death is a product of mind development. Bodies in the planes beyond death differ, as on the earth, in accordance to what has been developed in the mind, just as we react according to the manner in which we have handled the problems of the earth in our prior existences."

The Squire was anxious to get in another question. "What is man's purpose on earth?"

Ketchum could hardly restrain a sophisticated smile, but there was no questioning the Squire's earnestness. He edged closer to the couch, and peered down intently at his son.

"We are here to find out why we are here, that which is the nature of the instrumentation that God desires for us, thus to find contentment on earth and to achieve the ultimate perfection that will make us perfect companions of God in his heavenly place. Our futures in the hereafter, and thereafter, depend largely on what we do with our spirit, that portion of God that is given to us for life, with the gift of individuality or separate existence from God. Our task is to perfect our individuality, then return to God. Our spirit and soul, or individuality, are joined to him, and there is no more need to return to the earth plane." He paused. "We have finished."

For the next few days, Edgar read everything he could about reincarnation and discussed it incessantly with Gertrude. She finally asked for a reincarnation or life reading, as distinguished from the normal health reading. She was interested in learning whether it would show the development of their rare togetherness in past lives, and why it was that she couldn't recall anything from their past, provided there was such a past.

"If our subconscious remembers," she asked, "then why don't we remember specific things from our former lives?"

The sleeping Edgar replied promptly:

"Because we must function on a clean slate. That's the only way we can learn anything. Otherwise, we'd carry over into our relationships from the past all our prejudices, weaknesses, strengths, likes and dislikes and have them dominate our active life. On this plane we have free will, and will to react to events as they occur. What we are, and are to become, manifests itself in the choices we make, the way we meet life's challenges. We are handicapped, or advantaged to begin with, karmically; then the rest, in this lifetime, is up to us. By the decisions we make, the options, we shape not only the future but the present as it applies to us. We cannot stop the rain, but we can carry an umbrella, stay indoors, or go outside and court pneumonia—or, better still, get drenched and stay well through cultivating a positive mental attitude."

They had at least two lives together of a meaningful nature. In the one, she was with Uhjltd, in the City in the Hills and Plains, and was governess to his two sons, just as she mothered his two sons in this lifetime. "'The entity then was a follower of the Bedouins, and given as the most beautiful of that group to which the entity then belonged. The name then is that of Inxa, and the entity then ruled many through the power of the eye over the minds of those whom this would subjugate to her way of thinking."

And, then, with the straight face that he always preserved, the sleeping Cayce said, "And in the personality as exhibited today, we find in it the persistence in pursuing the condition thought or felt to be right. Still able to control many through the eye and the expression of the same."

Cayce's breathing continued in its regular rhythm, but he almost seemed to manage a sigh.

They had had their most significant and fascinating life together in ancient Egypt. This was just before the experience in the City of the Hills and Plains, where Gertrude first developed her loyalty to the entity known as Uhjltd.

The Egypt of that period was in turmoil. With Atlantis breaking up, many refugees from that prehistorical continent had migrated to the land of the Pharaohs, affecting the culture and introducing a new political faction. The entity known as Edgar Cayce was in that time a high priest, known as Ra-Ta, in the temples of King Arart. Gertrude was the daughter of a priest, who caught his eye because of her unusual beauty. In violation of the law of monogamy for priests, he took her as his wife, and the two with their followers were banished to the Nubian lands of Sudan.

From Cayce's own reading, it became obvious that this entity, known as Isris, had been secretly employed by the enemies of Ra-Ta, a liberal for his period, to charm him with her feminine wiles and bring about his disgrace and ruin.

"Among those, then, of the priest's daughters was one of the king's favorites—that made for the entertainment of the king and his council, and his visitors. She was more beautiful than the rest, and she was induced to gain the favor of the priest through the activities of herself in body, and in the manners that would induce some fault to be found. This was not by her own volition, but rather by the counsel of those that made for the persecutions of her own peoples that were being protected by the activities of the body, Ra-Ta. And the divisions arose that were even unknown then to Ra-Ta, for he being among those that trusted all, believed all, and—as it were—for the time the gods laughed at his weakness."

Ra-Ta had been vulnerable as an outsider himself. A leader from the Carpathian sector of east-central Europe, he sought to make his adopted land more spiritual-minded, and bring about a purer race. The Atlantean faction fought him as bitterly as the native element, breathing easily only when they thought they had undermined him.

Ra-Ta, as befitted his station, had his own entourage in exile. The relationship with Isris, beginning as a plot, had matured ironically into a strong union. They had one child, which they were compelled to leave behind in their exile. It died shortly thereafter.

"With the number that went into exile, of the two hundred and thirty-one souls, many were in the capacity of guards, defenders, interpreters—not to interpret languages or speech or activities, but to give to those that were unable to approach the priest, or when it was impossible for the priest to reach all about him directly."

Eventually, the high priest's friends were able to bring about his return. But by this time, he had aged considerably and was quite decrepit, no longer a suitable physical partner for the incomparable Isris. But on his return, he exposed himself to the rejuvenating color light therapy of the Temple Beautiful, and was fully restored.

"With the return then of the priest to the Temple Beautiful, there first began the priest to withdraw himself from the whole that regeneration in body might become manifest, and the body lay down the material weaknesses. From those sources of regeneration were re-created the elemental forces for the carrying on that which these material positions gave the opportunity for."

In a separate reading for Gertrude, confirmation of this joint past-life was obtained.

"Yes, we have that record as made in that experience," said the sleeping Cayce. "In the entering as a record, in the household of him raised to the position of priest, becoming a favorite of the king in his household, and a dancer in the temple service. And with the associations became a mother in the king's household, and was banished with the priest to the Nubian land, where she was in exile with him for nine years, returning finally with those gathered about the priest. Beautiful of body and figure, many are the casts that were made during the period as a dancer in the temple service. In the latter days, she became more active in the issuing forth of those tenets as were carried to the various groups or peoples, as the kingdom extended its appeal to other lands."

Like most other people, Gertrude wondered what there was in the past that influenced her positions and attitudes in this lifetime, the only lifetime, as Edgar Cayce had said, that one could do anything about. "What karma does the entity bring to the present from this Egyptian period," she asked, "and how may I work this out?"

Cayce touched on a facet of Gertrude's personality that may have influenced her attitude toward Wesley Ketchum. He replied:

"Easily holding grudges where there are misunderstandings, by those who apparently injure the body in thought or deed. In working out same, it becomes necessary in overcoming karma to strive for an ideal. Well to learn that lesson. For in building, the soul passes from experience to experience, developing by what it has held as its standard. Thus, as one builds in self that ideal as removes the errors of material things, so does the soul become like His."

"How may I better fit myself to aid in Edgar Cayce's work, which seems to be so influenced by this Egyptian period?"

"In drawing nearer and nearer to that mind as was in Him, the Son of Man, who crystallized the experiences of the period more than ten thousand years later." She was told, as so many others, to observe and heed Christ's teachings. "So may a soul, meditating on those tenets, come to know how self may apply self's ability in daily contacts with individuals, bring forth that as makes for the exemplifying of those laws, loves, and truths that He spoke about and lived."

"How can I develop my mental forces to the greatest extent in the present?"

"By more constant meditation, and putting into action day by day, a little more patience, a little more love, a little more forgiving, a little more prayer. Being made in the flesh, heir to the weaknesses of same, one becomes more spiritual by the even balance that is obtained by making personal application, doing that—even though it hurt—that will aid another. Not that self is to be crucified that another may have ease in the material sense. But that another may have understanding in the mental and spiritual sense. For 'My yoke is easy, my burden is light,' is seldom understood. When the desire and the purpose, the application, are one, then it becomes easy. But when they are at variance, one to another, hard is the way, and the call of the flesh becomes strong."

Could Gertrude have been thinking of Wesley Ketchum when she next asked, "How can I overcome antagonistic forces in self and others?"

"By actually manifesting forgiveness, more and more. As has been given, 'Is it easier, thy sins be forgiven or to say Arise, take up thy bed and walk? But that ye know that the Son hath the power to forgive'—meaning to forget the weakness and give strength to those that falter. Even so, in overcoming antagonistic feelings, forgive as ye would be forgiven, remembering them no more. This overcomes antagonism and antagonistic influences. The thoughts held create the currents upon which the wings of experience must pass, and then, as these are made in positive contacts, so is antagonism overcome and love made manifest, glorying in thine own ability in Him, and not in self."

Gertrude had one last and vital question:

"How does the life of Ra-Ta, the high priest, and his wife, Isris, have bearing on the present?"

The answer came back in a dull monotone:

"That same entity Ra-Ta that was taken in exile is at present in this earth's plane, the companion and mate as should be in this sphere. As they worked together then, so do they now. In this court, we find there was the study of the religious cults, the isms, the schisms in beliefs as would be termed in this day and plane. The High Priest who gave the elements of the religious force. And in the reign of this Pharaoh, the son of King Arart, did the religious cult reach its height as given through this priest, though he became the outcast. But the good that was accomplished by this individual was recorded in the resting place of the King. And this is manifested in the present in the delving into the whys and wherefores of all who express the hope that lies within the human breast of another

240

life after the passing from the earth's plane. This, we see, manifests itself in the present, in these very readings. Again, we find that the karma of each must be met, and in this plane overcome if each would enter into the spirit of the Creator, and become living souls. Be not deceived. Be not overcome. But overcome evil with good. We have finished."

Gertrude found these intimate sessions very reassuring. However, womanlike, she could not resist a complaint. "Edgar"—she pouted prettily—"I want to know why, if I was very beautiful and exotic once, I'm not that way now."

He kissed her lips closed. "But you are," said he staunchly.

She smiled impishly. "Men don't trail after me in the streets and send me orchids."

"You didn't make use of your beauty properly when it was yours," he said solemnly. "Whatever virtue you misuse, you lose. So I'm poor, because I didn't handle wealth well, and you don't get flowers."

Her smile widened. "So my husband admits I'm no great beauty."

Cayce became flustered. "You're the most beautiful creature ever to me."

With time and thought, he became increasingly convinced, not only of the plausibility of reincarnation, but of its reality. Nevertheless, he remained tolerant of those who did not share his belief, remembering his own early feelings of incredulity and disapproval. He spoke openly of his new belief in reincarnation, impervious to the looks of disbelief and scorn that often greeted his remarks. When Gertrude commiserated, he responded philosophically:

"Nobody seems to be appreciated until after they are dead. Christ was killed on the Cross, a prophet without honor in his own land. Peter and Paul were persecuted to their deaths, and so were many of the other apostles and their spiritual successors. Who am I to complain of being misunderstood or mistreated?"

Even though he was now dealing with the headiest subject of all, reincarnation, and all its remarkable implications, Cayce pursued his life in a normal way. He usually gave two health readings a day, with the Squire conducting the sessions, put in a good five or six hours at the photographic studio, and tended his garden of fruits and vegetables in the yard back of the house, often speaking encouragingly to plants which were slow to grow. He was so busy that Gertrude often chided him about his appearance, practically leading him into a clothing store so that he could buy a suit and a pair of shoes. She scolded him about his hair, and he finally ducked into a barbershop, around the corner from his studio, after she threatened to trim his neck with gardening shears.

On this one occasion, the barber looked up and nodded amiably as Edgar came in. He was in the middle of shaving a young man with a scraggly beard, and he had one eye on his three-year-old son who was dozing off in the adjacent barber's chair, a bag of cookies tightly clutched in his hand.

"His mother is out shopping," the barber explained wearily.

As Cayce sat down and began riffling through a newspaper, the boy suddenly awakened, gave Cayce a curious glance, then toddled up to him, and offered him a cookie with a great show of concern.

Cayce was amused. "Thank you, but I'm not hungry."

The boy insisted, until his father turned to him irritably. "You don't know that man. Leave him alone."

The boy's eyes rested knowingly on Cayce, then moved back to his father. "But I do," he said, with a solemn expression. "We were hungry together on the big river a long time ago."

11

A Very Secret Thing

For months now, Edgar Cayce had been troubled with blinding headaches which blurred his vision, brought on waves of nausea, and made it difficult for him to function. Gertrude had become increasingly concerned, as no plausible explanation for his condition presented itself. Edgar had his eyes checked, and had an overall checkup as well. He got a clean bill of health.

"If everybody in Hopkinsville was in your shape," said Dr. Janson, "we doctors would all be public charges."

When the attacks came, he would seem distracted, restless; his gray-blue eyes took on a dull glaze, and he would put his food away untouched.

Gertrude's health was better now, and she concentrated on handling this new problem. They were so much in tune, their lives so closely meshed, that every day seemed a glorious confirmation of the old cloth-of-gold dream. Relatives, particularly her mother, wondered how she could adjust to the uncertainties of life with a hopeless eccentric. But hers was a simple formula for marital bliss:

"Whatever Edgar wants, I want for him."

Without anything tangible to go on, she was beginning to associate the headaches with Dr. Ketchum.

As some women do with their own cycles, Gertrude had taken to marking her husband's headaches on her kitchen calendar. They lasted two or three days as

243

a rule, during which time he not only found it difficult to take pictures but to relax sufficiently to conduct his psychic readings. Nevertheless, even with a throbbing head, Edgar was amused by his wife's efforts to correlate his problem to certain dates.

"You know, dear"—he smiled—"it's not quite the same thing."

She blushed. "Edgar, Southern gentlemen aren't supposed to know about such things, leastwise talk about them."

One morning, at breakfast, he watched as she circled several calendar dates. He leaned over her shoulder. "Now, what are you trying to prove?"

"I'm not quite sure," she said with a frown, "but I feel it has something to do with the readings."

He groaned. "There you go, picking on poor Ketchum again."

"Poor Ketchum," she said derisively. "You should be so poor, Edgar."

He looked at her hazily through his latest headache, which centered just over the eyes. "Is that me for today?" He nodded at the latest circle, drawn in red crayon.

"Yes, and I'll wager you gave an emergency reading last night."

He looked at her curiously. "I'm always giving emergency readings."

"And you're always getting headaches."

He shook his head. "I usually wake up refreshed and rarin' to go."

She regarded him thoughtfully. "You haven't always felt that way, even before these headaches came on."

He tried to think back. "But that was when people abused the power, when I was asleep, trying to get stock market information, or winners at the racetrack. It wasn't for the ordinary health reading."

"And how, dear husband," she demanded, "did you know what you were being asked?"

"I got so that I knew when the reading wasn't right."

Gertrude's eyes lit up. "Exactly. You would feel

out of sorts for days, and sometimes have headaches."

He still didn't see what she was driving at. "But that was when the doctors were experimenting with me, before I realized how I was to help people."

She took the calendar off the wall and pondered it. "You might compare these dates with the dates of recent readings, Edgar."

Cayce looked at her indulgently. "What for? Either you, or Pa, or Ketchum, have been conducting the readings, so there's no chance of anybody slipping something over on me."

She searched her memory. "Do you remember that man in New York, who claimed the work was fraudulent because somebody had died despite a reading?"

He laughed. "These people don't understand that I can't make anybody immortal. Everybody dies on this plane."

She felt she was on to something. "Didn't you finally give him a test reading?"

He thought a moment. "That was the last of the test cases, I believe."

"Yes, he challenged you to trace his movements from his home to the office. You described his entering a cigar store, tracked him down the proper streets to his office, read off snatches of his morning mail as he was perusing it, and reported the gist of a telephone conversation."

Cayce chuckled. "Oh, I remember that fellow. He was a stockbroker. He came busting down right after that, and wanted me to go back to New York with him."

Gertrude's eyes sparkled. "What was it he said to you, Edgar?"

" 'I'll make you a millionaire—we'll clean up together on Wall Street.' "

She closed her eyes and thought a moment. "I'm trying to remember who was there at the time."

"Well, I was there, Gertrude, and so were you."

"And so was your father, and Wesley Ketchum."

He was still puzzled. "I don't see what you're trying

to prove—every reading is accounted for, and there's a transcript to show for it."

"Not every reading. Ketchum has called on you for emergency readings."

"Oh, sure there was a boy with a bad leg, and a girl who was pregnant, and things like that." He put his arms around her. "I love my little girl, but she's barking up the wrong tree on this one."

Gertrude made a sudden resolution. "Edgar, I'm going into the studio with you this morning. There is something I would like to check over."

His eyes twinkled. "As you say, Gertrude. And while you're there you may as well get out a few bills for me."

She gave him a rueful smile. "I didn't know you sent any out, Edgar."

She rolled up the marked calendar and slipped it under her arm.

"They'll be calling you Mrs. Sherlock Holmes," he said with a grin.

"I don't care what they call me if it gets to the bottom of these headaches, Edgar."

They walked out through the kitchen door to a small stable back of the house. Edgar hitched up his horse to the family buggy and helped Gertrude into a seat next to his.

She regarded the aging rig with an expression of distaste and thought of the newly married Ketchum. "Wesley Ketchum doesn't take Katy out in this kind of contraption."

He started to laugh. "Oh, Gertrude, is that what it's all about? Why didn't you say so—we can get another buggy."

Like other young husbands, Edgar Cayce had frequently dreamed of the time he would have a fine home, perhaps with servants to spare Gertrude the drudgery of the chores, and money to travel the world together, just the two of them, or with the children as they came. He was not dedicated to poverty, and didn't like being poor. He just didn't know how to make money, with or without his gift.

At this time, Gertrude saw even more clearly than he the pitfalls of his unique gift, with all its temptations for easy money. And so she was careful to make her position clear. "That's not what it's about," she said firmly. "I don't mind how I live, Edgar, as long as it's with you, but I don't like to see anybody taking advantage of your good nature."

They were now riding along easily, Edgar allowing the mare to set its own pace.

"Haven't you wondered," Gertrude pursued, "where Dr. Ketchum is getting the money for expensive cars, a splendid new house, and even a racing stable? What is a doctor in Hopkinsville, Kentucky, doing with a racing stable?"

Edgar slackened the reins a bit, and flicked the horse on the hindquarters. "We shouldn't begrudge our fellow man the fruits of an honest day's toil."

"Your toil, Edgar."

"I don't want any of that money. That's between Pa and Ketchum. They charge twenty dollars a reading, and what they do with it is their business. I have my studio, and it's the best-equipped in town."

Gertrude said with spirit, "Well, you don't buy racing stables on forty dollars a day, particularly when you have expenses, and are splitting it anyway."

Cayce nodded to a neighbor driving past the other way.

"You forget, Gertrude dear, that Ketchum now has an extensive practice. Besides," as if to close off the conversation, "Ketchum tells me he's been winning a lot of purses with his horses around the state. You know, Kentucky is great horse country."

She smiled thinly. "Don't change the subject, Edgar Cayce. I'm from Kentucky, too. I knew what kind of country this is, long before Wesley Ketchum arrived with his little carpetbag."

He gave her a tiny plunk under the chin. "Gertrude, you look so beautiful when you get your dander up. Just stay that way for a while."

She had to laugh despite herself. "I feel this way,

Edgar, only because I can't stand anybody hurting you. And when I see you racked with pain, with those terrible headaches, I know somebody has to be doing that to you."

"Who would do a thing like that, Gertrude?"

"Not deliberately, but not caring enough to care what is happening to you."

Something that he had said just a few moments before now struck her belatedly. "You said Ketchum was winning a lot of races around the state?"

"So I did, and bringing him some handsome purses."

She nodded thoughtfully. "Along with whatever he is wagering on the side."

"Nothing wrong with that, Gertrude. Andy Jackson did it all the time, and they made him President."

She laughed scornfully. "There's no danger of that happening to Wesley Ketchum, believe me."

"I believe you."

They had now arrived at Edgar's office. They could see Ketchum's red Brush parked down the street, near his own office.

Edgar helped his wife down from the rig. "You see, dear," he said with a grin, "Doc Ketchum is an early bird, and an early bird catches the worm."

"Well, you're no worm, Edgar, remember that."

The Squire was at his massive desk, obviously brimming with news when they walked into the psychic studio, where the records of the readings were kept on file.

The Squire gave Gertrude a perfunctory bow, and drew Edgar aside. "There's something I'd like to discuss with you, son."

With a look at Gertrude, Edgar said, "Won't it keep a while, Pa? Gertrude has something she wants to go over with me."

Intent on comparing the dates of headaches with the recent readings conducted by Ketchum, Gertrude was just as well pleased to have some time to herself. "I know my way around the files," she said. "I'll drop into the photographic studio when I'm through." She had kept her conversation deliberately cryptic, not trusting anybody at this point.

The Squire gave her a routine smile. "Let's go next door to your studio, Edgar, and I'll tell you all about it." He was like a boy with a new toy.

There were no photographic appointments for an hour, so Edgar sat down at his desk and gave his father his full attention, wondering what new scheme he might have concocted out of his wild dreams of ambition.

The Squire's face was bright with excitement. "Old Man," he cried, "you've really arrived. Charlie Meacham himself has asked for a reading. Imagine that!"

Edgar looked at his father bleakly. "Charlie Meacham, the Mayor? Why, he thinks of me as the Freak, and said so in his newspaper."

The Squire triumphantly held up a slip of paper. "Not any more. He's checked around, and has come up with an unsolicited testimonial. Listen to this:

" 'Edgar Cayce possesses a power that is out of the ordinary, being what is known as a psychic diagnostician. Some of my personal friends and acquaintances have had Mr. Cayce to diagnose and prescribe for them or some members of their families, proving in each case to be highly satisfactory and effecting a cure. I witnessed some of his work a short while ago, and while it was an out of town case and made at long distance, the patient was highly pleased and pronounced his work correct. I do not understand Mr. Cayce's work or how it is accomplished, but so far as I can learn, where the treatment is followed that he prescribes, the patient gets the desired results. He is a wonder to all who have seen his work.' "

The Squire radiated good will. "Now isn't that handsome?"

Edgar felt reasonably flattered, but still suspicious. "What does he want a reading for? He looks like a pretty healthy specimen to me."

"He just called, and said he wanted a reading right away, and how much would it cost?"

Edgar shrugged in annoyance. "You know I don't charge for the readings myself."

"But Ketchum and I do—twenty dollars—that's part of our arrangement with you, son. We got a lot of fancy equipment to pay for, Old Man. Expensive cameras don't grow on trees."

Cayce was startled. "I just hadn't thought of that, Pa," he said lamely.

"I don't know what you're so surprised about," his father said. "We said we'd give you the finest photographer's studio in Hopkinsville, and we have. Your five hundred dollars didn't go very far. That was just on account."

Edgar brushed a hand across his eyes. "But I didn't want any more than that," he protested.

"That's what you said," his father rejoined, "but I didn't see you sending any of the camera and darkroom equipment back, and there was no reason why you should. You've earned every last penny of it."

Edgar studied his father closely. "And how have I earned it, Pa?"

"By your readings. Sometimes you come up with some very interesting stuff."

"What kind of stuff?" Edgar's tone had sharpened.

The Squire grew vague. "Oh, there's no telling what you may say at times. You're just a fount of information."

"Pa, I'd like to know what's going on."

The Squire chuckled. "That's a little difficult when you're sleeping. Now about Charlie Meacham."

The younger Cayce sighed, making a note to resume this conversation after he had Gertrude's report. He had been tinkering with a camera throughout the discussion and now he put it away.

"Why would Charlie Meacham want a reading, Pa?"

"Beats me, but he was talking with Doc Ketchum about something. You know, Ketchum is your biggest booster."

"Then why didn't Ketchum call? He always has before."

The Squire gave his son a puzzled look. "I don't know why you're making such a fuss—it's just another reading."

The conversation with Gertrude had had its effect. "I don't think so. I smell a rat, and I don't like it."

His father shook his head in bewilderment. "Why don't you wait till he gets here?"

"You mean, you already made an appointment?" Edgar's voice was rasping.

"His money is as good as anybody else's."

Edgar felt a rising irritation. "That's the last thing I wanted, a business arrangement with you people, and apparently that's what I got."

His father drew back with an injured expression. "Son, there's times I don't understand you."

Edgar slapped the desk in his frustration. "You know, Pa, that I agreed to read only for people who had something wrong with their health. I don't want to get into other areas."

The Squire bridled the least bit impatiently. "You read for the boy who wanted to play the market, and it didn't seem to bother you when he won a lot of money."

"It did when I saw what happened to him."

"He would have wound up a ne'er-do-well, anyway," the Squire said. "He was not a very stable young man." The Squire looked at his son with a candid eye. "Would it have changed your mind any, Old Man, if he had given you a share of the profits as he was supposed to?"

Edgar blushed to the roots of his hair. "I didn't see anything wrong at the time with helping somebody make money, as long as they didn't do it at another's expense. But I'm beginning to think now that it's hard to mix the material with the spiritual."

"Well," the Squire said wryly, "I don't think Charlie Meacham will bother you for a money reading. He has all the money he needs."

Edgar laughed mirthlessly. "That doesn't mean

anything. I've noticed it's the rich who always seem to be wanting to get richer."

The Squire gave his son a long look. "Why not wait until you see what he wants before you get so fired up?"

Edgar's face set grimly. "I know what he wants."

The Squire's jaw dropped. "How would you know that?"

"Because I know Charlie Meacham, and what he's interested in, and I know Ketchum, and what he's interested in."

"Wesley Ketchum is your friend," the Squire protested sharply.

"Wesley Ketchum," said the younger Cayce, "is a climber. He's interested in getting on the good side of the Mayor, for whatever good it may do him."

"Then why didn't Ketchum call you directly?" said his father logically.

"Because he suspected what the answer would have been."

As the Squire was about to ask the obvious question, there was a cursory knock on the outer door, and a dignified-looking gentleman, looking very much the prototype of Southern plantation owner, stepped into the room with an expansive smile.

"I trust I'm on time." He grabbed the Squire's hand and nodded amiably in the general direction of the son. "Quite a studio you have here." His eyes flickered to the pictures on the wall, then back to the younger Cayce. "You'll have to take my pictures for the next campaign," he said with a gracious wave of the arm.

The Squire beamed and gave his son a knowing glance. "That would be wonderful, Mr. Mayor."

The Mayor neatly hitched his striped gray trousers, revealing matching velvet spats. He took out a long cheroot, and cut off the end, proffering two of the choice Havanas to the Squire and his son. Edgar shook his head, but the Squire accepted gratefully, putting the cigar safely away in his breast coat pocket. "If you don't mind, I'll smoke it later, Mr. Mayor."

Meacham peered over his cigar, at the younger

Cayce. "I've been hearing nice things about you, as I told your father."

Edgar returned his gaze evenly. "I haven't read about it in your newspaper."

The Mayor inhaled deeply. "You will," he said. "Just keep up the good work." He gave the cigar a loving tap. "If we don't get rid of these Night Riders, these cigars and pipe tobacco, too, are going to be hard to come by—not to mention what the boycott is doing to our economy."

He had caught Edgar's attention. "The opposing factions are close to settling, from what I read," the psychic responded.

"That may be," the visitor said judiciously, "but we'll never have peace until we bring these outlaws to justice."

Edgar shook his head slowly. "Didn't the good Lord say that vengeance was his?"

"I'm not talking about vengeance, but justice." He uncrossed his legs and leaned forward, bringing his face close to Edgar's. "I'm here, Edgar, to bring the leader of the Night Riders to book, and I'm enlisting your support."

Edgar drew out his pipe, and carefully tamped the tobacco into the bowl. "Now what good would that do, Mr. Mayor?" he said mildly.

The Mayor regarded Edgar equably, teetering back in his chair. "Not until recently have I put much stock in this psychic business. But—" He hesitated, giving Edgar the opportunity to finish the sentence.

"I don't blame you," said Edgar. "It's hard to accept, unless you've had an experience of your own."

His father gave him a chiding glance. "Remember, Edgar, when you named the killer in that Midwestern murder. That was really something." He bobbed his head at the Mayor. "Edgar had the details of a murder so accurate that the police were ready to arrest him. They figured only the killer could have known what he did about the murder."

The Mayor made an impatient noise with his nose.

"I'm more interested in what happens in good old Hopkinsville and you should be, too, Edgar, since you have lived here practically your whole life."

Edgar remained safely noncommittal. "That sounds reasonable, Mr. Mayor."

"Then," said the Mayor, probing this chink in the younger man's armor, "you should be interested in my proposal, particularly since you had some knowledge of the event in question before it occurred."

Edgar sat waiting, and the Mayor went on with an air of resignation.

"I understand from an unimpeachable source that you foresaw the Night Riders' dastardly raid to the last violent, murderous detail."

Edgar chewed on his unlighted pipe, waiting patiently for the Mayor to get to the point. "I didn't anticipate what they did to your newspaper plant, Mr. Mayor."

With the recollection of that disaster, the Mayor's face turned a brick red. "The ruffians! I'll see every one of them in jail before I get through." He took hold of himself with a visible effort. "That's what brings me to you, Edgar. If you could correctly foresee what was going to happen, why not, now that it's past, tear the masks of anonymity from that cowardly crew?"

Edgar Cayce considered the older man dispassionately. With the tobacco war apparently reaching a solution, he had hoped there would be an end to bitter recriminations that would only prolong the vendetta. He sucked on his pipe thoughtfully. "What," he asked abruptly, "did Ketchum have to say about it?"

The Mayor looked startled. "Why do you say Ketchum?"

"He told you about McCool, didn't he?"

The Mayor quickly recovered his normal aplomb. "Be that as it may, Edgar, you owe it to the community to use whatever special ability you have to unmask these scoundrels."

Edgar briefly pondered this novel notion of community responsibility. "I try to do my best by my fellow man in my own way," he said at length.

His visitor gave him a sharp look. "What does that mean?"

"I try to help people on an individual level, the only way I truly react. Every man is an island unto himself, and he must learn to live with himself, first and foremost."

The last thing the Mayor wanted was a philosophic discussion on man's ultimate purpose in search of happiness. "We've got to stand for law and order," he said bluntly, "and put the culprits where they can cause no more trouble."

"I don't rightly think that's my role, Mr. Mayor."

The Squire had been following the proceedings with a sinking feeling and was beginning to regret his earlier optimism in booking an appointment. "What Edgar means," he suggested tactfully, "is that he has no interest in politics."

Edgar saw no point in contradicting his father, and prolonging the discussion. But recognizing the Mayor to be an honest man, truly dedicated to maintaining the peace, he felt constrained to explain his position. "Every time I have been instrumental in bringing some offender to justice, as you call it, I have suffered as a result with subsequent headaches or twinges of conscience. I think I am being told something."

The Mayor was incredulous. "How can you feel remorse for putting a lawbreaker in jail?"

"I can judge only by my own intuitive response, and that has been negative."

The Mayor rose from his chair in his indignation. "Shouldn't something be properly done about men who terrorize a town and almost burn it to the ground?"

Cayce nodded sympathetically, then jumped ahead of the conversation, picking out the man who was Meacham's particular concern. "You don't have to worry about Sanders, Mr. Mayor. He's got his own problems."

The Mayor's jaw dropped. "Sanders, what do you know about Sanders?"

"Everybody knows he led the raid."

"But there's no evidence unless we put him on the scene and show that he masterminded the diabolical scheme."

There was a glint of amusement in the psychic's eyes. "You don't think a court of law would consider anything I turned up as evidence?"

"No, but you might turn up names and circumstances that we could later confirm. You seem to have the ability to look inside an event or a person, and know exactly what's taking place."

The Squire, silent till now, felt the conversation needed a push. "The boy is amazing," he said enthusiastically. "He can see anything, sickness, the insides of buildings, activity of all sorts, past and present, the horses, the stock market—"

Suddenly, he stopped short, feeling the reproach in his son's eyes. His face slowly took on a red hue, and he added weakly, "I mean there is just no limit to his range of activity, not that he does all these things as a rule."

The Mayor sensed a change in the atmosphere. A new tension seemed to have developed and Edgar appeared intent on bringing the conference to a close.

"I wish I could do something, Mr. Mayor," he said, standing up, "but whatever gift I have, I'm finally realizing, is intended to help people sick in body or soul. Not for the private or personal gain of anybody, including myself and my family." His eyes traveled from the Mayor to his father. "I had the idea once that the devil might be tempting me to do his work, though I wanted to believe that the good Lord gave me this special power. I've prayed that I would do only good, and I've watched and waited to see what would come of it. I've become convinced that it's a good force, and that it would never allow me to misuse it in any way, knowingly."

His gaze rested evenly on his father, and he said placidly, without accusation:

"There were times when readings for unworthy purposes, for gain or other material advantage, were taken without my knowledge. I suspected something was wrong because I was given warnings that I didn't fully comprehend at first. I began to feel bad after some of these readings; I would have headaches, and sometimes double vision. I would be sick to my stomach for days, with a feeling of malaise. Contrarily, when I've given my best and someone has been helped, mentally or physically, I wake up feeling fresh and vigorous. That's the way I want to keep it."

The Mayor looked completely befuddled. "I frankly don't understand you," said he, "but I respect a man for the courage of his convictions." He regarded Edgar quizzically for a moment. "If you could see what was going to happen to McCool, can you tell what will happen to Sanders?"

Cayce smiled and shook his head. "Whatever I see in the waking state, I see spontaneously. When you have made an inquiry about a certain person on a conscious level, I can only respond on that level. Trying to read consciously, I don't see any more than anybody else would. But it is my belief, as Jesus said, that everybody pays for his transgressions, in this world or another."

The Mayor's hand stopped at the doorknob. "What other world, Edgar?"

Edgar's eyes rose imperceptibly. "Do you remember what Jesus said to the Pharisee, Nicodemus?"

It was purely a rhetorical question, and the Mayor took it as such, as Cayce went on:

" 'Verily, verily, I say unto thee, Except a man be born again, he cannot see the Kingdom of God.' "

The Mayor obviously didn't know what to make of this strange young man. He was attempting to frame a suitable reply, and make a graceful exit, when the Squire pushed forward.

"Edgar's a Sunday School teacher,'" he hastened

to explain, "and his enthusiasm gets the better of him at times."

"I like enthusiasm," the Mayor said jovially, "and I like Edgar. He's a fine boy, and he may amount to something one day. He may be right too," he added resignedly, "about leaving Sanders to his Maker. In the end, He decides everything."

Edgar smiled boyishly at the Mayor's apparent about-face. "Thanks, Mr. Mayor, that entitles you to a free picture, anytime you drop in."

After the door closed on the Mayor, there was an embarrassed silence for a minute or two. Then slowly, and deliberately, reluctantly almost, Cayce faced his father. The Squire returned his gaze, nervously wetting his lips.

"Pa," said Edgar, "do you know anything about these headaches I've been getting lately?"

The Squire had regained some of his composure. "Just that you've been complaining about them, son."

As he examined his father's face, Edgar saw the tired lines of defeated middle age. He sensed the nervousness and uncertainty with which his father was narrowly watching him, the almost pleading look in the pale blue eyes. His father had always wanted to be someone, to be looked up to in the community. He had gone unsuccessfully from one business to another, always striving for more than he could attain. Now, whatever ambitions or dreams remained were jumbled together in his feelings about his son. As the silence lengthened between them, compassion welled up inside the son for the father. He could find no word of criticism. "Pa," he said finally, "I have decided to end the readings for the present."

His father gulped uncertainly. "But, Old Man, you have an agreement with Ketchum." Edgar noted his father's conspicuous omission of his own part in that agreement, just as his father added, "Of course, I don't care for myself."

Cayce's mind went back a while as he contemplated his father thoughtfully. "Do you remember Jeb Hawkins?" he asked.

The Squire's face brightened at the apparent digression. "The young fellow who asked for the reading for that New York stockbroker?"

"That's the one."

The Squire, though still not entirely comfortable, chuckled reminiscently. "Yes, we telegraphed that reading to New York, the broker was in such a sweat for it. And he came barging down here, hell-bent-for-election, after you mentioned the three letters on his desk, including one from his best girl, and even gave the first line of that letter."

Edgar didn't seem impressed at this time by his own omniscience. "I gave Jeb Hawkins three or four readings after that; I remember them now, all on the races. I hadn't figured out yet how this thing worked, and he convinced me that if he won he was going to put the money to good use."

"Yes, I remember Hawkins. You picked four winners for him in a row, and he kept doubling up and wound up with thirty thousand dollars, and didn't give you a dime."

"I didn't mind his not giving me anything, Pa, I really didn't. That's not the idea. I wound up with rotten headaches after each reading, and in the end it all turned out horribly all the way around, and he wound up in an insane asylum."

The Squire looked his disgust. "Jeb Hawkins was a fool. He had all that money, and didn't know enough to hang on to it."

"He wasn't much different from the average young fellow who stumbles on easy money," said Edgar tolerantly. "He was going to do so much for the needy, and he ended up squandering most of it on himself. This gift of mine just doesn't seem to lend itself to the material."

The Squire remained aloof from any philosophical conclusion. "What didn't go on wine, women and song," he said reasonably, "went back to the races."

"After the fourth reading, I finally refused him. I could see what it was doing."

"He sure went bad," the Squire agreed. "Even so, I never understood his going off the deep end."

"That was the last step. He didn't have anyplace else to go, Pa." Edgar's mouth had dropped mournfully. "I'm the one that got him started. I'm as much to blame as anybody."

"You thought you were doing good. There's nothing wrong with money, son. It's what people do with it that makes it bad."

Edgar smiled grimly. "Or what it does to them."

His father watched him uneasily, at a loss for words for once in his life.

Edgar shook his head sadly. "That was my last reading for speculation or for gain of any kind. At least to my knowledge," he added as an afterthought. He closed his eyes and took a deep breath. "With these headaches I've had recently, I'm not so sure any more. And neither is Gertrude. She's checking out the dates of some recent readings, to see whether they correspond to the headaches."

The Squire's discomfort weighed on him like a heavy cloak. "I wouldn't know about that, Old Man," said he faintly.

Edgar managed a smile. "That's good." Suddenly, he wanted to end the conversation, and with it his father's defensiveness. "Pa," he said, "I'll discuss it all with Ketchum. You don't have to bother with it. Everything will be all right." Impulsively, he threw his arms around the Squire's shoulders. "Just don't worry about it. I'm sure you felt you were doing right."

Tears had come to the Squire's eyes. He turned away quickly to hide his emotion, then fervidly gripped his son's hand. "Thanks, Edgar, thanks more than I can say." Without looking back, he slowly opened the door, and walked out into the hall, his sagging figure all at once showing the burden of time.

Edgar Cayce plopped himself into a chair and put his head in his hands. "God," he groaned, "why must helping people be so difficult?"

Gertrude had quietly come into the room at this

moment with the rolled-up calendar in one hand and a sheaf of stenographic transcripts in the other.

He looked up dolefully. "Must we go into all that?"

A look of solicitude crossed her face. "Not if you'd rather not, Edgar."

He shrugged. "I know what you must have found."

"Yes," she said, "they do correspond, the hearings conducted by Ketchum and the headaches."

"But it's not in the stenographer's transcripts; I've gone over all of them."

"One question about a horse race or the stock market—how long would that take to answer? And of course, who edited the stenographer's notes before they were typed out?"

He looked down unhappily at his shoes. "I guess that would be Ketchum," he said slowly.

She kissed him lightly on the forehead. "Don't let this discovery discourage you, Edgar dear. Think of it as making you free."

He gave her a wan smile. "I just hate to see what people do to themselves for gain."

"I know," she said soothingly. "But you don't have the same freedom because of your gift."

He looked at her curiously, his head cocked to a side and resting on his hand. "I don't understand."

She smiled tenderly. " 'As a man thinketh in his heart, so is he.' You couldn't use this God-given force for wrong purposes without one or two things happening: The power would be lost to you, or the information would cease to be right. In the one your soul would remain uncorrupted by withdrawing within itself, and the readings would stop. In the other, it would be corrupted by the contagious greed of others and the information would become distorted just as the motivation was distorted."

Edgar gave a wounded cry. "Pray God that never happens, Gertrude."

"Never fear," she said. "The world needs your gift, and you need a world to give it to."

12

Ketchum Returns a Favor

Edgar Cayce was more sad than angry. "I trusted you, and you let me down."

Ketchum saw no reason to be apologetic. "It was for the good of the cause. We weren't getting anywhere."

Cayce looked at him sharply. "Not getting anywhere? Who wanted to get anywhere? Certainly not me."

"That is the problem," Ketchum said smoothly. "There was no real public recognition. We need a hospital, or a clinic, to treat people you gave readings for. You would recommend a certain type of manipulation, and there wouldn't be an osteopath to do it. You would recommend certain herbs, and there wouldn't be a drugstore to sell them. You would recommend a wet cell appliance, but nobody knew how to put it together. To do this thing right we needed the proper facility, and that takes money."

Cayce moved over to the window, looking down on the human traffic window-shopping below on busy Main Street. "The ends," said he slowly, "do not justify the means. You had no right to go off on a tangent without consulting me."

"Where did we do anything so awful?" said Ketchum stoutly. "So I asked about the races occasionally, and the stock market. What was wrong with that, if it was to help people?"

262

Edgar turned on him coldly. "Who did it help? You've got automobiles, a fine home, even a racing stable; a large practice. You consider yourself a success. Well, I'm not so sure about that."

"Neither am I," said Ketchum urbanely. "Nobody outside of Christian County even knows I'm alive."

Cayce whistled in his incredulity. "You really are something, Ketchum. You don't even see how wrong you have been."

Ketchum gave him a mocking smile. "How wrong I have been, Edgar? Are you saying that you're all white and I'm all black? You like money just as much as anybody else does. You gave a reading on the racetrack knowingly, thinking you might profit yourself, and you sat still, or rather lay still, for readings on the stock market, and on buried treasure. You even read for a reward for a missing woman from Pittsburgh."

Edgar was struck to the core. "I didn't profit by any of it," he said.

"Not directly, but some of that money went to your father, and he siphoned it all into equipment for your photographic studio. Thousands went into that studio."

"I didn't ask for it." Edgar was on the defensive now.

"No, but you took it, knowing where it was coming from. So you're not all that blameless, if you're to judge yourself by the same standard you've set for me."

Edgar's face showed that Ketchum had scored a direct hit. In a troubled voice, he said, "Perhaps I have been confused in the past about what I'm to do with this thing. I do admit there have been times when I thought it would be wonderful to find a gold mine, or turn up an oil well, or make a mint out of the stock market. But I have learned the hard way that there are things I can do with this gift that I shouldn't do, if I want to continue helping people who are ill."

Ketchum's smile had turned to one of gratification. "So you will go on with your readings for the sick?"

Edgar shook his head. "Not right now. It's time I took inventory of my life, and what I want to do with it."

Ketchum was leaning back in a swivel chair, his feet hoisted comfortably on Cayce's desk. His voice, friendlier now, took on a persuasive note. "I admit we haven't been doing as well as we should. But we're getting five, ten, sometimes twenty dollars for health readings, and more often than not, nothing at all. If it hadn't been for some of these other readings that you object to, we wouldn't be where we are today."

"And where are we?" Cayce was genuinely puzzled.

"We have established a fund for research, and for that clinic I was talking about."

"What kind of fund?"

"Five to ten thousand dollars. You can do what you want with it."

An expression of amusement suddenly brightened Cayce's face. "Are you trying to bribe me, Doc?"

Ketchum laughed. "Just say you'd be receiving the rightful fruits of your labors."

Cayce shook his head slowly. "No, Doc, it's time we went our separate ways."

Ketchum pushed back a little more in his chair, and took out a cigar. "You're a little upset now, but you're not looking at the total picture. You're not thinking of the people who have been helped, including a lot of children who might not otherwise be walking around. You're not considering the transcripts we have in our files, many dealing with diseases thought to be incurable, and outlining the treatments that brought relief or a cure. What a reservoir of material for the medical researcher!"

"Oh, yes, I have thought about all that. I've thought about it through headaches that rocked my head, while sick to my stomach and aching all over."

Ketchum wagged his finger and smiled. "You can be mad at me, and disappointed in your father, but you can't just quit. You have a gift nobody else has, and you can't withdraw it on a whim. How can you turn away sick children? Didn't Jesus say, 'Suffer little children to come unto me'?"

Cayce had been pacing the room in his agitation. He stopped and gave Ketchum a burning look. "Don't worry about Jesus and the little children, Doc. It doesn't become you."

Ketchum laughed, pulling on his cigar. "Overall, the pluses far outweigh the minuses, Edgar, and that's what life is all about—balance. You have to balance one thing against the other."

"You're talking compromise. And I won't compromise what I do. Contract or no contract, I'm through."

Ketchum detached himself from the chair and leisurely stretched. "Think about it, Old Man," he said benignly. "I promise there will be no more readings that produce headaches."

The resentment and anger suddenly drained out of Cayce, leaving him ineffably weary and washed out. He took the outstretched hand.

Ketchum paused at the door, and there was an unaccustomed softness in his voice. "Think it over, Old Man. Don't act hastily."

Cayce turned back to his desk. He stared for minutes at the door that had closed behind Ketchum, and then with a sigh prepared for his first photographic assignment of the morning. "That'll be the only work I'll be doing for a long time," he mused unhappily.

All through the day, as he took his pictures, Cayce ruminated ruefully over the session with Ketchum. The doctor had hit him on a sensitive spot, his wistful desire at times for the money that would liberate Gertrude and himself from a life of chores. He had been rough on his father, and now Ketchum. He was not better really than either of them, and if it hadn't been for Gertrude, and her constant urging that the readings should always be spiritually motivated, he would have probably gone along with them openly. He was obviously an unworthy instrument of the gift a gracious God had entrusted to him.

At dinner that evening, his face was grim, reflecting

265

the guilt that had been welling up in him all day. His features were drawn and pale. Gertrude silently poured him a glass of his favorite red wine and waited for him to break the silence. She was familiar with his moods. He maintained his silence through the meal, and then as she was clearing away the dishes, he reached over and kissed her gratefully on the cheek. "Gertrude," he said, contritely, "how do you put up with an old grouch like me?"

She returned his kiss. "I love you, Edgar, because I can't help myself." Her tone changed suddenly, and she looked at him with concern. "It's Ketchum, isn't it?"

He sighed. "Yes, it's Ketchum. I walked out on him and Pa today."

"Good," she said vehemently. "That should cure the headaches."

They settled down by the fireplace, sitting close to one another near the glowing embers.

"Don't worry about it, Edgar," she said tenderly. "You made the right decision." Her voice softened, and she added, "Though I do like Katy ever so much and think she's a fine woman."

Cayce rubbed his hand through his hair, and the troubled look came back. "I'm not so sure that I'm any better than Ketchum. Perhaps he just had the courage that I lacked, and it's as simple as that." He almost seemed to be making a case for the doctor he had repudiated just a few hours before. "He has helped a lot of people who wouldn't otherwise have been helped."

She looked at him sharply. "You're not weakening, Edgar Cayce?"

"I'm just giving him his due," he said lamely.

Knowing her husband as she did, Gertrude knew that he would never be happy unless he was using his gift to help people who would not otherwise be helped.

"You can always give readings on your own, Edgar, helping whoever needs it, as you did Aunt Carrie, her baby, and me. I will conduct the readings for you, and you'll know then that you won't get any headaches from them."

He shook his head. "Maybe, after a while. I'm not ready for that yet."

She leaned back, satisfied, feeling the idea would take root. "Anyway," she said, "you're rid of whatever's been troubling you."

He had been thinking of the case Ketchum had made for himself. "I suppose," said he, "that the Doc felt justified by his own lights."

Gertrude looked at him in astonishment. "You have a sneaking fondness for that man, don't you?"

"Wesley Ketchum," he said gravely, "is a very fine doctor, with or without me."

Gertrude was adamant. "Nevertheless, I trust you will never speak to that man again."

"Remember the Good Book, Gertrude. 'Forgive us our debts, as we forgive our debtors.' What sort of hypocrite would I be, teaching Sunday School and all, if I could not forgive Wesley Ketchum, hoping at the same time that he can forgive me for being so pious."

"Oh, Edgar." She sighed. "You're almost too good to be true. Forgive then, dear Edgar, but don't forget, or you will be hurt again."

"Forgiving is easy, forgetting is hard. But without forgetting, there is no forgiving. So I guess it's my Christian duty to forget as well." He stretched out his arms and yawned luxuriously before she could register a further protest. "I've got a tough day tomorrow taking pictures, and I need my sleep."

The days passed into weeks, without any communication between Cayce and Ketchum. The Squire had sought to serve as an intermediary. Edgar, gently but firmly, had discouraged any meeting that might lead to a rapprochement. "Pa," he said, "I know you mean well, but it's better this way."

His father gave a rueful look. "Aside from anything else," he said, "Wesley Ketchum is your friend. He'd like you to get the recognition you so richly deserve."

Cayce came as close to impatience as he ever did

with his father. "You don't seem to understand, Pa, I don't want recognition. I just want to be left alone, to live my life with Gertrude, take my pictures, and raise a family."

The Squire shook his head disconsolately. "Old Man, that's like Rembrandt refusing to paint any more masterpieces, or the Wright brothers deciding that they had enough of flying. You just can't stifle a great gift such as yours. Don't you remember what the Good Book said?" The Squire shook with emotion. " 'Neither do men light a candle and put it under a bushel, but on a candlestick, and it giveth light unto all that are in the house.' "

Edgar was moved in spite of himself. "Thank you, Pa, for the encouragement, but I have to do it my own way. I hope you will understand that, and respect my decision."

The Squire had encountered defeat often enough in his lifetime to know that he was up against an immovable force. "At least," he said, "you don't mind Ketchum singing your praises."

Cayce had no idea what the Squire was talking about, and perhaps it was just as well.

For one Hopkinsville resident, at least, Dr. Ketchum's practice would hardly be the same without Edgar Cayce. That resident was Boze. He looked at his master as if he were completely deranged. "You can't get rid o' Mr. Cayce," he said in an aggrieved tone. "He's the backbone o' this here office."

"Never mind that," said Ketchum, rather sharply. "I didn't leave Cayce, he left me."

Boze wore a long face. "You my boss, and I'm loyal, 'deed I am, but Mr. Cayce musta had a good reason, 'deed he must."

Ketchum found the subject disagreeable. "Well, you just have to get along without him." He looked around the office critically. The last patient had gone, and with the sun sinking below the horizon darkness was beginning to close in. "Give the place an extra cleaning tonight. There's dust under the chairs in the waiting room."

Boze picked up a broom and began muttering to himself.

"If you have something to say," Ketchum said irritably, "say it, man."

Boze looked at him uncertainly. "I said there'll be a lot more dust 'round here with Mr. Cayce outa the place."

Ketchum didn't know whether to blow up or laugh, but Boze's face was so reflective of his disappointment that he didn't have the heart to chide him. "I got good news for you, Boze. I'm taking you to Boston next week."

Boze's broom slid from his hands. He did a little jig in his elation. "Boston, ya don't mean it? It can't be true. Dr. Wesley, I been thinking of Boston all my life, an' now I'm goin' there." His eyes filled with tears, and he unashamedly wiped them dry. "That's where the foks lived that set my people free. That's heaven to me, Dr. Wesley. That Boston."

"You really like Mr. Cayce, don't you?" Ketchum said almost wistfully.

Boze's bony face lit up. "He's a wonder, that man. Last Sunday, he tell us about Moses an' the Promised Land." Boze's dark eyes were shining. "And he done tell that we all can reach that land, 'cause"—he looked up brightly at Ketchum—" 'cause that Promised Land is right here in Hoptown. Can ya beat that, Dr. Wesley?"

Ketchum looked at his hired hand curiously. "How does he figure that, Boze?"

Boze placed a hand over his heart. "Here it is. What ya do with this, that's what takes ya to the Promised Land. It can be right 'round the corner, in what ya done for your neighbor, and your fella man. You really should come to church, Dr. Wesley, Mr. Cayce might even help ya."

The doctor's lips parted in a bleak smile. "That's not my style, Boze, though my new missus gets me there once in a while. I'll have to find the Promised Land my own way."

The following week, resplendent in a tailor-made

269

banker's gray, and with his valet extraordinaire at hand, Wesley Ketchum, M.D., traveled to Boston for a meeting of the American Society of Clinical Research. The invitation had come from a Boston colleague, who had overheard Ketchum talking about his Wonder Boy. The Boston physician could not begin to believe that anybody could diagnose a case and prescribe a remedy without examining the patient. It seemed not only incredible, but impossible. However, the doctor gave Ketchum the name and address of a patient and Cayce did the rest. It was a precise diagnosis, and the recommendation curiously coincided with the treatment the doctor already had prescribed.

"Tell us about your Wonder Boy," he pleaded, and Ketchum accepted. "It will give me a chance," he told the Squire, "to make it up to the boy. The medical fraternity in Kentucky will sit up and take notice for sure."

The Squire had been enthusiastic, regretting only that he couldn't make the trip to Boston.

On the train north, sitting in his compartment with Boze, Ketchum had considered the nature of his talk, deciding that he would make a straightforward account of his experience with Edgar and let the chips fall where they might.

Katy had not made the trip with him because of her classes at the college, but Boze kept him constantly entertained with his window-seat observations of the shifting panorama.

As they stopped over briefly in the Philadelphia depot, and then again, New York City, Boze noted the black porters grappling with travelers' bags on the station platforms.

"They sure got all the good jobs up here."

Ketchum agreed dryly. "Yes, they tote the load in the liberal North."

His irony was lost on the simple Boze.

At the Boston depot, Ketchum was greeted warmly by a committee of three, including the doctor who had extended the invitation. Boze's presence seemed to dismay these sons of fiery New England abolitionists, but only for a moment.

"Boze is a consultant of sorts," Ketchum explained with a smile. "He's a veteran of some of my most difficult cases, and an inveterate admirer of my subject tonight. He can testify to one of the most spectacular recoveries, a case of dementia praecox, if you gentlemen care for an eyewitness account."

The doctors were understandably taken aback.

"It won't be necessary," they assured Ketchum. "You will have a responsive audience. All of Boston's leading medical lights will be listening tonight, and the press as well."

Even as he made note of this, Ketchum found himself relishing his hosts' confusion. "Do you have a place for Boze on the platform, or elsewhere in the hall?"

"We'll find a place."

After freshening up at his hotel, attended only by Boze, Ketchum went downstairs to the meeting room. He had not felt like dinner after a late lunch in the railroad dining car. Although there were a few stragglers in the hotel lobby, the auditorium had already started to fill up.

Many eyes followed him curiously as he took the dais, alongside the chairman of the meeting and other distinguished guests in the medical field. He was easily the youngest man on the platform, being little more than thirty at this time, but the company of so many venerable and distinguished figures in medicine had no visible disconcerting effect on the young doctor from the hinterlands. Indeed, his whole personality seemed to expand with the attention he was receiving.

The chairman greeted him warmly. "I know some of your teachers from Cleveland, they speak very highly of your ability and enterprise."

Wesley Ketchum bowed respectfully in acknowledgment of these kudos.

"You are the youngest speaker to appear before this group of medical specialists," said another graybeard, whose name he did not quite get.

Again Wesley Ketchum bowed, thinking wryly to

himself, I wonder if they'll be as happy with me by the time I'm through tonight.

He listened patiently as he was being introduced, trying to appear completely detached, as if the introductory remarks were for somebody else. His searching eyes found Boze sitting uncertainly in a corner of the room, then swept over his distinguished audience, sensing a quickening interest as the chairman predicted this would be a meeting long remembered in Boston. "Dr. Ketchum is not our usual speaker, and his subject is even more unusual. I trust you will waive your usual orthodoxy for the evening and give him a resounding welcome."

Ketchum slowly rose, at his name, and, to a smattering of applause, moved to the lectern. For a split second, on the verge of his first talk, he regretted the impulse that had brought him to Boston. And then his natural insouciance reasserted itself, and he quickly took command. He would show these stiff-necked New Englanders a thing or two, and jar them out of their staid smugness, even if it was only for an hour or so. He adjusted his pince-nez—a good touch, he thought—and glanced down at his notes, another device, since he knew precisely what he intended to say.

His voice seemed to fill the meeting room.

"I have come from the scene of my practice in Christian County, Kentucky, to discuss with you learned physicians and surgeons My Most Unusual Case. I made the acquaintance of this young man about four years ago, when I found myself an alien doctor in an alien land—a Yankee seeking to practice medicine in a county still waging the Civil War. My Most Unusual Case, though a Southerner born and bred, was an alien also, but in a different sense than myself. Because of his unique difference, he had a reputation as a freak. Some said he was an imposter, a fake, others that he told wonderful truths while he was asleep, truths of engrossing interest to me because I am a doctor, and truths that should be of interest to you for a similar reason."

There was a slight stir in the scholarly audience,

272

and some gray heads craned forward, the better to concentrate on the speaker.

"When they first told me about this man and his medical prowess," he continued, "I couldn't accept it. I was from Missouri from start to finish. I had to be shown. When it comes to anything of a psychic nature every layman is a disbeliever from the start. And most of our chosen profession will not accept hypnotism, mesmerism, or any other *ism* unless it is vouched for by some M.D. way up in the profession, whose orthodox standing is unquestioned. My subject, I might add, is a psychic, a psychic diagnostician, if you please."

Ketchum looked out over the audience, picked out a few shocked faces with secret satisfaction, and with the feeling that he was sitting in on medical history.

"My subject simply lies down and folds his arms, and by autosuggestion goes to sleep. While in this sleep, which to all intents and purposes is a natural sleep, his objective mind is completely inactive and only his subjective mind, the subconscious, is actively at work.

"By suggestion he becomes unconscious to pain of any sort, and, strange to say, his best work is done when he is seemingly 'dead to the world.' In this state he can correctly diagnose illnesses of people he has never seen and effectively recommend cures."

Over the notes, which he peered at occasionally, Ketchum could see some looks of incredulity turn to horror, but for the most part the gathering appeared fascinated.

"All I do," said he, directing his remarks to a horrified graybeard in the first row, "is give him the name of my subject, who has requested medical help, and the exact location of same. And in a few minutes, while asleep or in trance, he begins to talk as clearly and distinctly as anyone. He usually goes into minute detail in making his diagnosis, especially if it is a very serious case.

"His language is usually of the best, and his psychological terms and description of the nervous anatomy would do credit to any professor of neurology. There is no faltering in his speech and all his statements are clear and concise. He handles the most complex jaw-breakers with as much ease as any Boston physician, which to me is quite wonderful, in view of the fact that while in his normal state he is an illiterate man, especially in the area of medicine, surgery, or pharmacy, of which he knows nothing in the conscious state."

A wave of doubt and disbelief that was almost a physical force surged up in the audience. A few interrogatory hands were raised, mostly by younger doctors, and Ketchum hesitated momentarily, glancing at the meeting chairman.

That gentleman rose and briefly stated, "I know there is much in this unusual talk that you doctors will want to question, but I would suggest questions be deferred until our speaker has finished. He may then be good enough to answer as he sees fit."

Ketchum was in no way disturbed by the interruption. I'm getting to them, he thought with grim satisfaction. And on he went.

"After going into detail with a diagnosis, giving etiology and symptoms, and then treatment of a case, My Most Unusual Case is awakened by the suggestion that he will see this subject or patient no more. And in a few minutes he will be awake. Upon questioning him, he knows absolutely nothing that he has said, or whose case he was talking about. I have used him in several hundred cases, and have never known of any errors in diagnosis, except in two cases where he prescribed a child in each case who had the same name, and who resided in the same house as the subject. With this confusion of name, he simply described the wrong person, but was right even then in his description of the child he saw."

By this time, many of the doctors were openly scoffing, and some were laughing conspicuously behind their hands. Ketchum stopped speaking and gazed at them until they turned red in embarrassment. His eyes roamed challengingly over the big room, and he proceeded vigorously, as if nothing had happened.

"Now this description of mine, although rather short, is no myth but a firm reality. The regular profession scoffs at anything reliable coming from such a source, because the majority are in the rut and have never taken to anything not strictly orthodox.

"The cases I have used him in, have, in the main, gone the rounds before coming to my attention." He paused dramatically, focusing on a distinguished-looking figure introduced to him earlier as a prominent surgeon. "And in six important cases which had been diagnosed as strictly surgical, he stated that no such condition existed, and outlined treatment which was followed with gratifying results in every case."

This was the supreme affront. Ketchum could feel the audience slipping away. Some were yawning, others exchanging amused glances. Two or three were already heading for the door. But Ketchum had expected no more. His quick eye had picked out three or four drably dressed young men, obviously reporters, who had been scribbling furiously as he talked. He knew with inner satisfaction that his words would carry to a far greater and more responsive audience than was in this room. Slyly, he struck back at his audience.

"Now, in closing, you may ask why has a man with such powers not been before the public and received the endorsement of the profession, one and all, without fear or favor? I can truly answer by saying they are not ready to receive such as yet. Even Christ himself was rejected, for 'Except ye see signs and wonders ye will not believe'."

As he quoted from Scripture, Ketchum smiled faintly. Cayce would be proud of me, he thought, stealing his stuff as I am. He looked to the rear of the room, and caught Boze's eye, and saw the latter bobbing his head in approval.

He put down his notes and injected a note of friendliness in his voice, almost of intimacy, in fact. His eyes traveled around the room, resting for a moment on faces that appeared halfway sympathetic.

"I would appreciate the advice and suggestions of my co-workers in this broad field as to the best method of putting my man in the way of helping suffering humanity, and would be glad to have you send me the name and address of your most complex case and I will try to prove what I have endeavored to describe."

He had finished his remarks and now looked invitingly out on the assembly. There were no volunteers at this time. The applause was perfunctory, but he had expected no better. He noticed with gratification that one of the reporters had his hand raised. Other hands were up, too, around the hall.

The chairman stepped forward, and perfunctorily shook his hand. "Thank you, Dr. Ketchum, for a most interesting talk." He looked around the audience. "Any questions before we conclude?"

Ketchum nodded to the young fellow who had been taking notes. "I'll take him first."

The young man, confirming Ketchum's appraisal, identified himself as a newspaper reporter. "I found your talk interesting, but without a name to check back on, it could all be highly imaginary," said he earnestly.

There were approving cries of "Hear, hear."

Ketchum, who had stepped back, moved forward to the lectern again. "I have not mentioned My Most Unusual Case's name as he is a very modest young man, and wants no part of notoriety."

There were groans of "Oh, sure," and knowing looks, but Ketchum held up a restraining hand.

"However, in view of the fact that practically everybody in Hopkinsville, including the medical fraternity, knows of this young man, I see no reason for not releasing it at this time." He paused and looked back again at Boze, whose white-toothed smile mirrored his pleasure. "This Wonder Boy, as I sometimes refer to him, goes by the name of Edgar Cayce." He spelled out the name. "It's pronounced Casey. He is a fine, upstanding young man, a credit to the community"—Ketchum smiled inwardly, wondering how Edgar could object to such a eulogy—"and a teacher in the Sunday School. By profession, he is a photographer."

The reporter had still another question. "What does he charge for these treatments?"

Ketchum turned bland. "Unlike the medical profession, he asks nothing for his services, though I must acknowledge that I have billed patients for his services as a psychic diagnostician, as for any other medical service."

The reporter was persistent. "Are you the only doctor using this Cayce professionally?"

"In Hopkinsville, yes, and elsewhere, so far as I know."

"If he's so effective, why don't other doctors in Kentucky make similar use of him?"

Ketchum was almost jovial in his response. "Because they don't know a good thing when they see it. I'd stand a patient on his head if I thought it would help him."

The reporter had other questions, but the chairman waved him down, giving a dark-haired, youthful-looking doctor the floor. "Dr. Montgomery has a question," he said.

Montgomery was one of the few doctors who had remained raptly interested throughout. "Granted this man has this rare ability, Doctor, how do you account for it?"

Ketchum beamed at this question. "This is something I constantly questioned myself. There seemed no answer, though the subject himself, like Christ, felt that his power came through God. As a man of science, like the gentlemen in this room"—he was never more urbane—"I was not quite satisfied with this answer. So, since the subject seemed so right about everything else in his subconscious state, I decided to put him under autohypnosis and ask him to give the source of his mystifying knowledge."

Ketchum, adjusting his pince-nez, now searched rapidly through his notes. "Ah, here it is," he said, finding the page he was looking for. "Now this is pretty much the way he said it himself, speaking of himself in the third person."

" 'Edgar Cayce's mind is amenable to suggestion, the same as all other subconscious minds, but in addition, thereto, it has the power to interpret to the objective mind of others what it acquires from the subconscious mind of other individuals. The subconscious mind forgets nothing. The conscious mind receives the impression from without and transfers all thought to the subconscious, where it remains even though the conscious be destroyed. Now this subconscious mind is in direct communication with all other subconscious minds, and is capable of interpreting through Edgar Cayce's objective mind and imparting impressions received to other objective minds, gathering in this way all knowledge possessed by millions of other subconscious minds.' "

As he put down his notes, Ketchum looked out cheerfully on a sea of disbelieving faces. "I don't mind your skepticism at all." He smiled. "I can hardly credit it myself. But that's what the man said, and I've never known him to be wrong in his sleep."

There was a sally of laughter at this, and the faces of some in the audience expressed relief, thinking that Ketchum might really have been pulling their leg and was about to make a clean breast of it.

His next words were quite shattering. "Gentlemen, all I can say is that this Wonder Boy, who never got out of grade school, knows more about medicine than I do, and I went to one of the finest institutions of medical training in the East."

Dr. Montgomery was still standing, waving for attention. "Another question please."

"Of course." Wesley Ketchum thoroughly enjoyed the spotlight.

"You made a remarkable statement, and I would like some clarification."

"Yes," Ketchum's tone had just the right combination of courtesy and reserve.

"You said that the subconscious mind forgets nothing, remembering even after the conscious mind dies."

He paused to allow the significance to sink in. "How, I ask, can memory or anything else survive after after death? Are you asking us to accept ghosts?"

A ripple of laughter ran through the auditorium. The question had again eased the atmosphere and made Ketchum's performance seem more an entertainment of frontier folklore than a serious medical discourse.

"Hear, hear," they cried.

Ketchum's manner was totally disarming. "I have no explanation of Mr. Cayce's explanation. But one far greater than you or I said many years ago that we too could cure the sick and the dying with faith in the Father. Where this curiously therapeutic ability of Cayce's comes from I can only conjecture."

Montgomery sat down reluctantly, obviously not satisfied. And another went up.

The chairman looked at his watch. "This will have to be the last question," he said with resolution. "We are wearying this young man who has so generously traveled hundreds of miles to be with us tonight." He nodded to another youthful-looking doctor. "The floor is yours, Dr. Framingham."

The questioner was in about the same mold as Montgomery, lean-faced, intelligent, earnest, and politely skeptical. "Doctor, you say you used this man in several hundred cases. Could you illustrate one case?"

Ketchum nodded at this question. "I would like to cite the case that first brought this unusual young man to my attention. The patient was a small child, daughter of the School Superintendent of Hopkinsville. She had been diagnosed as incurable by the best doctors in the Central States. They sent her home to die. One diagnosis from my man, as a last resort, completely altered the situation. Within three months, the child, who had deteriorated to a vegetable state, without comprehension of any sort, was restored to perfect health. The doctor merely followed my man's directions. This case can be readily confirmed with a visit to Hopkinsville, or by correspondence. The father will discuss it with any responsible person."

To a silent room, Ketchum bowed and sat down. The meeting had ended in a serious vein, leaving many in the audience with a vague sense of discomfort.

The chairman stepped forward quickly. "The meeting," he said, "is dismissed."

To Boze, the Ketchum talk was a great success. In the hotel, as he packed the bags, and later on the train, he covertly studied his employer from time to time.

"What is it?" Ketchum said finally.

"You sure wowed 'em," said Boze admiringly.

Ketchum was mildly perplexed. "Did you understand all that?"

"I'm talkin' about all that Bible talk. I was sure wrong about you."

"How is that?" said Ketchum as Philadelphia slipped by.

"You is a spiritual man, whether you know it or not."

"Thanks, Boze," said Ketchum, recalling his last conversation with Cayce. "I'm glad somebody thinks I'm ready for an angel's wings."

Ketchum's words had gone on before him. Before he got back to Hopkinsville with Boze, the wire services had flashed the account of Cayce's strange power all over the country. The various newspapers carrying the reports were careful to point out the solid qualifications of the source.

"It is well enough to add," said *The New York Times,* "that Dr. Wesley H. Ketchum is a reputable physician of high standing and successful practice in the homeopathic school of medicine. He possesses a classical education, is by nature of a scientific turn, and is a graduate of one of the leading medical institutions of the country. He is vouched for by orthodox physicians in both Kentucky and Ohio, in both of which states he is well known. In Hopkinsville, where his home is, no physician of any school stands higher, though he is still a young man on the sunny side of Dr. Osler's deadline of forty."

280

Then came the usual medical disclaimer, expedient even for a revolutionary:

"Dr. Ketchum wishes it distinctly understood that his presentation of the subject is purely ethical, and that he attempts no explanation of what must be classified as mysterious mental phenomena."

The trip home was uneventful for Ketchum. But even as the train brought the two travelers to a jarring stop at the Hopkinsville station, the subject of the Boston talk was already experiencing the perilous byproducts of fame.

Cayce missed the first assault. He had already left for the studio when the reporters descended on his home. They took the pictures off the living room wall and even raided the family albums, as Gertrude looked on, speechless.

"Your husband is a famous man," they explained, as if that was all the justification needed.

When Edgar arrived in response to Gertrude's summons, they had already trampled the lawn and hedges and were firing away at Gertrude with a verbal barrage.

Edgar faced them on the front porch, recognizing the inevitability of an avalanche. "All this," said he, indicating a headline, "has been done without my knowledge or permission. But ask your questions, and get it over with."

There were about a dozen reporters in the group, and all began asking different questions at the same time. It was bedlam.

As Cayce wearily held up a hand, he saw a familiar rig pull up in front of his house, and a familiar figure hitched his horse to a stone post. It was the Squire, and he was enthusiastically waving a newspaper in his hand.

"Edgar," he cried, "you're famous."

As Edgar groaned, the newsmen demanded to know who the newcomer was.

"It's my father," sighed Edgar. "He'll be glad to tell you anything you want to know. Anything."

The Squire was in his glory. "Gentlemen," he said, "fire away."

As the medley resumed, he called out, "You, with the green press card in his hat, let's hear from you."

The dark, sallow-faced reporter, in a faded brown suit had traveled five hundred miles to ask one question framed by his publisher. "Can your son go to sleep and find a lost gold mine? That's what I want to know."

Edgar Cayce, his hands over his ears, safely fled into his house and locked the door. In the Squire, he knew, the reporters had met their match.

13

A Majority of One

Wesley Ketchum still carried his shotgun wherever he went and made no secret of it. When he progressed from a horsedrawn rig to a horseless carriage, he merely transferred the weapon from one conveyance to another and kept it conspicuously by his side. He would not budge, retreat or yield one iota. As a boy in the rough-and-tumble of Ohio, he had learned that even the biggest bully didn't relish tormenting a smaller target, if it meant a bloody nose or black eye in return. "I couldn't afford *not* to fight," he said once, recalling his boyhood. "They would have been all over a fractious little fellow like me."

He felt vastly different about the alienated Cayce than he did about the adversary doctors. For Cayce, he had a genuine affection and respect, tinged with regret that this simple fellow—he did not mean it demeaningly—had no true insight into the practical exploitation of his great gift.

To both his wife and the Squire. he was emphatic in reaffirming that he saw no harm in using the psychic power to win money on the market or the races. "Exactly who have we hurt?" If there was any deception—though he didn't admit any—he saw this essentially as Edgar Cayce's fault. "If the boy wasn't so confused about what he wanted, it wouldn't have been necessary to cover up things a little."

The Squire, as usual, championed his son. "You

can't get away from Edgar's headaches," he said earnestly. "It must have been bothering his subconscious, which may be a better judge of what the boy's doing than his conscious."

"I don't doubt that," Ketchum rejoined wryly.

The Squire recalled the time that Edgar's subconscious had not let him finish a reading on buried treasure. "I guess this was similar to the headaches."

"Edgar would like the same things we like, Squire, it's just that he has this confused feeling about putting everything on a spiritual basis."

This conversation had taken place two or three days after the doctor's return from Boston, with the city now full of the lame, halt and blind, clamoring for young Cayce's attention.

The Squire was every bit as frustrated as Ketchum. "Edgar would have liked to profit, if he could, and still keep his gift. But Gertrude keeps telling him it's not possible, and he's come to believe her."

Ketchum was ever the pragmatist. "Well, she's with him more than we are, so it isn't much of a contest. I guess I better kiss the boy good-by."

"He's fond of you, Doc, it's just that he thinks we pulled the wool over his eyes a bit."

"Let him be poor for another ten years," said Ketchum sardonically, "and he may change his tune."

"I wouldn't be a bit surprised," said the Squire with a worldly smile, "but right now there's no moving him."

Ketchum blamed Edgar for not coming to the phone or returning his calls. "You would think that I had suddenly become a leper."

"I just think he would like to avoid temptation. You know, you can be very persuasive, Doc."

"And what of our contract?"

"Let's forget it. You're not a loser. You're well-established now. And with all that publicity in Boston, you're about the best known doctor in the state today."

This reminded Ketchum of still another grievance. "You'd think the boy would thank me for all the credit I gave him."

The Squire puffed contentedly on a long cheroot. "That's what you don't understand, Ketchum. He doesn't want any of that. If Edgar could do it all under a bushel basket, that's the way he'd want it."

The Squire had called on Ketchum in a spirit of friendly concern, almost forgotten in listening to the doctor. "Oh, by the way," said the Squire, "did you know Sanders and company were holding a special meeting of the medical society to discuss ways and means of tossing you out?"

Ketchum was not as startled as the Squire would have thought. "Oh, some wisenheimer stopped me this morning to tell me about it. He could hardly wait to give me the word."

The Squire was again impressed by the doctor's pugnacity. "You don't back up an inch, do you, Doc?" he said almost wistfully.

"I can't afford to," Ketchum rejoined, "Or those Reb"—he broke off with a look at the Squire—"or those wolves would just tear me apart, limb by limb." His underjaw shot out. "I aim to see that doesn't happen."

"They're upset about Boston, particularly with your remarks about the medical fraternity here."

"Nonsense." Ketchum's voice was razor sharp. "They're sore because of my success, and because I'm a Yankee, and a brash one at that. And I don't give a hoot for the bunch of them."

The Squire held out an admonishing hand. "I've been around here a lot longer than you, Doc, and I know these people. Just admit you may have been wrong. What difference does it make now?"

Ketchum looked at him in amazement. "Not on your life, Squire. I wouldn't admit I was wrong, if I was. I'd use Edgar Cayce for the rest of time if he'd let me."

The Squire held his ground. "I've grown fond of you, Doc, and I just don't want to see your career ruined. You're too good a doctor."

Ketchum was genuinely touched. "Thanks, Squire, I appreciate your kindness. I've enjoyed our association, despite that dumb son of yours." He got up with a sigh. "Now I have to start taking care of the sick."

Regardless of how it appeared, Ketchum did not take the action against himself lightly. All that day, as he talked to patients, his versatile mind was at work mapping a counter-attack. He had developed many friends, the Daltons, Davises, and numerous others, but none with a say in a medical conclave. He could look to no resources but his own. But as his Presidential favorite, Andrew Jackson, had once said, any man by resolute action could become a majority of one.

Boze usually sensed any change in his master's mood. Cleaning up, after the last patient had left, he kept darting looks at Ketchum, who was staring contemplatively out of a window. It was not like the doctor to sit still for long. "Wha's the matter?" said Boze, curiosity getting the better of him. "Don't you have a home anymore, Dr. Wesley?"

Ketchum looked up with a start, then gave Boze a friendly smile. "I've got lots to think about, old fellow. Your friends, specifically the hounds of Hippocrates, are hot on my trail, and I have to make sure they don't get me treed."

Boze's eyebrows tilted to his hairline. "What these friends ya talk about? I got no friends but you, Dr. Wesley, an' maybe Mr. Cayce. I dunno what ya talkin' about. Nosirree." He shook his head dolefully. "I have no truck with any hound dogs, neither."

Ketchum's laughter eased the tension slowly building up in him. "I was just making a facetious comment, Boze. Please forgive me."

Boze was too proud to acknowledge any shortcomings in his vocabulary, but he wanted it clearly understood that his loyalties were not divided.

"I'm as different from these doctors as black 'an white," he said solemnly.

Ketchum gave him a curious look. "Are you pulling my leg, Boze?"

"I dunno what you is talking about, Dr. Wesley. If you is in trouble, I wanna know about it."

Ketchum looked at his hired man contritely. "Boze,

no man ever had a better partner in a watermelon hunt, I can vouch for that. But nobody can help me now but myself."

Boze regarded him doubtfully out of troubled eyes.

"How about Mr. Cayce? I knew there would be trouble once you two split off."

Ketchum found this observation particularly ironic at this time. "Obviously," he said dryly, "I didn't split off soon enough."

Boze, essentially, was single-minded.

"Maybe, Mr. Cayce should know about this, so he can help you."

Ketchum laughed the least bit harshly. "He'd be the last one to help, I'm afraid."

Ketchum had grown accustomed to using his loyal servitor as a sounding board, and the ring of his words carried conviction. "Boze," he exclaimed, "I'll show them."

Boze shook his head. "There's a lot more o' them than there is o' you, Dr. Wesley."

Ketchum rose and put on his hat. "I, Boze, shall constitute a majority of one."

Boze blinked uncertainly at his master's receding back. "I dunno what's comin' over that man," he said woefully.

There was little doubt in Ketchum's mind of the motivating forces in the action against him. Sanders had long bided his time to get back for the typhoid incident and nurmerous other slights. He had the support of Benson and others like him in the Christian County medical society, comprising some forty-five members. Ketchum could count on Dr. House, Janson, perhaps Dr. Board, with whom he had been friendly since the pellagra matter, and possibly Dr. Williams, impressed by the Dalton case. Four out of forty-five, and at that, he could hardly expect any of them to stick their necks out defending a Yankee.

Dr. House telephoned him that evening. "I'm surprised," said he, "that you weren't at the medical meeting this morning."

"I wasn't apprised of it."

287

"Well, they're going after your license. I don't like to say 'I told you so,' but I did warn you about Cayce."

Ketchum overlooked this perfectly human tendency to assert one's superior judgment. "What is their next step?" he asked with his usual practicality.

"There's to be a general meeting of the county medical society Friday morning at the courthouse, at which time a committee will be designated to go to the state capital at Frankfort and request that your license be revoked."

"Don't I get a hearing?" Ketchum asked.

"Why, yes, after the committee is chosen, you will be permitted to answer the charges."

Ketchum laughed into the telephone. "After they've tried and convicted me, they're inviting me to appear and defend myself."

"Your hearing will take place before the State Medical Board meets in Frankfort."

"That's nice of them," Ketchum said dryly. "But I may have a few surprises of my own for these gentlemen."

Dr. House's natural prudence asserted itself. "I wouldn't do anything rash. That's what got you in trouble in the first place."

"Do anything rash? Why, my house is burning down, and you're asking me not to yell Fire! Not on your life. You can tell your friends that Wesley Ketchum has just begun to fight."

There were other concerned telephone calls from influential friends, reflecting the inroads Ketchum had made in the community in a short time.

George Dalton, recently voted Hopkinsville's most beloved citizen, was his usual hearty self. "Doc," he said without preamble, "I hear you're in trouble with the doctors. Just tell me what I can do, and I'll do it. I'll be only too glad to stand testimonial for you."

Ketchum was more touched than he would acknowledge. "Thanks, Mr. Dalton, but this is strictly a private fight, and I want it that way."

A speculative note crept into Dalton's voice. "By the way, Doc, did you use that freak on my leg?"

Ketchum chuckled. "You were one of the first," he said readily enough. "And it was a good thing for you —and me."

Dalton took it in good grace. "Well, you had enough sense to use him, that's the important thing." He seemed to be mulling something over. "And you still had those nails made, and you punched them in. So you deserve the credit." There was affection in his voice. "You're a fighter, Ketchum, that's what I like about you. Go get 'em."

Dietrich had also telephoned, offering to provide an affidavit on his daughter.

Ketchum saw the immediate weakness. "That would be a defense of Cayce, not me, since I did not handle that case." But he was duly grateful. "Don't worry about me, Professor," he said, with more confidence than he felt. "I've just begun to fight."

"Keep your wits about you, Ketchum," Dietrich advised, "and you'll win out. I know these people down here. They're essentially decent-minded and fair. They'll give you your day in court."

One man, the one call he was waiting for, had not been heard from. Ketchum had hoped against hope that Edgar Cayce, remembering their friendship, would come forward. It had been a slim hope, no more. And he realized more than ever that his future relied on the efforts of one man, himself.

Within twenty-four hours, the whole town was alive with rumors of Ketchum's threatened ouster and disgrace.

As chance would have it, he ran into his principal adversary, Dr. Sanders, in the street the following morning.

Sanders was in a cheerful mood. "Well, Ketchum, you're finally getting your comeuppance." There was a swagger almost in the way Sanders stood. "You finally shot yourself down, when you went up to Yankee-land, and ran off at the mouth about that freak Cayce." Sanders' voice hardened. "You've gotten all this publicity, and filled up the town with hypochondriacs. It's a fake. And you know it's a fake, and pretty soon they'll know it in Frankfort."

Ketchum looked squarely into the other man's eyes. "I don't scare easy, Sanders, especially not from cowards who ride at night with hoods over their heads."

The color deepened in Sanders' face, and he advanced a step, his fists clenched.

A thin smile played on the smaller man's lips, and his blue eyes turned cold. "I wouldn't, Sanders. I also carry a hand gun, and I wouldn't hesitate to use it."

Sanders' eyes had become narrow slits. "We should ride you out of town on a rail."

"My Smith and Wesson has six bullets. I promise you it will be a costly ride. And by the way"—his hand had conspicuously gone to his pocket—"have you had any typhoid cases lately?"

The veins in Sanders' neck stood out. "You've signed your death warrant in this town."

Ketchum backed off a half-step, as if assuring himself room for a quick draw. "That remains to be seen, Mr. Night Rider."

Sanders restrained himself with a visible effort, then turned on his heel and strode off, formidable even in retreat. The tautness suddenly drained out of Ketchum. The hand poised so provocatively in a pocket brought out a big handkerchief and mopped his brow.

Ketchum was well aware that not all the doctors were unalterably opposed to him. The disinterested majority, as is invariably the case in any showdown, were usually willing to abide by the will of the interested few who would energetically prosecute the matter.

Ketchum had decided, in keeping with his character, that in boldness lay his best hope of blocking his adversaries.

Friday finally came.

Just before the meeting, scheduled for nine that morning, Ketchum stopped off at the First National Bank. From the street, through the plate glass window, he signaled the cashier, Bailey Russell, and that worthy slowly came to the door.

"What is it, Doc?" he said, opening the door a wedge. "We're not open for an hour."

"I need a favor," whispered Ketchum, as the bank tellers looked on curiously.

Bailey Russell remembered that the Yankee doctor had removed his youngster's tonsils at a reduced fee. "Whatever I can do for you, Doc, short of looting the till." Russell laughed feebly at his own joke.

"No, Bailey, I'll be happy to walk away with my own money."

The cashier was conscious of the scrutiny of passers-by. "Come on in, and we'll talk it over."

He led the doctor to a teller's window. "Now, Doc, what can I do for you?"

Ketchum had an air of special urgency about him. "I want to withdraw one thousand dollars, and I want it in new bills, two separate packets of five hundred dollars each."

Bailey Russell had issued large sums to the doctor before, with a knowing wink that let the doctor know that he knew that it was being invested in sound horseflesh. But this was the first time new bills had been specified. "What the dickens you got on?" he asked.

Ketchum looked around quickly, then put a finger to his lips. "Mum's the word, Bailey. I don't want anyone to get wind of my activities. But I can tell you it's very important, or I wouldn't be using new money."

"How do you want it, Doc?"

"In five-dollar bills," Ketchum decided. "That will make a sizable stack, without making it too bulky to carry around."

He didn't count the money, but put the separate packets in a side pocket. "Thanks, Bailey, I'll remember you."

"That's all right, Doc," Bailey said agreeably. "I owe you a favor or two." He let the doctor out the door, which he had previously locked after him, then stood watching a moment as Ketchum marched down the street. That man is up to something, he thought. But then he's always up to something.

Ketchum knew that the special session, convened for the business of drumming him out of medicine, was taking place in the county courthouse building, in a courtroom normally vacant at this time of the year.

Ketchum had worked up a plan after a fashion. It was not operable without Cayce's cooperation, and he had no reason to believe this would be forthcoming. However, it might not come to that eventuality if he made a bold enough thrust to forestall a showdown. He sighed. How much more effective it would be with Cayce at this side. But he would do his best. That was all a man could ever do, he paraphrased Edgar Cayce without realizing it, the best where he was, with whatever was available to him.

By the time Ketchum walked into the courthouse and found the meeting room, the session was under way. He slipped in unnoticed, through a swinging door, and took a seat quietly in the last row of the dark chamber. He looked around the room quickly. There were some forty-five to fifty doctors there, practically every M.D. in the county, and their eyes were glued on the chairman.

Ketchum's lips came together grimly. As he surmised, the chairman was his old friend Sanders.

His eyes traveled around the room—there was Benson, Williams, House, Janson, Board, they were all there.

As the first order of business, the secretary, Benson, read off the minutes of the previous meeting.

"At least," ruminated the uninvited guest, "I'll get an idea of how they intend to railroad me back to Ohio."

Benson, in an oratorical voice, named the three members chosen for the mission to the state capital. Ketchum laughed at the names. Sanders, Benson, and Smithers. How could any panel be more heavily loaded?

"It is the purpose of this meeting," Benson said

in stentorian tones, "to ratify the selection and approve a formal petition duly listing the charges against the aforesaid Dr. Wesley Ketchum. I could read off the document in full, but it would perhaps be better, since we all have to get away to patients, to give the gist of the charges."

He looked over the paper; then with a nod from Sanders, seated at the judge's bench, he ran over the accusations briefly. "Dr. Ketchum not only used the freak Cayce as an accessory in the treatment of patients, but then went north and bragged about it before a group of Yankee doctors. At the same time he belittled respectable physicians in Christian County because they wouldn't taint their profession with similar quackery. We know Edgar Cayce to be a faker, at most an unscrupulous mentalist or mind reader, and the quicker the medical profession eliminates the two, the better standing doctors in the county will have, as some may have mistakenly thought this evil practice sanctioned by this society."

Ketchum sat fuming, waiting for the propitious moment to make his presence felt. He had slumped in his seat, his head barely above the bench ahead of him, and Benson did not see him as he finished and called for questions.

One doctor, whom Ketchum didn't recognize, got up. He was apparently from the outlying areas of the county. He was gray and grizzled, with a stern, honest countenance. "When," he asked, "is this committee going to Frankfort?"

"It is scheduled to leave Monday."

"And this man, Ketchum—I am not making a brief for a Yankee, mind you—but isn't he entitled to know of these charges and answer them in some fashion?"

A faint look of annoyance crossed Philip Benson's handsome face. "He will be duly notified before the committee leaves, and will have his opportunity to present his defense."

"Isn't that like locking the barn door after the horse had run off?"

"That will be for the State Board in Frankfort to determined. They will consider his rebuttal."

Sanders rapped his gavel. "I would like to point out to you doctors outside Hopkinsville that Dr. Ketchum has openly bragged about using this faker."

Ketchum was squirming at the edge of his seat, barely able to contain himself.

Dr. House rose slowly now. What he was about to say might cost him the respect and affection of many who had been lifelong friends, but as he thought about his wife, Carrie, and his son, alive today because of Edgar Cayce, he could not do otherwise.

He was a gentle man, and he reacted passively to life. It was not his style to deliver fiery polemics. He was no Zola defending Dreyfus, no Cicero lashing out at Catiline. He was a small-town doctor, with a love of tradition and tranquillity, caring enough for his fellow man to get out of a warm bed at three in the morning and plow through snow drifts in a horse and buggy to perform emergency surgery on a kitchen table.

"Gentlemen," he said, looking around mildly, "as some may know, Edgar Cayce is a relative of mind through marriage." There were starts of surprise among the doctors not resident in Hopkinsville. "I am not speaking out because of this kinship. However, because of this kinship, through this same Edgar Cayce, my wife and child were spared when doctors could not help them."

Ketchum, pleased at this turn of events, could see Dr. Janson humbly bow his head. Janson was a good sort, one of the four votes he was resonably sure of. House might turn over a few more, but he lacked the authority which made men follow after somebody like Sanders.

House was speaking as casually as if he were addressing a patient. He mentioned the test Edgar had submitted to at the Literary Club. "The chairman was present, and so was Dr. Benson, when the man they call a freak correctly diagnosed a case, a young man ill at a student dormitory." His gaze took in both

294

Sanders and Benson. "If there was collusion on this occasion, it must have been with Dr. Benson's consent. Dr. Benson not only confirmed the diagnosis, it being his patient, but verified that Cayce had correctly read the patient's pulse and temperature from a distance."

He paused. "I make no brief here for Dr. Ketchum's use of a psychic as an adjunct to his practice, but I can sympathize with his making use of something that none here understand, when ordinary medicine does not appear to help. Knowing Ketchum's heart to be right, I would suggest a vote of censure, rather than expulsion, as more in keeping with the offense. Let us tell him, Go and sin no more."

Dr. House sat down amid a buzz of conversation.

As Dr. Janson now strove for attention, Sanders rapped the judge's gavel sharply. "There seems to be some misunderstanding," he said caustically. "Cayce is not being charged with conduct unbecoming a physician, but Ketchum. Let us remember that."

Janson would not be waved down. "But if Ketchum was helping people with Cayce, that would certainly put a better face on his behavior."

Benson shook his head scornfully. He read from a newspaper, which he had suddenly produced. " 'And Dr. Ketchum, asked why other doctors didn't use Cayce, said it was because they were in a rut.' " He looked around the room with a withering glance. "Gentlemen, am I to understand that we are backward because we use the latest medical facilities instead of a freak who never went beyond grade school?"

There were murmurs of indignation. Dr. House, looking around at the unsympathetic faces, could see whatever ground he had picked up for Ketchum had been lost by this one sally.

The chairman's gaze now roved around the courtroom. "If there is no other comment from a member we will proceed to the vote of expulsion, subject of course to its ratification by the Medical Board in Frankfort."

His gavel was poised, ready to reinforce his remarks, when a resolute voice spoke up from the rear.

"I am a member in good standing in the medical society of Christian County, and I have something to say in my behalf before judgment is unjustly and illegally passed on me."

Wesley Ketchum could not have contrived a more dramatic entrance. Heads were craned from every direction, with embarrassed gasps of surprise.

Even Sanders showed a certain discomfiture. His gavel came down sharply. "You are out of order," he cried.

Ketchum's voice rose sternly. "You, Mr. Chairman, are the one out of order. I am fighting for the sacred right of a fair trial before one's peers."

He had walked down the aisle, swinging past the gate which separated the magistrate's bench and counsel tables from the spectator benches. He now stood, half-facing the bench and the courtroom.

Sanders again moved to gavel him down. But Ketchum's appearance had aroused not only curiosity but a sense of fair play. Cries of "Hear, hear" emanated from the benches.

Sanders' gavel slid reluctantly out of his fingers.

Ketchum made a good impression as he stood there, his head up, his eyes clear and resolute, his manner respectful, but in no way defensive. "Gentlemen," he said in a firm voice, "I will make it short, as I know you are all busy men, with practices to get back to. Let me say first that I am sorry that I have brought any problem to the doctors of Christian County. You were born and raised in these parts, the majority of you. I was not. I was raised north of the Ohio River, and I came here a few years ago at the suggestion of one of your distinguished doctors. I stayed at the encouragement of some leading citizens, George Dalton, for one, whom you all know and respect, and the head of your school system, Dr. Dietrich. Both are familiar with my work with this freak, as some call him, and would be here today, to speak in my behalf, if this were not a session closed to the public, as it rightfully should be.

"It was Professor Dietrich who first told me about

this boy, who grew up among you. He is from a well-known family, the well-respected and numerous Cayce clan, one of your old families, who fought in the Revolutionary War and the Civil War after that. At any rate, Professor Dietrich told me that this boy had cured his daughter, when doctors here and elsewhere had given her up, and suggested that I investigate, and that is what I have been doing, investigating. And in the process I have been helping people like George Dalton, the Davis boy, and others."

Ketchum had decided against a direct confrontation, and he was glad of it now, as he sensed the readiness of many in the audience to hear him out.

"I am still investigating this man Cayce. And I am here not only to defend myself, but to enlist your support in this research project. Of course, if the only aim of this meeting is to kick me out of the profession, it would be meaningless for me to suggest this little experiment to you."

He had again held their interest. By labeling his own activity research, he made it an easier pill to swallow. Identifying Edgar Cayce with their own backgrounds made the clairvoyant a familiar, acceptable figure.

Ketchum patted his pockets now, as if to reassure himself of the contents, then edged closer to the long counsel table, just below the judge's bench. He faced the courtroom, allowing his eyes to flick over each and every countenance. As he did so, peering into the last row, where he had been sitting but a few minutes before, he started for a moment, his poise briefly shaken. But he recovered quickly, continuing wth his customary aplomb.

"Here, gentlemen, is a suggestion I would respectfully submit to you. I would like you to appoint six men from your numbers and I would want to be one of the six. Each man choose one of his most complex cases; then have Edgar Cayce lie down as is his practice, and go to sleep and diagnose each case, with two stenographers sitting one on either side of him, taking it down verbatim. After his diagnoses have been made, we will all examine these cases, checking them against what he said."

Now with a dramatic flourish, he reached into his suit pocket and took out the two stacks of bills and spread them out on the counsel table.

"There's a thousand dollars here in cold cash," he announced. "This says that Edgar Cayce is right in all six cases. But if the diagnoses that he makes are not absolutely correct in every detail, then after the fee for your regular examination of the patient is deducted, I will turn the residue over to any charity that you name in Christian County."

He now stared deliberately at the back of the room, in what was for Ketchum a rare appeal, a look that could be read properly by only one person.

Dr. Janson, unmindful of the secret drama, stood up, hoping to help Ketchum. "Mr. Chairman, I make a motion the charges be laid on the table."

For a moment, Ketchum's heart leaped hopefully. But it was not to be that easy.

Undirected, the majority might have readily consented to indefinitely putting off an unpleasant business. But Sanders and Benson were not so easily dissuaded.

From the bench, Sanders quickly countered. "We don't intend to make a sideshow out of this meeting. Obviously, it's only a delaying action on Ketchum's part and will solve nothing. As I understand it, even the Freak won't have anything to do with Ketchum any more. Even he is fed up with his lack of ethics."

Obviously, the story of the break had leaked out; it was virtually impossible to keep anything quiet for long in a small town like Hopkinsville.

With this thrust by Sanders, the natural buoyance that had kept him on the offensive seemed to ooze out of Ketchum. He still stood straight and defiant, hoping there would be no request to produce Cayce on the spot.

As so often happens, it almost seemed as if his secret fear promptly evoked the undesired consequence.

One doctor spoke up. "I, for one, would be willing

to go along with Ketchum's proposal if he could produce this Cayce at this time."

There were cries of approval from many sides, and Sanders appeared to acquiesce in what seemed the wish of the majority. "All right, Ketchum, you produce Cayce, and we'll give him one case, not six, and we'll decide it here and now."

Ketchum temporized. "But you'd have to get him here."

A tall, slim figure stood up in the last row.

As Ketchum's gaze turned to this figure, the others in the room followed.

There were murmurs of astonishment, and Sanders and Benson exchanged shocked glances.

The figure spoke in a clear, high-pitched, yet strong and resolute voice. "My name is Edgar Cayce, and I am here to state, to my knowledge, that what Wesley Ketchum has said here is true, and that he has tried at all times to help the sick of this community to the best of his ability."

This was more than Ketchum could have hoped for. For the first time in his life, his eyes moistened, and he blinked unashamedly. It was all he could do to disguise his emotion as he stood there, more surprised, if the truth be known, than anybody else in the room.

Cayce now began walking toward the front of the chamber, taking his position by Ketchum's side.

"As Dr. Sanders proposed," he said, with a glance to the bench, "I stand ready to diagnose any case that anyone submits, though I am not to be asked to recommend a cure, as I am presently undecided how this ability should be used."

No matter how the reading or the meeting went, Ketchum felt a reassuring glow in Cayce's espousal of his cause. He wondered for a moment how he had known of the meeting. It had to be Boze, it could have been none other. And he would have confidently wagered where Boze was at that moment.

Benson had stepped forward with a self-satisfied smirk. "In my pocket," he said, "I happen to have the diagnosis, confirmed by two specialists, of a very difficult case." He now addressed himself to Ketchum. "Am I to understand, given the name and address of this patient, that your—your Mr. Cayce"—his voice was faintly disdainful—"will duplicate this diagnosis?"

"I don't know about duplicating it," said Ketchum, "but he will make the correct diagnosis."

"There is no possibility of an inaccuracy in this diagnosis. So I must insist that his diagnosis correspond to that made by the two most distinguished doctors in their field."

Ketchum quickly saw that the majority thought Benson's stipulation reasonable.

"All right," he agreed, not having any other recourse.

The name and address of the patient was given to Ketchum on a slip of paper. "We neither need nor desire any other information," he explained.

His look settled on the long counsel table. "Gentlemen, for want of a sofa or couch, Mr. Cayce will stretch out on this hard table, using his jacket for a pillow. I will conduct the questioning, standing at his side."

Many of the doctors moved forward for a better view of the proceedings.

Sanders looked down with a contemptuous smile from the judge's bench. "Please proceed," he said. "The members are waiting."

Cayce slipped off his coat, tie and shoes. He loosened his belt and rolled up his shirtsleeves, then lay down on the hard table, stretching out on his back.

Ketchum quickly made the suggestion, giving the patient's name and address. "Go to sleep," he said, "and find the body, which is requesting help through his doctor. After you find the body, tell us what is wrong with it physically. When this is done, without passing on to a remedy, you will wake up fresh and vigorous, not remembering a word that you have said."

Dr. Benson had taken the patient's diagnosis out

of his pocket, and it was being passed from one doctor to another. They shook their heads wonderingly.

But their attention was soon regained. Edgar Cayce had started to speak. His voice, as usual, was expressionless, a dull monotone.

"I have the body," he said "The trouble with this man is all with his eyes."

For a bare moment, Ketchum had nervously doubted. But he was almost exultant now, for Cayce had at least tuned in to the problem area, as Ketchum had been able to discern from his own fleeting glimpse of the diagnosis.

"A very unusual case," said Cayce. "There are few like it. The central axis cylinder of the subject's eyes is blank. He can only see out of the sides of his eyes, through the filaments around the edges. The optic nerve seems to be only active around the edges. Most unusual. The central part of his optic nerve is dead. This man has been to many doctors and to many clinics and obtained no help whatsoever. He will continue to see out the sides of his eyes." He paused. "I have finished with this body. He is deserving of help."

Nearly everybody had seen the diagnosis Benson had pulled out of his pocket. There were gasps now of wonder.

As Ketchum was returning Cayce to consciousness, a middle-aged, well-dressed doctor stood up. He was a well-known eye specialist. "This is the most amazing demonstration I have ever witnessed. I examined the patient, and did not properly diagnose his affliction at first, because I had never seen a case like it before. Later on, after another diagnosis had been made, I went over the man's eyes again, and discovered indeed that he did see out the sides of his eyes. Every word that Cayce has said is absolutely true." He looked around the room at his colleagues, and his eyes finally rested on Sanders. "Some day, gentlemen, in fifty years or perhaps a hundred, men will be talking of what was done here today. And, who knows but what clairvoyants or psychics may one day play a special role in medicine? Meanwhile, I think we all owe an apology to Dr. Ketchum, and a word of thanks to his protégé, Edgar Cayce."

There were cries of "Aye, aye." Then, with Sanders and Benson silently recognizing defeat, Dr. Janson rose again. "I propose anew that the subject—not Edgar Cayce," he added quickly—"be laid on the table, indefinitely."

There was a loud assenting chorus, and before its echo had faded, a furious Sanders, trailed by a subdued Benson, had stalked out of the courtroom.

Ketchum took Cayce's hand gratefully, "Edgar, what can I do for you? Name it, and you can have it."

Cayce gave him an amused glance. "How about some milk and crackers, Doc? I'm hungry."

In the corridor outside, Boze happily went into a dance as he saw the two men emerge together. As Ketchum had correctly surmised, it was Boze who had gone for Cayce.

"You two is sure an unbeatable combination." he said with an ear-to-ear grin. "I'm goin' out an' get you both the biggest an' bes' watermelon that ol' Farmer Jones can grow."

In parting, the two men again shook hands.

"Thanks again, Old Man," said Ketchum. "I'll never forget you."

Each knew he was going his separate way, for Ketchum, with the sensitivity that was part of his incongruously brash facade, knew that nothing essentially had changed between them. Cayce was still his friend, but never more his partner. The men who had once come to an agreement were no more. Time and events had changed that.

Gertrude was waiting as usual when Edgar came home that evening. "Did you have a good day, dear?" She kissed him affectionately.

"The usual children and their fond mothers," he said, looking for the newspaper.

"Is that all?" she asked, with an innocent look.

He looked at her and smiled. "Now, Gertrude, don't chide me for doing a good deed."

"Edgar, I heard that you were marvelous."

"And who have you been listening to?"

"Oh, Aunt Carrie called."

"As I suspected, and she got it from Tom House."

"Dr. House put in a few words, too, I understand."

"That was before I got there, Gertrude. I didn't know about the meeting until Boze came and fetched me."

"You're not going back to Ketchum, Edgar?" She made an effort to sound casual.

"None of us can go back, Gertrude. My problem is going ahead."

She gave him a serious look. "Whatever happens, I think we must reconcile ourselves to being without money."

"Why do you say that?"

"Your gift has shown you that you can't make money with it and yourself prosper."

He laughed. "That seems to be a paradox."

"In a way I suppose it is. But still we'll never be poor, Edgar, just broke. There's a difference. Poverty is a state of mind. People in love are never poor."

"I wonder," he sighed, "if I will be able to help people without getting confused again about what the readings are for."

She gave him a caressing smile. "You will, when you are ready. What you have recently passed through is similar to a rebirth."

"You mean I'm being reincarnated in this lifetime?" He was half-jesting.

"Not exactly."

He turned to his favorite book. "Nicodemus asks Christ how a man can be born when he is old. 'Can he enter the second time into his mother's womb and be born?' "

"And what did Jesus say?"

" 'That which is born of the flesh is flesh; and that which is born of the Spirit is spirit.' "

Her face was radiant. "Your gift is from God, Edgar; it is of the spirit. Always remember that, no matter the temptation."

"Yes, Gertrude," he said dutifully. "But will people ever stop thinking of me as some sort of nut?"

"You're just different," she said.

Even she was not fully aware of how different.

Often, before their marriage he had thought sadly of how every man was an island unto himself. It was still very true. There were so many things he would have liked to talk about, but the thought of them dazzled even his mind and he feared to give them expression.

Loving him, bound to him closely, she had caught glimpses of things welling up in him that she had never shared. She had waited patiently, hoping one day that he would speak out of his own accord. But he had not been ready.

He seemed to read her mind now, as he had so many other times.

"Why should I burden you with what I have seen?" he said with a wan smile.

"Sharing lightens a load," she said, "and that's what soul mates are for, to make things easier for the other person from one life to the next."

He brushed a hand over his eyes and veiled them against the light.

"In the beginning the little people told me of things that would happen, and they often happened. Later, I had dreams and visions, and they came to pass as well. During my reading at the courtroom for Ketchum, I had a curious dream, as sometimes happens, as you may remember, in a reading. This dream was more curious and comprehensive than the rest. In it, I saw not only our future, but the future of many peoples." His eyes were closed, shielded from hers. "In the dream I saw men fighting in trenches, in airplanes, and on the seas. I saw men dying horribly on battle-scarred fields. I saw Germany in ruins, its great cities demolished in rubble. As the dream continued I saw great turmoil in Wall Street, stocks plunging to the bottom. I saw great chaos and riots in the streets of our land, with brother turned against brother in bitter racial conflict. I saw China, now a divided vassal state, as a great power, rivaling the United States, and Russia, with a united population twice that of both combined."

He fell silent for awhile, and she willed him to go on, knowing that in the catharsis of unburdening himself he would find a certain peace and tranquility.

"In this country, I saw distructive earthquakes, the cities of Los Angeles and San Francisco, and of New York tumbled in their own debris. But all this not before the turn of the century."

Gertrude could not grasp the magnitude of what she was hearing. Wifelike, she asked:

"But, Edgar, what's going to happen to us?"

He smiled appreciatively. "I saw us walking together on a sandy ocean beach where I seem to have been before. And as we were walking, the deserted beach suddenly became a boardwalk with swarms of bathers and huge hotels. It was a very remarkable thing."

As she looked at that lean, troubled face, with its familiar lines, her eyes shone with the love that passeth normal understanding, a legacy perhaps from the lives they had shared together. She, too, quoted form her husband's favorite source. It seemed to be the answer he was waiting for, for he smiled serenely as she spoke:

" 'He that receveth a prophet in the name of a prophet shall receive a prophet's reward; and he that receiveth a righteous man shall receive a righteous man's reward.' "

Epilogue

by Hugh Lynn Cayce

As Edgar Cayce predicted, the years ahead saw many drastic changes. The First World War, which he foresaw, was followed by the stock market crash of 1929, the Depression and then World War II. He also forecast racial strife thereafter which he said would break into open violence before the death of the second President to die in office—Kennedy, that is to say, following Roosevelt. He predicted forty years of tremendous political, social, economic, scientific and earth changes beginning in 1958, reaching a crescendo toward 1998. Already we have seen the discovery of the laser beam, hypnosis in medical therapy, startling new methods of diagnosis through blood analysis, expansion of the radio telescope, the birth of new nations and space travel.

For Edgar Cayce there were also constant changes. In 1912, he left Hopkinsville, Kentucky, and after a brief stay in Anniston, Alabama, settled in Selma, Alabama where he tried to give up psychic readings and concentrate on photography. But people continued to seek him out for psychic help.

In Selma, at age six, I had reason to thank the Lord for my father. I was playing with some flash powder one day, and it blew up in my face, blinding me. Doctors proposed that one infected eye be removed to save my sight. In pain, with my eyes heavily bandaged, I asked my father to go to sleep and give me a reading. In the sleep state, he recommended packs, internal medicine and a special diet. Weeks later, the bandages were removed, and I could see. There was no need for the operation.

After Selma came a period of groping for oil in Texas, as my father again tested his gift, hoping that his goal of building a hospital would be made possible by this psychic exploration. The search for oil was not successful.

After the petroleum fiasco, the family moved to Dayton, Ohio, and then, as he had dreamed, to the sparsely settled sand hills of Virginia Beach, Virginia, which have become a great resort area as he predicted. In Virginia Beach a hospital, using information from his readings, functioned successfully for three years, until the Depression.

But research continued. The Association for Research and Englightenment, Inc., a psychical research society with an open membership, was formed in 1932 to preserve and study the material based on thousands of Cayce readings. The national headquarters are in the original hospital building, which was repurchased in 1956. The Association is collaborating with medical groups, parapsychological organizations and archaeologists.

To meet the interests of young people, an embryo Atlantic University has recently grown from his principles and philosophies, and is currently conducting classes in Virginia.

From Virginia Beach, his work has spread around the world. Edgar Cayce had said, "First, there would be the few, then the many." Before his and Gertrude's death in 1945—hers following by a few months—they saw the first study group dedicated to the philosophic and psychological study of his readings take root in Virginia Beach; then similar groups branched out by the hundreds (more than two thousand in 1973), in this country and abroad. Millions have been fascinated by the books and articles that have become part of his legacy.

His unconscious mind missed very little. In 1961, at Virginia Beach, I showed researcher Jess Stearn three separate readings my father had made thirty years before, in 1931. By name, they apparently foreshadowed Stearn's coming, indicating he would help bring the Edgar Cayce work to the masses. This happened with *The Sleeping Prophet,* a world-wide best seller, and now *A Prophet in His Own Country.*

Ahead lie intriguingly unexplored areas of the unconscious mind as vast as space itself. For me, in this adventure, Edgar Cayce looms as an early astronaut of the unconcious mind, blazing a trail of inner space that others can follow by merely heeding the markers he has plainly left.

About the Author

Jess Stearn was for many years a prizewinning reporter for the New York *Daily News* and later an editor for *Newsweek*. Currently living in Malibu Beach, California, he is an expert on various forms of ESP and has researched the whole world of psychic phenomena. Mr. Stearn has long been a pioneer of many subjects for the popular audience. His *The Door to the Future* was one of the very first best-selling works on psychic phenomena, similarly *The Sixth Man* on homosexuality, and his book on drugs, *The Seekers,* was publicly recommended by the then Director of the Federal Bureau of Narcotics. Of all Jess Stearns' best-selling books, the most popular has been *Edgar Cayce, The Sleeping Prophet,* his portrait of the mature life and work of the preeminent mystic and healer. In *A Prophet in His Own Country,* he turns with equal eloquence and appeal to a highly dramatic account of the young manhood of Cayce. Publishing plans for the future include a second collaboration with famed novelist Taylor Caldwell—their first joint work was *The Search for a Soul; Taylor Caldwell's Psychic Lives*—on a book dealing with Lost Atlantis which will appear in early 1975.

THE A.R.E. TODAY

The Association for Research and Enlightenment is an open-membership, nonprofit organization chartered under the laws of the Commonwealth of Virginia to carry on psychic research. It cooperates in the fields of medicine, psychology, and theology. The active membership of the A.R.E. is made up of people from all walks of life, of all religious faiths, and many nationalities.

In 1975, a modern library—conference center was completed. There, available for examination and study, are 14,256 Edgar Cayce readings. The readings are the clairvoyant discourses given by Cayce while he was in a self-induced hypnotic sleep-state. Copious indexing and cross-indexing make the readings readily accessible for study. In addition, a large collection of psychic literature is available to the public with books on loan to members.

The Edgar Cayce material has proven valuable when worked with in an A.R.E. Study Group. Over 1600 groups flourish throughout the United States and other countries.

For an introductory brochure, write A.R.E. Dept. I, Box 595, Virginia Beach, Va. 23451.